Policies and Procedures for the Electronic Medical Practice

Edward D. Jones, III and Carolyn P. Hartley, MLA

AMA
AMERICAN
MEDICAL
ASSOCIATION

Internet address: www.ama-assn.org

Additional copies of this book may be ordered by calling 800-621-8335 or from the secure AMA web site at www.amabookstore.com. Refer to product number OP 602909.

ISBN 978-1-60359-106-5

BP0209P033:12/09

Library of Congress Cataloging-in-Publication Data

Jones, Ed (Edward Douglass)
  Policies and procedures for the electronic medical practice/Edward D. Jones III and Carolyn P. Hartley.
      p. ; cm.
  Includes bibliographical references and index.
  Summary: "This book provides insight and advice for an electronically connected medical office from workflow processes, ePrescribing and security guidelines. Book also includes policies and procedures in a customizable format that can establish a platform for an electronically connected medical office"—Provided by publisher.
  ISBN 978-1-60359-106-5 (alk. paper)
  1. Medical informatics. 2. Medical offices—Automation. I. Hartley, Carolyn P. II. American Medical Association. III. Title.
  [DNLM: 1. Medical Records Systems, Computerized–organization & administration—United States. 2. Computer Security—United States. 3. Confidentiality–United States. 4. Office Management–United States. 5. Physicians' Offices—organization & administration—United States. WX 173 J76p 2010]
  R858.J665 2010
  610.285–dc22
                                          2009030231

Dedications

In honor of my wife, Ann Maynard Jones, and in loving memory of our son, Brett Ashley Maynard (1971–2008), known fondly in Charleston, South Carolina, as the Rock Star Chef.

For Kathy, Jim, and Dad. And for Doctors Steve and Sarah.

About the Authors

Ed Jones is managing member and CEO of Cornichon Healthcare Solutions, LLC, located on Seabrook Island, South Carolina, and president of HIPAA, LLC, located in Atlanta, Georgia. Ed and his business and technical colleagues at Cornichon consult with health care stakeholders on electronic business strategies related to the Health Insurance Portability and Accountability Act (HIPAA) and Health Information Technology for Economic and Clinical Health Act (HITECH Act) regulations and with providers and vendors on certification and implementation of electronic health record (EHR) systems. Ed and his business colleagues at HIPAA, LLC, owner of hipaa.com, provide documentation on HIPAA and HITECH Act regulations at a single site and provide online training related to those regulations in order to mitigate privacy and security risks.

Ed brings considerable health care industry and business leadership to both companies. He was elected by his peers for two terms as the 2003–2004 chair of the board of directors of WEDI–the Workgroup for Electronic Data Interchange, an association of more than 300 corporate and government members that was founded by former secretary of Health and Human Services (HHS) Louis W. Sullivan, MD. WEDI is an advisor to the secretary of HHS and National Committee on Vital and Health Statistics (NCVHS) on design and implementation of HIPAA administrative simplification standards and on electronic business and clinical tools in health care. Ed also was a founding commissioner of the Electronic Healthcare Network Accreditation Commission (EHNAC) and an architect of its accreditation criteria, serving from 1994 to 2003.

Until it was acquired in December 1999, Ed served as senior vice president and member of the CEO's Executive Operations Committee of the Centris Group, Inc., headquartered in Costa Mesa, California, which comprised seven subsidiary companies with a core focus on underwriting and reinsuring self-funded health plans for US employers. Before joining Centris in 1993, Ed served as executive vice president and as a member of the board of directors of Medical Review Systems, a firm that he co-founded in 1990 and that was acquired in 1995 by Equifax. Before that, he served as a consultant to the National Research Council of the National Academy of Sciences, the US Sentencing Commission, and firms in insurance and other industries and held senior positions in the US Department of Justice and Central Intelligence Agency.

Ed holds degrees in economics from the University of Chicago and Washington University in St. Louis. This is the sixth book he has written with Carolyn Hartley. Ed can be reached at edj3@me.com.

Carolyn Hartley, MLA, president and CEO of Physicians EHR, Inc, has been in health care since 1982 and in health information technology (HIT) for more than a decade. Her publishing history speaks to the trust she has established with health care provider organizations. She is lead or co-author of 13 textbooks on privacy, security, and EHR implementation. She also is EHR technical advisor for several national medical societies that represent oncologists, gastroenterologists, nephrologists, dentists, and community health centers.

She and her team of HIT implementation consultants serve as project managers and management coaches to assist medical practices through the complexities of EHR implementation by helping them achieve implementation milestones, such as EHR software and hardware selection, contract negotiation, interface scheduling and testing, training, installation, Go-Live, post–Go-Live, and implementation repair. Frustrated with the vast amount of information needed for client policies and procedures and for her writing and speaking engagements, she joined colleagues at HIPAA.com and regularly posts comments. She also maintains a blog at ehr.ascoexchange.org, emrjobs.com, and at physiciansehr.com.

Carolyn is a certified implementation consultant and holds an undergraduate degree in education with a master of liberal arts degree with an emphasis in medical anthropology from Baker University. She can be reached at Carolyn@physiciansehr.com.

Brief Table of Contents

Table of Contents

Introduction

The health care industry is undergoing a global revolution driven by a force it can no longer resist: information technology.[1]

Why Build Policies and Procedures?

Policies and procedures in a medical practice "happen" every day whether they are written or unwritten. A written policy and procedure gives everyone a fair shake at knowing what to do and how to do it. It also spells out the consequences of what happens if you repeatedly break a policy or incorrectly follow a procedure.

The way in which you operated your office in a paper world is about to get shaken up as you transition to an electronic office. Your practice will sift through a significant number of new security issues. You will redesign workflow processes, especially as you begin transmitting computerized physician orders between your practice and labs, pharmacies, imaging centers, and other providers, and as you begin receiving data into your patients' records. You also will need to instruct your staff on how to create, store, and transmit confidential information as it electronically moves to your health exchange partners, such as laboratories, imaging and pathology labs, hospitals, and patients.

The good news is that electronic security has been tested in other industries, including banking, retail sales, transportation, and manufacturing, that have already transitioned into an electronic environment. Although these industries don't often handle protected health information, lessons have been learned from their successes and missteps.

To some, security may be easily relegated as a technical network activity, but the creation and handling of electronic health information has more to do with administrative and human decisions than network management. That's why your staff must have specific guidance on

---

[1] Amar Gupta, "Prescription for Changes," *Wall Street Journal,* Oct. 20, 2008, p. R6.

- how they will handle computer equipment,
- who can access and revise patient records, and
- measures that will need to be taken to maintain the confidentiality, integrity, and availability of health information.

When policies aren't written, physicians tend to randomly react to new quality issues or internal squabbles, resulting in inconsistent results. All too often, a medical assistant will say, "Well, this doctor wants me to do things this way, but if it's this doctor, then we do it another way."

This kind of uncertainty and inconsistency results in internal security issues, bickering, cliques, and playing favorites; ultimately weakening the delivery of quality care to patients and workflow processes. When the process or the procedures break down, you have a proven formula for staff turnover, workflow inefficiencies, and medical errors.

Stepped Up Enforcement of Privacy and Security Rules

The American Recovery and Reinvestment Act of 2009 (often called the Stimulus Package, or ARRA) provides incentive funding for physicians who adopt electronic health records and demonstrate they are *meaningful* users. At a high level, meaningful *user* means the physician practice can demonstrate it can participate in

- ePrescribing,
- clinical decision support, and
- quality reporting.

ARRA also comes with advanced Health Insurance Portability and Accountability Act (HIPAA) privacy and security requirements, which are detailed in Chapter 2 and Appendix B.

Security is of interest to agencies inside and outside the US Department of Health and Human Services (HHS). A privacy complaint can be registered with the Office for Civil Rights (OCR), the office within HHS responsible for enforcing the Privacy Rule and, effective July 27, 2009, the Security Rule as well. If there appears to be reason for a criminal investigation, OCR may refer the breach to any of several additional regulatory agencies, such as the Department of Homeland Security, Department of Justice, Department of Labor, Department of Commerce, Department of Defense, Internal Revenue Service, Social Security Administration, Federal Trade Commission, and Veteran's Administration. OCR also may elect to refer a complaint to your state's attorney general, who may have more resources available to resolve the complaint.

Lessons Learned from Privacy Complaints

In response to inquiries to learn where the majority of privacy breaches have occurred, OCR agreed to release generalized data, comparing 2003 activities with those from 2004–2007. Of concern to physicians are the categories of grievances that consumers are posting against ambulatory care givers. The top five complaints that involved corrective action are listed in the table below.

Complaint	What It Means (high level)
Impermissible uses and disclosures	An unauthorized person viewed, received, altered, or could have otherwise accessed the patient's record.
Administrative and physical safeguards	Broad category that refers to anything from establishing and implementing policies and procedures to protecting the physical environment containing the medical charts.

continued next page

Complaint	What It Means (high level)
Access	Providing the right information to the right person at the right time. Access controls in an electronic health record (EHR) means mechanisms for protecting sensitive communication over open or private networks so that they cannot be intercepted and interpreted by anyone other than the recipient.
Minimum necessary	The minimum amount of information should be accessed for a person to do his/her job.
Notice of Privacy Practices (NPP)	Another broad category that may indicate a patient did not receive an NPP or is filing a complaint based on the NPP's content.

These 2007 complaints come from the same categories of complaints filed in 2003, possible signs that

- OCR has fine-tuned its bell curve of privacy breach investigative tactics.
- Providers continue to make the same mistakes and should focus on training and security reminders.
- Patients are becoming educated about their privacy rights.
- The complaint categories are too broadly defined.

In 2008, the authors were called to be expert witnesses for a practice that was responding to an OCR inquiry. On a daily basis, the provider took home and stored in his home-safe the practice's daily backup file of electronic protected health information, which was on the provider's laptop. The data on the laptop were encrypted, essentially rendering any file content inaccessible to an unauthorized user. Before the laptop could be secured at home, it was stolen from the provider's garaged car. The provider followed his own policies and procedures that said in the event his electronic media was stolen, he would notify patients of the incident as well as provide the phone number and address of the OCR in the event anyone wanted to file a privacy complaint.

Of the several hundred notified patients, one took action, contacted OCR, and filed a complaint. This triggered an investigative letter from the office of the secretary of HHS. The provider wisely contacted his health law attorney.

Part of the legal defense strategy was to hire experts to evaluate the provider's policies and procedures and ensure that they were in compliance with HIPAA privacy and security requirements and that in reporting this security incident, the provider followed his own policies and procedures on mitigating a privacy breach.

The practice's policies and procedures were found to be in good order. HHS did not pursue an on-site investigation, rather HHS asked that he develop and implement a plan to remediate the problem so that no backup files could be stolen again. Case closed. Frazzled nerves mended; and now, the provider thinks twice before leaving the laptop in his car.[2]

In his deposition, the clinician explained that his practice had begun with a template of policies and procedures, similar to the ones included in this book. Using a risk assessment, the practice identified risks that were relevant to its location, size, and budget and then customized its policies and procedures according to the risks identified in the practice's risk assessment.

Your customized policies and procedures will keep you on safer ground for any number of reasons. Here are some examples:

- A police officer requests a medical record for a 19-year-old male with a history of driving under the influence. What do you do?

---

[2] For additional information on the importance of securing electronic media, see Huffman, Steve. "A Laptop Lost: Securing Mobile Devices–That sinking feeling in your stomach tells you something is horribly wrong." *ADVANCE for Health Information Executives*. August 2009, pp26 and 28.

- The mother of a 15-year-old girl wants to know why her daughter has an appointment with an obstetrician. What do you do?

- An employee in your practice wants to know about the medical care of another female employee and searches the medical record to see how she's doing. What do you do?

Policies and Procedures You Can Customize

This book includes policies and procedures in a customizable format that can establish a platform for your electronically connected medical office. Each chapter is formatted according to the following structure:

- learning objectives,
- new terms introduced in the chapter,
- case study,
- background supporting the set of policies and procedures presented in the chapter, and
- policies and procedures for you to customize.

Organization of This Book

What follows is a brief chapter-by-chapter overview of the policies you'll find in this book.

Chapter 1: Getting Started With Your Policies and Procedures

In this chapter, you will learn how to get started building or revising your policies and procedures; how technology energizes, increases efficiency and quality, and poses new risks; and the basics of building a policy and procedure, including the seven layers of a policy and procedure. Sample exercises are provided to help you create your own policy and procedure. Then, you will build the administrative components that support the creation, storage, and transmission of electronic health information.

Chapter 2: Your Roadmap through the Decade of Health Information Technology

Use this chapter for future planning. You will learn how the Decade of Health Information Technology will affect your policies and procedures and forthcoming regulatory modifications will change the way you manage billing and clinical documentation, claims, and remittance. There are no policies and procedures accompanying this chapter. Appendix B discusses the forthcoming enhancements to privacy and security compliance as a result of the HITECH Act, which was enacted as part of the American Recovery and Reinvestment Act of 2009 that was signed by President Obama on February 17, 2009.

Chapter 3: Evaluating Safeguards for Technology Adoption, Updates, and Health Information Exchange

In this chapter, you will learn how to develop new work processes that protect your systems, facility, and electronically protected health information; how to customize physical and technical policies and procedures for your environment that also make sense to your workforce; and how to evaluate physical and technical safeguards of health exchange partners.

Chapter 4: Performance Measurements and Their Effects on Your Policies and Procedures

Do you participate, or plan to participate, in reimbursement incentives offered by payers, both public and private? You will learn the basics of performance measurements and how they impact your policies and procedures; how integration of your practice management, laboratory, pharmacy information systems, and electronic medical records impact your performance measurements and therefore your policies and procedures; and how patients' increasingly involved financial participation affects your policies and procedures.

Chapter 5: Managing the Personal Health Record

It has taken a long time for the personal health record (PHR) to evolve. Consequently, these records come in many varieties. Most recently, the PHR has been adopted by disease-specific medical societies as a way to assist patients in disease management. You'll see this in the care of diabetes, cancer, asthma, and heart disease. In this chapter, you will learn how to prepare your practice for patients who want to be involved in managing their health information; key components of a personal health record; recent guidance that clarifies health information you can provide to family, friends, and caregivers; and standards that are waived in a presidential-declared emergency.

Prerequisites for Policies and Procedures for the Electronic Medical Practice

A few steps must be in place before the policies and procedures can be developed for an electronic medical practice, including:

- The ambulatory care practice has already implemented its privacy policies[3] and procedures and provides ongoing training on those policies.

- The privacy and security officials (may be the same person) confer on policies and procedures to ensure they are not in conflict.

- A notice of privacy practices is presented to each new patient.

- Business associates (see Chapter 2 and Appendix B) are now preparing to be covered entities.

Start Now

The policies and procedures in this book are designed to get you started. They are meant to be generic and do not represent legal advice. In developing your policies and procedures for the electronic exchange of health information, review and rewrite them to fit into your environment. It is recommended that you present all policies and procedures to a health law attorney for review before presenting them to your staff. Finally, highlight the core points from each policy and procedure and present them during training and regular security reminders.

Good luck. We hope you'll let us know how you're doing.

Carolyn Hartley and Ed Jones

---

[3] Compliance date for HIPAA's Privacy Rule was April 14, 2003.

CHAPTER 1

Getting Started With Your Policies and Procedures

IN THIS CHAPTER, YOU WILL LEARN

- How to get started building or revising your policies and procedures
- How technology energizes, increases efficiency and quality, and poses new risks
- What policies and procedures are
- The seven layers of a policy and related procedures
- Sample exercise to create your own policies and procedures.

Key Terms

> **Biometrics:** An identification system that identifies a human from a measurement of a physical feature or repeatable action of the individual, for example, hand geometry, retinal scan, iris scan, fingerprint or finger-image patterns, facial characteristics, DNA sequence characteristics, voice prints, and hand-written signature.

1

Covered entity: (1) A health plan; (2) a health care clearinghouse; (3) a health care provider who transmits any health information in electronic form in connection with a transaction covered by Health Insurance Portability and Accountability Act (HIPAA) Administrative Simplification standards

Designated record set: A group of records maintained by or for a covered entity that includes (1) medical records; (2) billing records maintained by the covered health care provider; (3) enrollment, payment, claims adjudication, and case or medical management record systems maintained by or for a health plan; and (4) records used in whole or in part by or for the covered entity to make decisions about the individual.

Digital signature: An electronic signature, which serves as a unique identifier for an individual, much like a written signature where an algorithm authenticates the integrity of the signed data and the identity of the signatory.[1]

Electronically connected practice: A solo or group practice that functions in an interfaced environment, bringing together its practice management system with electronic medical record software, allowing ePrescribing, clinical decision support, internal and external communication with its referring network, and exchange of health information with its community of caregivers.

Electronic health record (EHR): Confidential, identifiable health information that is used, disclosed, stored, retrieved, analyzed, and owned by the entity that created it. It is a longitudinal electronic record of patient health information produced by encounters in one or more care settings. Included in this information are patient demographics, progress notes, problems, medications, vital signs,

---

[1] US Department of Commerce/National Institute of Standards and Technology (NIST). *"Digital Signature Standards (DSS),"* FIPS Publication 186-2, Jan. 27, 2000. Available online at: http://csrc.nist.gov/publications/fips/fips186-2/fips186-2.pdf.

past medical history, immunizations, laboratory data, and radiology reports. The EHR automates and streamlines the clinician's workflow. The EHR has the ability to independently generate a complete record of a clinical patient encounter, as well as support other care-related activities such as decision support, quality management, and clinical reporting.[2]

Electronic medical record: The software that allows a health care provider to create, edit, add to, store, transmit, exchange, and disclose medical information about a patient.

Electronic signature: A unique identifier of the signatory individual that ensures the integrity of a document's content and provides for no repudiation, that is, strong and substantial evidence that will make it difficult for the signer to claim that the electronic representation is not valid. Currently, the only technically mature electronic signature meeting the above criteria is the digital signature.

ePrescribing: Electronic prescribing, which enables a prescriber to electronically generate a prescription directly to a pharmacy from the point of care. ePrescribing was included as a provision in the Medicare Modernization Act of 2003.

Health information exchange (HIE): The electronic mobilization of health care information across organizations within a region or community. HIE provides the capability to electronically move clinical information between disparate health care information systems while maintaining the meaning of the information being

---

[2] HIMSS EHRVA Definitional Model and Application Process, October 2006. Available online at: www.himssehrva.org/docs/EHRVA_application.pdf. HIMSS is the Health Information Management Systems Society, EHRVA is the Electronic Health Record Vendor Association. The American Recovery and Reinvestment Act of 2009, signed by President Obama on February 17, 2009, defines *electronic health record* in the context of *privacy* as "an electronic record of health-related information on an individual that is created, gathered, managed, and consulted by authorized health care clinicians and staff." See p. 145 of the *American Recovery and Reinvestment Act of 2009*, which is available online in portable document format (pdf) at http://frwebgate. access.gpo.gov/cgi-bin/getdoc.cgi?dbname=111_cong_bills&docid=f:h1enr.pdf.

exchanged. The goal of HIE is to facilitate access to and retrieval of clinical data to provide safer, more timely, efficient, effective, equitable, patient-centered care.

Health information technology (HIT): An approach that allows comprehensive management of medical information and its secure exchange between health care consumers and providers. The US Department of Health and Human Services (HHS) promotes countrywide adoption of electronic health record systems by 2014 with the expectation that hundreds of thousands of health care information technology systems throughout the United States will be able to exchange information. Broad use of HIT will

- improve health care quality,
- prevent medical errors,
- reduce health care costs,
- increase administrative efficiencies,
- decrease paperwork, and
- expand access to affordable care.[3]

Information system: An interconnected set of information resources under the same direct management control that shares common functionality. A system normally includes hardware, software, information, data, applications, communications, and people.

Personal identification number: A number or code assigned to an individual and used to provide verification of identity.

---

[3] The American Recovery and Reinvestment Act of 2009, signed by President Obama on February 17, 2009, defines *health information technology* in the context of *improving health care quality, safety, and efficiency* as "hardware, software, integrated technologies or related licenses, intellectual property, upgrades, or packaged solutions sold as services that are designed for or support the use by health care entities or patients for the electronic creation, maintenance, access, or exchange of health information." See p. 115 of the *American Recovery and Reinvestment Act of 2009,* which is available online in portable document format (pdf) at http://frwebgate.access.gpo.gov/cgi-bin/getdoc.cgi?dbname=111_cong_bills&docid=f:h1enr.pdf.

Policy: A plan or course of action, as by a government, political party, or business, intended to influence and determine decisions, actions, and other matters.

Privacy breach: The intrusion into the personal life of another, without just cause, that can give the person whose privacy has been invaded a right to bring a lawsuit for damages against the person or entity that intruded. Under the Health Insurance Portability and Accountability Act, the most common privacy breaches fall into unauthorized use and disclosure of health information, inappropriate access to health information, and inadequate safeguards protecting confidential health information.[4]

Procedure: A manner of proceeding; a way of performing or affecting something; a series of steps taken to accomplish an end.

Requirement: The policies and procedures that a covered entity must follow to comply with a standard.

Security incident: The violation or imminent threat of violation of computer security policies or procedures over a core security requirement that impacts the confidentiality, integrity, and availability of confidential health information.

---

[4] The American Recovery and Reinvestment Act of 2009, signed by President Obama on February 17, 2009, defines *breach* in the context of *privacy* as "IN GENERAL–The term 'breach' means the unauthorized acquisition, access, use, or disclosure of protected health information which compromises the security or privacy of such information, except where an unauthorized person to whom such information is disclosed would not reasonably have been able to retain such information. EXCEPTIONS–The Term 'breach' does not include (i) any unintentional acquisition, access, or use of protected health information by an employee or individual acting under the authority of a covered entity or business associate if–(I) such acquisition, access, or use was made in good faith and within the course and scope of the employment or other professional relationship of such employee or individual, respectively, with the covered entity or business associate; and (II) such information is not further acquired, accessed, used, or disclosed by any person; or (ii) any inadvertent disclosure from an individual who is otherwise authorized to access protected health information at a facility operated by a covered entity or business associate to another similarly situated individual at same facility; and (iii) any such information received as a result of such disclosure is not further acquired, accessed, used, or disclosed without authorization by any person." See *Ibid.*, p. 144.

Standard: A rule, condition, or requirement that describes the following information for products, systems, services, or practices by (1) classification of components; (2) specification of materials, performance, or operations; (3) delineation of procedures; or (4) governs the privacy of individually identifiable health information.

Telephone call-back procedure: A method of authenticating the identity of the receiver and sender of information through a series of questions and answers sent back and forth in order to establish the identity of both the receiver and the sender. For example, a communicating system exchanges a series of identification codes as part of initiating a session to exchange information or a host computer disconnects the initial session before the authentication is complete, then the host calls the user back to establish a session at a predetermined telephone number.

Case Study

At the end of each day, the nurses at a practice in Ohio return their tablet PCs, each to its own cradle at the main nursing station. Twice a day, they charge the battery and sync data that has been gathered into the main server. This is done so that they never put more than 3 hours of medical information at risk of being lost by low batteries or dropped or lost laptops. At the end of the day, all cradles are relocated to a locked cabinet.

Because physicians often want to access medical information outside the practice's offices, each laptop is equipped with a small global positioning system (GPS) receiver. The receiver is installed so that the laptop can be quickly located if it is misplaced or stolen. The practice's policies require that the laptop be checked out so that the practice administrator can account for all computers each day.

Policies also require that resident health care providers change passwords every 60 days, which means frequently updating—and remembering—passwords to the electronic medical record (EMR) and the practice management software (PMS). To help providers with password management, finger-image identification software was added to the laptops so that, at the touch of a finger, the physician could access his or her own laptop. A program on the back end facilitates password updates while maintaining the finger image as the primary user authentication. If the doctor's finger is injured, a quick call to the software company, accompanied by responding to a few security questions, will restore access.

The practice's policies and procedures were designed to mitigate risk. So, when a disgruntled employee made off with five tablets on a Friday afternoon and posted them for sale on the Internet, the practice administrator received a GPS alert and immediately put a contingency plan in place. Not only did these actions prevent access to the health information on the tablets, but all passwords on the practice's server were immediately changed. Since the portable computers were encrypted, the practice was not required to notify the media of the breach. They did, however, immediately retrain appropriate staff on termination procedures.

Communication is required because the Health Insurance Portability and Accountability Act of 1996 (HIPAA) Security Rule states that a covered entity is required to "[i]dentify and respond to suspected or known security incidents; mitigate, to the extent practicable, harmful effects of security incidents that are known to the covered entity; and document security incidents and their outcomes."[5]

When an event like this happens to you, what would be your practice's mitigation strategy and procedures?

---

[5] Department of Health and Human Services, Office of the Secretary, "45 CFR Parts 160, 162, and 164: Health Insurance Reform: Security Standards; Final Rule," in *Federal Register (Part II)*, v.68, n.34, Thursday, February 20, 2003, pp.8333-8381. Hereinafter, citations are in the format of volume *Federal Register* page, as in this case: 68 *Federal Register* 8377. The American Recovery and Reinvestment Act of 2009, signed by President Obama on February 17, 2009, in the context of *privacy breach*, specifies additional policy and procedure requirements related to a security incident. These requirements are discussed further in Chapter 2 and in Appendix B.

Technology Energizes, Increases Efficiency and Quality, and Presents Different Risks

The sizzle of technology as well as the promise of improved quality and efficiency of care motivate us to get up and running in an electronic environment. Improved efficiency will carry you through a dozen demonstrations, through the interface discussions, and through contract negotiations.

Like most practices, you're eager to get rid of those clunky paper records and bring your practice into a much more cost-effective environment. At some point, the sizzle will morph into real-life operations, and the trained computer users will find comfort in using automation. The benefits are plentiful, but the risks also must be reviewed, balanced, and monitored so that confidential health information is accessible to the right person at the right time.

Computer-related tasks that you perform at home should not be allowed on a laptop connected to electronic protected health information. Laptops must be locked at night, especially in practices in which the nursing staff uses them interchangeably. Failure to account for all laptops during the day puts your health information at risk.

Security and privacy reminders will always be necessary. But reminders tend to be put in place when a policy has been tested or after an unfortunate event takes you down a pathway you hadn't intended to go.

One of the most exciting components of automating your office is that once you get involved in health information technology (HIT), new doors will always be opened to you. Unfortunately, this can then become a new concern. While technology can be captivating, it also puts your practice at some measure of risk because technology will usually be ahead of your policies.[6]

At the base of new technology adoption are good business processes, common sense, and privacy/security rules. Each of these components is addressed in this book. Keep in mind that common sense to a practice owner may not be common sense to an employee. When these rules and processes are put into a policies and procedures manual, your practice's policies (or business rules) serve as the behavioral platform that guides your staff through situations that may be somewhat new to them. These include

- how they can and cannot use the Internet,
- how to manage multiple passwords,
- how and when to access confidential health information,
- how to report an accidental disclosure of health information, and
- how to restore health information after a disaster, and so much more.

See following boxed-texts, which describes a situation and a sample policy and procedures to manage the situation.

---

[6] For a current discussion of this and other issues related to electronic health records, see the March-April 2009, v.28, n2. issue of *Health Affairs,* especially the section entitled: "Stimulating Health IT." *Health Affairs* is published by Project HOPE, and can be accessed at www.healthaffairs.org.

Records Checkout in Paper and Electronic Offices

When old and new technologies are at odds with your implementation process and when the practice owners are trying to make the most of their technology investment, a lack of policies and procedures can trip you up if you haven't spelled out expectations to your clinical and administrative work-force. For example, compare the policy for checking out a medical record in a paper-based practice versus a policy for accessing the same record in a paperless practice.

Records Checkout in a Paper Office

Others may see portions of the medical record while it's checked out, but it can only be physically present at one place at a time. Physicians may feel secure knowing no one else can see the record while it is locked up in the doctor's office. However, the health information necessary for clinical decision-making also is locked up, making assessments and plans nearly impossible to complete, even by the physician, without traveling back to the office to open the record.

Sample policy: It is our practice's policy that the medical records clerk or librarian is the only person who can release a medical record to a clinician.

Sample procedures: In our practice, a nurse, mid-level administrator, or doctor will come to the medical records library, write the patient's name, and then sign and date a log indicating the workforce member who has checked out the record. If the medical record is moved to a new location, the name that appears on our log is the person responsible for tracking and returning the medical record to the library.

Records Checkout in an Electronic Office

In an electronic environment, the patient record can be securely accessed using multiple search criteria. The appropriate user can call up a patient's record using the chart number, the patient's last name, the date of last visit, the patient's Social Security number or other personal identifier, or any combination of these data elements.

When preparing for the next day's visits, the scheduler component of the PMS or EHR module automatically calls up the next day's patient records into the queue. In the electronic office, access is permitted by user authentication built into the system during installation. The authentication typically includes the user's name and unique password or the user's finger image. Because the record is stored in an electronic format, it can be securely accessed via the practice's network from multiple locations. So, in setting up authentication, the policy might read something like this.

Sample policy: Workforce members are responsible for complying with the practice's policies and procedures for accessing confidential patient records, workstations, transactions, programs, processes, or other mechanisms used in the practice.

Sample procedures:

- Our system administrator will grant access so that clinical, administrative, and billing teams each have appropriate access to electronic protected health information.

- Workforce members will be granted access to only the minimum amount of electronic protected health information needed to complete assigned tasks.

- Physicians in our practice will be granted access to all clinical information, including payer information.

- Each member of the workforce will be assigned a unique user ID and an initial password, which the workforce member will change when signing onto the system for the first time.

What are policies and procedures?

You have been following policies and procedures since the day you were born. Someone said to your mother, "Feed the baby every three hours," or "Nurse the baby whenever he's hungry." That's a policy. It tells you what to do.

The procedures are what your mother did to meet the requirements of that policy. A procedure is an efficient way to standardize how something should be done. Wash bottles, measure 3 ounces of water with 2 scoops of formula, and shake well. For bottle-fed babies, the procedure involves more measurements than for nursed babies. A procedure for nursing moms would be to drink plenty of fluids, practice good hygiene, and allow the baby to nurse 15 to 25 minutes on each side. Because measuring fluid intake was quite a bit more complex, nursing mothers may spend a good amount of time guessing what the cries meant. Is the baby getting enough nourishment? Did I eat too much spicy food last night? Should I nurse him again? Is he colicky? While most moms work through multiple indecisions with the first child, they also have built a more trusting relationship with the procedures, learned what worked and what didn't, and can rely on best practices (what worked) and be more comfortable with the procedures with subsequent children.

How to Build Your Policies and Procedures

HIPAA's administrative simplification privacy and security rules provide a solid business infrastructure to categorize policies and procedures according to what needs to be done, define job roles to perform tasks, and establish ways to complete the tasks. You can use these rules to develop your policies and procedures, as described in the following paragraphs.

What to do:

Learn the infrastructure upon which you will build your policies and procedures.

As quoted earlier in this chapter, according to HIPAA's Security Rule, 45 Code of Federal Regulations (CFR) §164.308 (a) (6): A covered entity is required to

> [i]dentify and respond to suspected or known security incidents; mitigate, to the extent practicable, harmful effects of security incidents known to the covered entity; and document security incidents and their outcomes.

According to HIPAA's Privacy Rule, 45 CFR § 164.530 (f),

> [a] covered entity must mitigate, to the extent practicable, any harmful effect that is known to the covered entity of a use or disclosure of protected health information in violation of its policies and procedures or the requirements of this subpart [Administrative Requirements].[7]

Note that the Security Rule covers electronic protected health information, whereas the Privacy Rule covers protected health information that may be in oral, written, or electronic format.[vii]

To comply with the Security and Privacy rules, as a covered entity, you make the decision as to what "the extent practicable" is for each incident. For example, a physician located in an area where tornados are common, such as Oklahoma City, the Texas Panhandle, or Wichita, Kansas, may identify risks that are different from a practice on the tenth floor of a building in New York City.

---

[7] Department of Health and Human Services, Office of the Secretary, "45 CFR Parts 160 and 164: Standards for Privacy of Individually Identifiable Health Information; Final Rule," in *Federal Register (Part V)*, v.67, n.157, Wednesday, August 14, 2002, pp. 53182–53273. The quotation is at 67 *Federal Register* 53272. We discuss privacy further in Chapter 2 and Appendix B.

"To the extent practicable" applies to reasonableness and scalability as key factors in determining security methods and measures to be implemented. In your risk analysis, identify vulnerabilities that compromise the confidentiality, integrity, and availability of health information. Note the following:

- Confidentiality. Measures you will take to ensure health information is not made available or disclosed to unauthorized persons or processes.

- Integrity. Measures you will take to ensure health information has not been altered or destroyed in an unauthorized manner.

- Availability. Measures you will take to ensure health information is accessible and usable upon demand by an authorized person.

In addition to HIPAA's privacy and security rules, the Patriot Act, portions of the Sarbanes–Oxley Act of 2002, the information security document published by the National Institute of Standards and Technology (NIST)[8], the Federal Trade Commission's (FTC) Red Flag Rule, and certain provisions of the Health Information Technology for Economic and Clinical Health Act (HITECH Act) that was enacted as part of the American Recovery and Reinvestment Act on February 17, 2009[9], now influence how you protect confidential health information. Each of these documents was considered when building the policies and procedures in this manual.

---

[8] US Department of Commerce/National Institute of Standards and Technology. *"An Introductory Resource Guide for Implementing the Health Insurance Portability and Accountability Act (HIPAA) Security Rule."* NIST Special Publication 800-66, Revision 1. October 2008. Available online at: http://csrc.nist.gov/publications/nistpubs/800-66-Rev1/SP-800-66-Revision1.pdf.

[9] See pp. 144–165: Subtitle D–Privacy, of the *American Recovery and Reinvestment Act of 2009*, which is available online in portable document format (pdf) at http://frwebgate.access.gpo.gov/cgi-bin/getdoc.cgi?dbname=111_cong_bills&docid=f:h1enr.pdf. We discuss provisions of Subtitle D–Privacy in Chapter 2 and Appendix B.

How to do it:

1. Research the framework, privacy, and security mandates that support your practice's policies and procedures.

2. The best way to research this is to read the final privacy and security rules that serve as the baseline for safeguarding confidential health information. Copies of those rules, as published in the *Federal Register* are available at www.hhs.gov/ocr/privacy/hipaa/administrative/index.html.

3. The Privacy Rule that safeguards electronic, oral, and written protected health information has been modified by the HITECH Act, which is available in Appendix B, but the policies and procedures included in this manual accommodate and complement those modifications. Further, states may continue to adopt more stringent privacy rules related to protection of health information.[10]

4. Computer security guidelines, incident management reports, guides to mobile computing, guides to encryption, security testing, and many other topics can be found at http://csrc.nist.gov/publications/PubsSPs.html.

5. Refer to Table A-1 in Appendix A. As you review each safeguard standard, you'll notice that some are required, while others are addressable.

6. You must comply with a required standard, to the extent practicable.

---

[10] A useful resource for checking privacy rules in the state where your practice is located is on the National Conference of State Legislatures (NCSL) HIPAA Resource page: "Impacts and actions by states—Medical record privacy, security and electronic transactions." This site is available online at: www.ncsl.org/programs/health/hipaa.htm. For an example of more stringent state privacy requirements, see Jaikumar Vijayan, "New health-care privacy laws heighten need for HIPAA compliance in California: Schwarzenegger signs two data privacy bills that use the federal HIPAA law as a baseline," *Computerworld*, Oct. 7, 2008. This article is available online via web link at the referenced NCSL web site.

7. An addressable standard is usually more complex than a required standard. Addressable does not mean optional. Rather, it means you must use a decision tree to evaluate how it will apply to your practice. See sample decision tree in Figure 1-1.

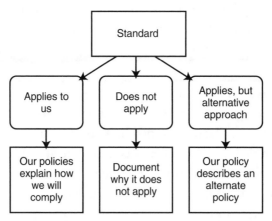

Figure 1-1 Compiance Decision Tree For An Addressable Standard

8. Conduct a risk analysis, sometimes called a gap analysis. A risk analysis helps you identify gaps in your policies and procedures in which a problem might arise. You cannot provide a detailed plan for every risk but you can identify and assess probabilities of risks likely to occur, based on previous events (fire, theft or vandalism, weather).

9. You cannot build your policies and procedures without first understanding where your risks lie. Your policies and procedures are built to protect your practice from those risks. In developing policies and procedures, you establish a road map that defines how you will mitigate outcomes if a security incident or privacy breach occurs. Judgment is required. For example, an audit trail will identify whose records have been downloaded to a laptop. If a laptop is stolen, you, as a covered entity, will determine how to mitigate the damage.

10. Several organizations make risk analysis outlines available for their members, including WEDI, NCHICA, as do several state health information technology associations. A sample risk analysis for a physician practice is available in Appendix A.

11. If you plan to participate in ePrescribing, you must assess the risks involved in prescribing and determine the following:

   (i) degree of confidence you have in the individual(s) ordering an ePrescription,

   (ii) degree of confidence that the person filing the prescription is the person identified in (i), and

   (iii) degree of confidence that the ePrescribing message was sent securely.

CRITICAL POINT

The risk analysis is at the heart of your policies and procedures for electronic protected health information. Your policies and procedures are built from your documented analysis of risks, including vulnerabilities and threats.

---

12. In complying with one standard, you also are likely to comply with several other standards at the same time. Rather than rewriting the policy in multiple formats, a cross-reference checklist of the process flow, *At A Glance* chart in Appendix A, is included to help you build on what may already be in place.

Seven Layers of a Policy and Procedure

The NIST has compiled years of empirical findings to determine how well the HIPAA administrative simplification standards are adhered to and how tools for compliance have evolved. Not surprisingly, its findings indicate that policies and procedures are ineffective without continual training, reminders, and sanctions. Findings also indicate that the benefits and outcomes of functioning policies and procedures result in improved communication and trust to improve employee performance.

With fairness and equity at the center of every policy and procedure, NIST has identified the following seven layers of a policy and accompanying procedures:

1. Writing

2. Reviewing and rewriting

3. Distributing and acknowledging

4. Ownership

5. Training and support

6. Testing

7. Measurements: knowing whether, when, or how to amend.

What to do:

Write policies and procedures that are easy to understand and also fit the roles of those people affected by them. Obtain buy-in from your workforce members so that they take ownership of the policies and procedures, then schedule recurring training sessions.

How to do it:

1. The privacy and security officials must take ownership of policies and procedures.

2. Allow members of the workforce to participate in the risk analysis, and in the design and content of your policies and procedures. Provide each with privacy, security, and other standards that are either required or addressable. Workforce member participation will be most useful in helping your practice define "reasonableness and scalability."

3. Ask workforce members to document why they believe a policy or procedure is or is not reasonable and scalable.

4. Write a policy and outline procedures that should be in place, not necessarily how processes work now. In adopting electronic medical record software, your policies will likely need to be updated to reflect new workflows and guidelines for health information exchange.

5. If you are transitioning into an electronic environment, your implementation consultant should map out your current paper-based workflows and compare them to the proposed electronic environment workflows.

6. Study the workflows and redesign them for the electronic environment.

7. Review and rewrite the policy and procedures.

8. Send the policy and procedures to department heads and ask them to review and respond. Each department leader may in turn ask for feedback from the workforce; this is a strategy that leads to better adoption of procedures. In a smaller practice, each individual may want to review a section of the policy and procedures that most closely relates to the workforce member's work.

9. Upon receiving the reviewed policy, analyze which revisions can be included and still safeguard protected health information processes identified in your risk analysis.

10. Distribute the policies and procedures and obtain written acknowledgment that they have been received.

11. Schedule departmental meetings and present the policies and procedures to the workforce. Include volunteers who handle confidential health information in the policies and procedures training and acknowledgment process.

12. Obtain a signed acknowledgment that the workforce member has received the policies and procedures and understands what they say.

13. Provide a physical location for the policies and procedures, whether they are in a three-ring notebook or on your Intranet, so that workforce members can easily access them.

CRITICAL POINT

Obtain written acknowledgment that each workforce member has received the policies and procedures and understands what they say.

Training and Support

1. Present the policies and procedures at an attendance-mandatory session in a way that engages the workforce's attention. This can be during a monthly "lunch and learn" with food and drinks provided or it can be during an in-service training. Do not expect compliance with policies and procedures if the workforce is not physically present for training.

2. After presenting the policies and procedures, solicit questions from attendees and document any objection or refusal to accept the policies and procedures, as well as the reason for refusal, which may include religious, gender, or race concerns.

3. Attendees must sign an acknowledgment that they have received training and were given an opportunity to participate in the development of the policies and procedures.

4. Recognize that your policies and procedures will be tested.

5. Policies and procedures are equalizers. They apply to everyone in the workforce, including management and your volunteers.

6. It bears repeating: your policies and procedures will be tested. When that happens, your policies and procedures serve as a point of reference. You can say, "Let's look up the policy to see what it says."

7. Policies and procedures come with sanctions or consequences. Workforce members who don't show up for work without cause may lose their jobs. And persons who access protected health information records that they are not authorized to see violate patient privacy.

8. Sanctions must be implementable to everyone on the workforce, from the doctor's favorite mid-level clinician to the front office receptionist, in-house pharmacist, lab director, and practice manager. Possible sanctions may include

   a. First offense: oral warning and reminder

   b. Second offense: oral warning and scheduled training

   c. Third offense: oral and written warning inserted into the staff's personnel file

   d. Fourth offense: time off without pay

   e. Fifth offense: release from duties inside the practice

9. You may have more or less patience with your staff, but sanctions that exist in most physician practices are a result of implementing the HIPAA Privacy Rule. Confer with the practice's privacy official to ensure sanctions protecting the security of electronic protected health information do not conflict.

In 2001, the Earnhardt Family Protection Act, named for NASCAR legend Dale Earnhardt, made autopsy photographs, video, and audio recordings confidential. Violators of the act could be charged with a third-degree felony, punishable by jail time and up to a $5,000 fine. The act, which was quickly drafted to prevent the media from obtaining post-accident photographs, was upheld in 2007 when media and curious hospital workers sought access to Anna Nicole Smith's autopsy and photos.[11]

Palisades Medical Center in North Bergen, New Jersey, investigated 40 workforce members and suspended 27 of them for a month without pay for allegedly accessing George Clooney's protected health information without authorization.[12]

"When a clear violation is established, the level of punishment will likely depend on one's employer," according to Reece Hirsch, a partner in the San Francisco office of the law firm of Sonnenschein Nath & Rosenthal LLP. Hirsch said the industry is divided as to what are sufficient sanctions.

He recalls asking some 300 privacy professionals at a conference whether they would terminate individuals who were caught improperly accessing protected health information or just discipline the workers. "About half of them said they would terminate individuals for (the breach), about half said they would discipline them," he says. "It all depends on the circumstances."[13]

In March 2008, 13 employees of the UCLA Medical Center were suspended for snooping in the confidential medical records of Britney Spears when she was hospitalized. An additional six physicians also faced discipline for peeking at her computerized records.[14]

---

[11] Williams, David E., "'Dale Earnhardt law' may shield Smith autopsy photos," posted 11:29 PM EST, Feb. 9, 2007, CNN.

[12] "27 suspended for Clooney file peek," Story reported on CNN, Wednesday, October 10, 2007.

[13] Report on patient privacy, reprinted in *Health Business Today,* Nov. 19, 2007.

[14] Ornstein, Charles. "UCLA workers snooped in Spears' medical records." *Los Angeles Times,* March 15, 2008. Available online at: http://articles.latimes.com/2008/mar/15/local/me-britney15.

Privacy violations caught the attention of Governor Schwarzenegger when hospital employees snooped in patient files, including those of California's First Lady, Maria Shriver. As a result, the governor created a new state Office of Health Information Integrity with power to review security plans and violations and assess fines of up to $250,000 against violators of patient privacy.[15]

10. Measure before amending. Know when, how, and why you are making an amendment.

11. A general rule of thumb is that if the same policy and procedures are tested more than three times by different people, it's time to take a look at the policy to see if it needs to be updated or revised.

12. Policies also will need to be amended if any of the following occur:

    a. Your practice is merging with another practice or acquired by a health care system.

    b. Your practice needs to implement policies for managing and safeguarding identified and de-identified information if your practice engages in clinical research or engages researchers to do so.

13. One of the by-products of quality improvement and error management is to impose new workflow procedures that may adversely impact what your practice is trying to accomplish. The benefit of electronic medical record software is that it can standardize the technical aspects of your business processes (workflows). You will want to evaluate whether new regulations outdate your existing policies.

---

[15] Paddock, Catherine. Schwarzenegger calls for stronger privacy of medical records. *Los Angeles Times,* April 8, 2008, reprinted in *Medical News Today,* www.medicalnewstoday. com/articles/103098.php. Also, see reference to new California privacy laws related to HIPAA in footnote 10 in this chapter.

14. New technology changes the way you do business. For example, when privacy and security mandates were first released, biometric tools such as finger-image authentication were not nearly as mature and affordable as they are now. Today, the physician's finger can act as the authentication tool and essentially "sit on top" of the user ID and password.[16]

Health IT Security Rule Attributes

Ten key attributes of the HIPAA Administrative Simplification Security Rule are listed below. Each workforce member in your practice should have a working knowledge of the terms in italics, because these are key components of your policies and procedures regarding the safeguarding of electronic health information in your practice. In addition, the HITECH Act that was enacted as part of the American Recovery and Reinvestment Act of 2009, and signed into law by President Obama on February 17, 2009, requires that your business associates comply with the Security Rule beginning on February 17, 2010. This is discussed further in the next chapter and in Appendix B.

---

[16] Effective Jan. 1, 2007, the Deficit Reduction Act of 2005 (DRA) was amended to strengthen protections regarding fraud and abuse with respect to Medicaid billings. Later in 2007, the federal Office of the National Coordinator of Health Information Technology (ONC) recommended to the electronic health record (EHR) certifying authority, the Certification Commission for Health Information Technology (CCHIT), that the CCHIT adopt requirements for EHRs that "require capability to capture a unique physical patient identifier, such as a photo or a biometric in the EHR and capture means used by a practice to validate identification by **2009**; and demonstrate in the EHR system the ability to support biometrics or tokens as the minimum e-authentication level in **2010**." See www.cchit.org/files/certification/08/Ambulatory/CCHITCriteriaAMBULATORY08FINAL.pdf.

1. The Security Rule is a set of standards and implementation specifications with which the practice as a covered entity must comply by federal law.

2. The Security Rule standards are always required for compliance by your practice, while implementation specifications can be required or addressable.

3. The Security Rule is scalable, taking into consideration the size of your practice, and flexible, taking into consideration the structure of the practice, costs of security measures, and probability and criticality of potential risks.

4. The Security Rule is reasonable and permits the practice to implement security safeguards that are appropriate.

5. The Security Rule is built on key principles of availability, confidentiality, and integrity of patients' health information.

6. The Security Rule is technology neutral: the choice of protection measures (inputs) is up to the practice as long as the safeguard performance measures (outputs) are achieved.

7. The Security Rule is based on risk analysis and mitigation of risk: identifying potential vulnerabilities in and threats to the practice and taking risk avoidance measures.

8. The Security Rule is built on a foundation of safeguarding electronic protected health information, so maintaining the availability of electricity is a key factor.

9. The Security Rule formalizes many of the policies and procedures that you likely use in your practice today.

10. The Security Rule is an investment in the future of your practice as a successful business.

Use the Action Plan here to begin assigning tasks to members of your security teams. Perform a weekly follow-up on the status of each assignment.

| TABLE 1-1 | Health Information Management Security Action Plan |

Task	Person Responsible	Date Completed
Practice Managers read Executive Summary, Chapters 1 and 2 of this book	PM	
1. Build Your Security Team	SO/PO	
Appoint a HIPAA Security Official (SO)	PM	
Appoint a HIPAA Security Team	SO + PM	
Read the Security Rule (in the Appendix)	SO + PO	
Make a list of how electronic protected health information is used, stored, or transmitted	SO + Team + OM	
Divide administrative, physical and technical sections into workgroups	SO	
Read assigned chapters in detail and other chapters in general		
Determine budget	SO + PM	
2. Determine Your Risk	SO + TEAM	
Conduct a risk assessment.	SO + PO + Team	
Assess and record vulnerabilities and threats.	SO	
Identify whether you already have a policy or procedure for each security feature	SO, OM	
Identify and prioritize measures to reduce risks.	SO	
Develop a budget to manage risks.	SO	

Task	Person Responsible	Date Completed
3. Develop a Plan	SO + Team	
Review Security Standards Matrix to determine tasks and resources you need to become HIPAA compliant.		
Determine a timetable for plan development and review		
Ask vendors about security features included in your information system	SO + OM	
4. Develop Policies and Procedures	SO + Team	
Document how you plan to implement each security standard	SO	
Study and evaluate budget as you evaluate specifications	SO	
Include sanctions, but be realistic about those sanctions.	SO	
Identify security controls to meet policy requirements. Discuss technical safeguards with vendors	SO + PM + Vendor	
5. Implement Administrative, Physical and Technical Controls	SO	
Plan enough time to install, test and certify any vendor upgrades	SO + Vendor	
Document procedures, develop necessary forms to accompany new controls	SO + Team	
Manage budget through implementation	SO	

continued next page

TABLE 1-1	Health Information Management Security Action Plan—continued

Task	Person Responsible	Date Completed
6. Develop and Present Security Training, Awareness and Ongoing Reminders	SO	
Provide all staff with security awareness training	SO	
Determine who needs specific training and at what level	SO	
Develop an ongoing security reminder plan.	SO	
7. Develop an Ongoing Monitoring Process	SO	
Determine how often you will conduct regular audits. Conduct audits when an incident occurs and as required by your policies.	SO	
Integrate privacy complaints and security incidents when appropriate.	SO + PO	
Monitor regulations and changes	SO + PO	
Refer to the Security Rule when you have questions.	SO	

Reproduced with permission from: Carolyn Hartley. *Physician's eHealth Report*. Cary, North Carolina: J Merrill Publishing; April 2005: Vol 2(3):p9.

OM indicates office manager; PM, practice manager; PO, privacy official; SO, security official.

Implementing a Security Plan

Use the Security Plan here to begin assigning tasks to members of your security teams. Perform a weekly follow-up on the status of each assignment.

TABLE 1-2 | Sample Risk Assessment Results and Overview of Mitigation Strategies

Risk/Mitigation	Level	Owner
Risk: Portable computers taken out of the practice **Mitigation:** Laptops are encrypted. All laptops/tablets must be accounted for at the end of each day. Encrypted laptops/tablets must be signed out before removed from the premises.	5	\<Name\>
Risk: Significant investment in information systems in last 2 years **Mitigation:** Protect with new procedures and consistently enforce safeguards to protect systems.	4	\<Name\>
Risk: Vendors have access to ePHI. These include \<PM System\>, \<EHR\>, \<lab\>, \<pharmacy\>, and \<other\>. **Mitigation:** Each has signed a business associate's agreement stored in the security official's office.	3	\<Name\>
Risk: Information system activity review **Mitigation:** Security team will authorize user privileges and conduct information system activity reviews at least weekly for the first six months. Thereafter, at least biweekly, as appropriate.	4	\<Name\>
Risk: Access – Volunteers may include being patients who have access to ePHI. **Mitigation:** Volunteers trained in privacy and security policies and procedures.	3	\<Name\>

continued next page

TABLE 1-2	Sample Risk Assessment Results and Overview of Mitigation Strategies—continued

Risk/Mitigation	Level	Owner
Risk: Not all supervisors address sanctions using the same procedures. **Mitigation:** Physicians will determine sanctions and implement sanctions as consistently as reasonably possible.	4	\<Name\>
Risk: Lack of written job descriptions **Mitigation:** Job descriptions will be written and developed for each position.	3	\<Name\>
Risk: Access to ePHI **Mitigation:** Establish minimum necessary standards and assign them to each workforce member role. Establish exceptions and explain why.	4	\<Name\>
Risk: Malicious software **Mitigation:** All software must be reviewed and approved by the security official or other security administrative member before it can be installed.	3	\<Name\>
Risk: Review of workforce member access to ePHI. **Mitigation:** Periodically, and upon promotion or new assignment of duties, the owners of this risk will evaluate the workforce member access to ePHI.	3	\<name\>
Risk: Security training **Mitigation:** Once each year, train all users on policies and procedures. Develop monthly security reminders.	4	\<Name\>
Risk: System access **Mitigation:** Train users on what to do if they cannot access the system.	3	\<Name\>

Risk/Mitigation	Level	Owner
Risk: Disaster recovery	4	\<Name\>
Mitigation: Disaster recovery plan filed with security official, with supervisors informed of location of written document and their duties for executing plan in event of disaster. Supervisors trained on how to access and protect ePHI in the event of a disaster. Identified threats as fire, theft, earthquake, electrical surges or outages, acts of God.		
Risk: Contingency Plan	3	\<Name\>

Mitigation: Physicians have reciprocal agreements with local practices to treat patients in the event of a significant disaster.
 	
\<Name\> has unique security user ID to be used in emergency.
 	
Staff trained on contingency plan, which resides in written form with security official and also can be retrieved electronically.
 	
Call list is in place.
  1) (Practice administrator) first to be contacted.
  2) Practice administrator calls lead physician, director of nursing, head nurses, department heads.
  3) Each contacts respective members of their clinical and administrative teams.		

Risk: Use of workstations and Internet access	4	\<Name\>
Mitigation: All users are trained on appropriate use of workstations. Sanctions in place for violations, especially written display of password or sharing of password with another workforce member.		

continued next page

TABLE 1-2	Sample Risk Assessment Results and Overview of Mitigation Strategies—continued

Risk/Mitigation	Level	Owner
Risk: Device and media controls **Mitigation:** Training on hardware and software reuse, destroying content on hard drives before donating to schools, elsewhere.	3	\<Name\>
Risk: Password sharing **Mitigation:** Training on use of passwords and sanctions for violations of written display of password or sharing of password with another workforce member.	3	\<Name\>
Risk: Email **Mitigation:** Training on appropriate use of emails containing ePHI. Sanctions on access to email through unsecure open Internet providers.	5	\<Name\>
Risk: ePrescribing **Mitigation:** Use tamper-proof/forge resistant prescription pads, verify ePrescribing certification of our EMR vendor; assure prescribers are who they say they are by using a user ID and password, digital signature, biometric tool, or all of the above; ensure security policies and procedures and sanctions for misuse of paper or electronic prescriptions are strictly enforced.	5	\<Name\>
Risk: Mistaken identity **Mitigation:** Digital signatures must accompany incoming and outgoing encrypted transmissions involving electronic protected health information.		

To implement a security plan in your practice, you must first conduct a risk analysis. Your entire implementation plan is built on the risks you identify and analyze in your practice. To conduct a risk analysis, delegate one person with responsibility to get the risk analysis moving. Because one of the required standards is that you assign a security official, this is a good place to start.

Step 1: Assign a Security Official

You'll notice the first policy in this chapter is to assign the lead person in managing the security of protected electronic health information. A security official will spend 80 percent of the time managing people and 20 percent managing technical components, usually working alongside information technology vendors. Your security official must work closely with the privacy official (often it's the same person, particularly in a small practice) so that security policies and procedures do not conflict with privacy policies and procedures already in place. In many practices, the office manager serves in both positions.

Step 2: Conduct a Risk Analysis

This is the heart of your security plan. If you are a small practice, engage everyone in the office in the risk analysis, and include vendors, business associates, and practice managers. For large practices, engage one person from each area as well as business associates, if necessary.

Step 3: Develop Policies and Procedures

After each standard's implementation specification, you'll find sample policies and procedures that you can use as reference guides. They are also available in PDF and Microsoft® Word documents in the enclosed CD-ROM. These policies and procedures are for demonstration purposes only and are not to be construed in any way as legal opinion.[17] If a patient believes someone in your practice has exposed protected health information to an unauthorized source, and he or she files a complaint, your required written policies and procedures are likely to be referenced and evaluated to ensure you are following them.

Do not adopt these policies and procedures as your own without first ensuring that you and your staff can live with the decisions you've put into writing. Undoubtedly, you will want to customize those policies and procedures for your practice.

Step 4: Provide Security Awareness and Training

The Security Rule requires you to provide periodic security updates; put procedures in place that guard against, detect, and report malicious software; monitor failed login attempts; and develop procedures for creating, changing, and safeguarding passwords.

As you read through the policies and procedures, we have tried to simplify the technology and make the implementation process as clear as possible for you. You may decide to engage a technology consultant at some point, but after reading this book, you'll have specific reasons for that engagement.

---

[17] Make sure that your practice's corporate attorney reviews your policies and procedures when they are initiated and if they are later modified. Remember, the Security Rule covers electronic protected health information only, while the Privacy Rule covers protected health information in electronic, oral, and written forms. Also, your state may have *more stringent* privacy provisions regarding the safeguarding of protected health information.

Summary

Your administrative policies and procedures set the framework for how you will develop or revise your existing policies. Most practices built policies and procedures when the HIPAA Privacy Rule was first implemented in April 2003. You will have to dust off those policies and revisit them as you move into your electronic environment.

For example, "access" generally means the same thing in both a paper and electronic environment, but the procedures are very different. In a paper record, your access is limited as much by the honor system as it is by who allows you to view the record and its present location. In an electronic environment, the system administrator establishes access, which is controlled by your assigned user ID and password, with access tracked via audit trail.

Build your policies and procedures after first conducting a risk analysis that identifies how you will protect the confidentiality, integrity, and availability of confidential health information to the extent practicable.

Sample procedures: Our practice designated <Name(s)> to be our Privacy and/or Security Official supported by our practice compliance team. The compliance team reports to <Name>, who is the practice's administrator. Members of the compliance team with designated administrative, privacy, and security duties may include:

<Name>

<Name>

<Name>

<Also, suggest head nurses <Name> and <Name>

<Other department heads (lab, pharmacy, imaging)>

Our compliance officer will delegate tasks and responsibilities but is ultimately responsible for protecting the confidentiality of protected health information. His/Her key responsibilities include:

- preparing and managing the budget allocated to the management of our privacy and security activities

- maintaining an up-to-date inventory of hardware and software

- developing and implementing policies, procedures, and guidelines to direct and carry out the objectives of our security program, including policies and procedures that govern:

  - ensuring the privacy and security of protected health information

  - implementing security risk management

  - performing security administration

  - ensuring security of the computer network, servers, and wireless networks

  - ensuring security of personal computers and portable computer devices

  - providing physical security

  - developing and implementing a disaster recovery program

  - developing an ongoing privacy and security awareness training program

  - researching and recommending new security measures for the practice

  - maintaining documentation regarding levels of access granted to each information system user, reviewing those levels periodically, and revising access as roles and duties change within the practice

  - investigating, responding to, and remedying privacy breaches and security incidents

- documenting and maintaining system authorization records
- supervising vendor personnel or business associates who perform technical system maintenance activities and ensuring that they have received training on our policies as they relate to their involvement in our practice.

All new technology will be presented to the compliance official for approval and for the security team to evaluate the impact to our system's integrity. Any new software must comply with the applicable policies and procedures of our practice.

Risk Analysis		
Safeguard: Administrative	*Federal Register*	Required/Addressable
Security management process	68 *Federal Register* 8377 45 CFR 164.308 (a)(1)(ii)(A)	Required

Requirement: Conduct an accurate and thorough assessment of the potential risks and vulnerabilities to the confidentiality, integrity, and availability of electronic protected health information held by the covered entity.

Sample policy: Our practice conducted a risk analysis before we implemented electronic health records. We will review that risk analysis at least every six months, and after that whenever a new regulation affecting the practice requires compliance.

Sample procedures: We modified the risk analysis provided for us in the appendix of the Policies and Procedures for the Electronic Medical Office, as the framework for evaluating our administrative, physical, and technical risks. We also reviewed NIST documentation.[19] Because we process credit and debit

---

[19] US Department of Commerce/National Institute of Standards and Technology. "An Introductory Resource Guide for Implementing the Health Insurance Portability and Accountability Act (HIPAA) Security Rule." NIST Special Publication 800-66, Revision 1. October 2008. Available online at: http://csrc.nist.gov/publications/nistpubs/800-66-Rev1/SP-800-66-Revision1.pdf.

cards, our risk analysis included payment card industry (PCI) data security standards (DSS)[20] and Federal Trade Commission (FTC) identity-theft prevention and detection "red flags" rules.[21]

We examined technical and nontechnical systems, including:

- hardware and software in use in the practice
- system interfaces inside and outside of the practice
- electronic systems for creating, storing, and transmitting data by our practice
- how business associates access our systems
- PCI security standards
- how identity is treated and protected in our systems

---

[20] All entities that transmit, process, or store payment card data must be compliant with PCI DDS. The new Data Security Standard Version 1.2 is effective Oct. 1, 2008. See the PCI Quick Reference Guide: Understanding the Payment Card Industry, Data Security Standard 1.2, published by the PCI Security Standards Council™ and available online at www.pcisecuritystandards.org/pdfs/pci_ssc_quick_guide.pdf. The security standards are outlined in Chapter 2.

[21] These rules apply to "creditors," which health care providers are deemed to be if they allow "deferred payment for services, including when hospitals establish payment plans for patients unable to pay their bills or even when physician practices and hospitals collect billing information and copayments and then bill patients later for the balance they owe." The FTC issued its ruling in November 2007, but deferred enforcement until May 1, 2009, to clarify the ruling and provide guidance to affected entities. See Gregg Blesch, "Yellow flags on 'red flags' rule," *Modern Healthcare*, Oct. 27, 2008, and FTC, "FTC Will Grant Six-Month Delay of Enforcement of 'Red Flags' Rule Requiring Creditors and Financial Institutions to Have Identity Theft Programs," Press Release, Oct. 22, 2008. Available online at: www.ftc.gov/opa/2008/10/ redflags.shtm. The FTC announced a second compliance date delay of three months on Friday, May 1, 2009, making the new compliance date August 1, 2009. Then, the FTC issued on July 31, 2009, a third delay for 90 days until November 1, 2009. These delays were to give affected entitites more time to develop and implement written identity theft prevention policies and procedures for compliance with the rule, which are based on enabling regulations of provisions in the Fair and Accurate Credit Transactions Act of 2003. Please visit the FTC Web site at www.ftc.gov for further updates. The identify-theft prevention and detection "red flags" rules are outlined in Chapter 2.

- ePrescribing capabilities of our EMR vendor, including certification
- biometric authentication capabilities of our EMR vendor and our practice's ability to use authentication tools.

We also analyzed our weaknesses in practice workflow and procedures, and consulted prior risk analysis reports, audit comments, security requirements, and results of security tests prior to completing our policies and procedures.

We identified any history of attacks to our practice, including those caused by natural disasters, disgruntled employees, water damage, electrical outages, and viruses, and evaluated the possible motivation, threat capacity, and current controls in place to offset and manage the impact of the attacks that occurred. Our findings are included in our risk analysis report.

We then rated the likelihood of each risk, including potential contingencies and potential disasters, on a scale of 1 to 5, with 1 being least likely and 5 being highly likely, and developed steps to mitigate the future likelihood of any potential risks that received a 4 or 5 rating.

We assigned one person to be the owner of each potential risk that exceeded a level 3 rating. For example, in migrating risk to an electronic medical record with an in-house lab, our security official owns the task of ensuring that the vendor's software will not hinder or harm information stored in our practice management system. All workforce members must seek the security official's permission before installing any new software.

A record of findings, risk owners, and mitigation procedures is filed with the system administrator and the security official.

Our policies and procedures were developed as a result of the risks we discovered in our risk analysis and the need to control and mitigate those risks.

Sanction Policy		
Safeguard: Administrative	*Federal Register*	Required/Addressable
Security management process	68 *Federal Register* 8377 45 CFR 164.308 (a)(1)(ii)(C)	Required

Requirement: Apply appropriate sanctions against workforce members who fail to comply with the security policies and procedures of the covered entity.

Sample policy: Our practice has implemented a security sanction policy to safeguard confidential health information in oral, written, and electronic forms. Workforce members are responsible for complying with the practice's policies and procedures. Failure to do so may result in disciplinary action, up to and including termination of employment.

Sample procedures: All workforce members will receive training on our policies and procedures prior to adoption of new policies or modification of existing policies.

As part of new employee orientation, all new workforce members will participate in a minimum 1-hour one-on-one policies and procedures training session with our privacy and security officials.

Sanctions on failure to comply with our policies and procedures are as follows:

1. Upon first noncompliant event, the workforce member's supervisor and one member of the physician staff will have a private conversation with the workforce member and review the appropriate policy and procedure to be certain the workforce member understands the policy.

2. Upon the second noncompliant event, the supervisor and office administrator will have a private conversation with the workforce member, and a letter of remediation will be placed in the employee's personnel file.

3. Upon the third noncompliant event for the same activity, the workforce member will be sent home for 3 days without pay.

4. Upon the fourth noncompliant event, the workforce member will be terminated as an employee.

Information System Activity Review

Safeguard: Administrative	*Federal Register*	Required/Addressable
Security management process	68 *Federal Register* 8377 45 CFR 164.308 (a)(1)(ii)(D)	Required

Requirement: Implement procedures to regularly review records of information system activity, such as audit logs, access reports, and security incident tracking reports.

Some patients in our practice are high-profile members of the community and others are workforce members of the practice, so we identified this as a level 4 risk for our practice. <Name> has been assigned as the owner of this policy.

Sample policy: Our practice will safeguard electronic protected health information and regularly review records of information activity, such as audit trails, system logs, access reports, and security incident tracking reports, for inappropriate use. Our practice does not accept unauthorized snooping or peeking into any patient's medical records, regardless of their public or private status. We will impose sanctions on any workforce member who violates this policy.

Sample procedures: Each supervisor is responsible for overseeing compliance of our practice policies and procedures by regularly reviewing records of information system activity for inappropriate use. Failure to do so may result in disciplinary action according to the practice's sanction policies and procedures.

Our practice has implemented audit control mechanisms to record and examine system activity, identify suspect data activities, and respond to potential system vulnerabilities.

Our practice maintains audit trails and activity logs of system logins, file accesses, and security incidents that pertain to the practice's critical application systems and any system written by a contractor, vendor, or workforce member.

At a minimum, supervisors will review audit logs at least monthly, with preference for twice monthly, and at any unannounced time.

Authorization and/or Supervision

Safeguard: Administrative	*Federal Register*	Required/Addressable
Workforce security	68 *Federal Register* 8377 45 CFR 164.308 (a)(3)(ii)(A)	Addressable

Requirement: Implement policies and procedures to ensure that all workforce members have appropriate access to confidential health information and to prevent those workforce members who do not have access from obtaining it.

Sample policy: Our practice will authorize access to protected electronic health information according to the roles within the practice. We also will supervise workforce members who have access to confidential health information in oral, written, and electronic form, regardless of its location and how it is accessed.

Because several of our physicians take laptops, tablets, personal data assistants, and other portable devices containing confidential health information out of the practice each evening, this is a level 5 risk for us, and <Name> is assigned ownership to manage this safeguard measure.

Sample procedures: In our risk analysis, we developed a checklist of risks associated with physicians, nurses, and mid-level front-office and back-office workforce members. We will update that checklist at least on a yearly basis. The checklist is stored in the security official's office.

After completing the checklist and role-based analysis, our practice tied levels of authorization to job responsibilities and specified levels of authorization in job descriptions of workforce members.

Physicians have been granted authorization to all clinical documentation. Other clinicians within our practice, including nurses and mid-level workforce members, may have access to physician orders, such as labs, pharmacy, imaging, as well as other components within the medical record. They also may have access to health plan payer information in order to identify a private or public health plan payer as it relates to the delivery of care to a beneficiary.

Nonphysician caregivers do not have access to individual patient financial details. Only physicians who are practice owners, the practice administrator, and billing staff may have access to the patient's financial details.

At the end of each day, all laptops will be accounted for. This policy is described in detail in our physical safeguards.

The security official will ensure that each member of the workforce is trained and understands these responsibilities.

Workforce Clearance Procedures

Safeguard: Administrative	*Federal Register*	Required/Addressable
Workforce security	68 *Federal Register* 8377 45 CFR 164.308 (a)(3)(ii)(B)	Addressable

Requirement: Determine that the access of a workforce member to confidential health information is appropriate.

Sample policy: At the security official's discretion, a background check may be authorized for any new employee or existing workforce member who engages in activities that cause the security official to question clearances. This is a level 3 risk for us. Our practice administrator is assigned the owner of this risk.

Sample procedures: In our risk analysis, our practice analyzed job responsibilities of workforce members. We incorporated those responsibilities into job descriptions as a prerequisite for issuing clearance to access electronic protected health information.

As part of our hiring procedures, we will:

- require a written application for employment
- require written proof of citizenship or resident alien status
- confirm prior employment history
- request professional/personal references and contact those references
- confirm educational history and practicing credentials
- verify licenses
- verify candidate's compliance history with any regulatory or medical requirements relevant to employment
- conduct a criminal background check using a consulting service
- confirm application statements, as appropriate.

Our practice also will require that workforce members provide and maintain the practice with up-to-date written documentation for:

- federal and state tax withholding
- Social Security number
- any change in immigration status if not a US citizen.

Each new employee will meet with the security official, who will provide an in-person or online training session on the policies and procedures and ask the new employee to sign a document acknowledging his or her understanding of the policies and procedures, along with notice on where written and electronic versions of the policies and procedures can be found for personal reference.

Each new employee will be assigned a workforce member as a "buddy" for 6 months, to whom he or she can go to with questions on internal policies and procedures. If the buddy cannot answer a particular question definitively, the new employee and the workforce buddy should go to the security official for clarification.

Our security official or system administrator will document all assigned clearances (such as password, building entrance pass, and office key) with each workforce member, as appropriate. Each workforce member will sign a receipt acknowledging receipt of clearances and immediately inform the security official of any change in job responsibilities.

The security official will cancel immediately any clearances upon notification to a workforce member that his or her employment is terminated.

Termination Procedures

Safeguard: Administrative	*Federal Register*	Required/Addressable
Workforce security	68 *Federal Register* 8377 45 CFR 164.308 (a)(3)(ii)(C)	Addressable

Requirement: Terminate access to confidential health information when the employment of a workforce member ends or as required by determinations made as part of our workforce clearance procedures.

Sample policy: It is our practice's policy to make every effort to preserve the relationship between employee and employer. We also acknowledge that there may be voluntary and involuntary reasons for termination of employment. Regardless of the cause, the employee's access to confidential health information will cease within 2 hours of termination.

Sample procedures: Our practice analyzed job responsibilities of workforce members in our risk analysis and incorporated those responsibilities into job descriptions prior to issuing a clearance for access to electronic protected health information.

We documented all clearances, including passwords and user IDs assigned to each workforce member. Each workforce member will sign an acknowledgment of receipt and understanding of policies regarding his or her clearance privileges.

In the event those clearances change through termination of employment or termination of access to electronic protected health information, the following will occur:

- Our practice will explain that authorization for access to electronic protected health information has changed and the user ID and password have been terminated.

- The workforce member will sign an acknowledgment of notification that access to protected health information is no longer authorized.

- The workforce member will be reminded of the practice's sanction policy for a security incident resulting from an unauthorized workforce member attempting to gain access to protected health information, and of the potential criminal and civil penalties for a privacy breach or unauthorized disclosure of protected health information.

Our practice will conduct an exit interview with a workforce member whose employment is voluntarily terminated. In the interview, the practice will:

- explain that passwords and other authentication tools are invalid effective immediately, authorizations are denied, and audit reports will indicate when an attempt to access protected health information has been denied.

- ask the departing workforce member to sign an acknowledgment of understanding of information conveyed during the exit interview.

If an employee is involuntarily terminated and the security official has not been involved in the termination process, the supervisor will contact the security official no later than 1 hour after termination of an employee so that access authorizations to the practice's information systems and its electronic protected health information can be removed.

Access Authorization		
Safeguard: Administrative	*Federal Register*	**Required/Addressable**
Information access management	68 *Federal Register* 8377 45 CFR 164.308 (a)(4)(ii)(B)	Required

Requirement: Authorize access to confidential health information consistent with your privacy rule.

Sample policy: Each workforce member is responsible for complying with our policies and procedures for accessing workstations, transactions, programs, processes, and other mechanisms used in the practice. Outside vendors who require access must be subject not only to the business associate agreement, but also must be counseled by the security official on the practice's security policies and procedures and the business associate's obligation to comply with the Security Rule no later than February 17, 2010, as provided for in the HITECH Act provisions of the American Recovery and Reinvestment Act of 2009, signed into law by President Obama on February 17, 2009.

Sample procedures: Our security official will collaborate with clinical supervisors in granting access so that our privacy and security policies are in agreement. <Name> and <Name> are the only persons who can grant access privileges.

Each workforce member is granted the minimum amount of information necessary to complete assigned tasks. Physicians who also are shareholders in the practice are granted access to all components of the patients' medical records. Nurses and nurse practitioners are granted full access to the clinical records and to payer information but do not have access to patients' financial information.

Establish and Modify Access

Safeguard: Administrative	*Federal Register*	Required/Addressable
Information access management	68 *Federal Register* 8377 45 CFR 164.308 (a)(4)(ii)(C)	Addressable

Requirement: Implement policies and procedures for how the workforce will be granted access (via workstation, transaction, program, or other mechanism).

Sample policy: Only persons authorized to modify electronic protected health information may do so. Unauthorized persons who modify electronic protected health information will be sanctioned. Outside vendors who require access are subject to our business associate agreement and also will be counseled by our security official on the practice's confidentiality policies and procedures. Business associates' access may be modified as needs for access change.

Sample procedures: <Name> and <Name> will provide written authorization to each person with access privileges. In our practice, the administrator also will counsel hardware and software vendors as well as consultants with access to the practice's information systems on the terms of our practice's business associate's agreement and on the practice's security policies and procedures.

The security official will document and maintain access authorization records, including workforce members granted access, permission levels, and times of such access.

The security official will counsel any workforce member who alters, modifies, or in any way changes electronic protected health information without authorization. Affected workforce members will receive sanctions according to our practice's sanction policy, up to and including termination.

Establishing and modifying access will be part of our security reminders training process.

Security Awareness and Training		
Safeguard: Administrative	***Federal Register***	**Required/Addressable**
Security awareness and training	68 *Federal Register* 8377 45 CFR 164.308 (a)(5)(i)	Required

Requirement: Implement a security awareness and training program for all members of the workforce (including management).

Sample policy: Securing electronic protected health information is more than a policy; it is a primary responsibility of each workforce member. Each workforce member is responsible for complying with our practice's policies and procedures. To demonstrate our commitment to security, our practice will provide a "Secure My PHI" reminder exercise at least once monthly.

This is a level 4 risk for us, at least during the first 12 months, or until our workforce develops new habits. <Name> and <Name> are the owners of this risk.

Sample procedures: Our practice provides a security awareness training session each year, scheduled at an event when workforce members are expected to attend. Those who are unable to participate in the annual training are required to meet with the security official in a follow-up session.

Our practice has posted security reminders throughout our physical location, including the nurse's station, in the lab, and in the lounge, where employees and business associates often gather for meetings.

As part of our monthly reminder campaign and also whenever passwords change, our security official will send a reminder to each workforce member, which may include any of the following:

- Simple reminders via e-mail
- Wall posters
- Updates on new viruses
- Security reminders about laptops, tablet PCs, PDAs, and other portable devices that contain or transmit electronic protected health information.

We encourage our workforce members to provide us with security topics, including making presentations on those topics.

Protection from Malicious Software

Safeguard: Administrative	*Federal Register*	Required/Addressable
Security awareness and training	68 *Federal Register* 8377 45 CFR 164.308 (a)(5)(ii)(B)	Addressable

Requirement: Develop procedures for protecting our assets and confidential health information against malicious software.

Sample policy: Our practice will guard against, detect, and report malicious software, including software that has not yet compromised the system but is suspect. This includes firewalls, virus protection software, and other measures to protect the confidentiality, integrity, and availability of protected health information. Our staff is responsible for complying with these policies and procedures regarding malicious software.

This is a level 3 risk for us. <Name> and <Name> are the owners of this risk.

Sample procedure: Our security official, in consultation with our electronic health record vendor and IT support staff, are the only members who can authorize installation of new software.

Our workforce members may not bring into the practice or download from the Internet any software without the express written authorization from the security official.

Each workforce member is required to install virus protection software that is presented by the security official.

Workforce members will report immediately any detected virus to the security official and office administrator.

Our practice participates in providing online consultation with patients through secure and protected e-mail as part of our business operations. We will make available computers connected to the Internet, other than those used to manage electronic protected health information records, for workforce members to check personal e-mails during breaks.

Our security official will make workforce members aware of sanctions in place for those who violate policies and procedures against malicious software attacks.

Login Monitoring		
Safeguard: Administrative	*Federal Register*	**Required/Addressable**
Security awareness and training	68 *Federal Register* 8377 45 CFR 164.308 (a)(5)(ii)(C)	Addressable

Requirement: Protect your assets and confidential health information by monitoring login attempts and reporting discrepancies.

Sample policy: Our IT vendors will assist us in setting up mechanisms that allow us to see who is logging into the system and also to file a report on repeated unsuccessful attempts.

Sample procedures: Our practice has established triggering mechanisms that immediately alert the security official after three failed login attempts from the same user within a 24-hour period. To be reinstated, the user must consult with the security official who will assign a new password.

Our practice will activate account lockout capabilities, except for physicians, when the workforce is out of the office, such as on weekends and holidays.

Our security official will review, on a weekly basis, a report on system login activity.

Password Management

Safeguard: Administrative	*Federal Register*	Required/Addressable
Security awareness and training	68 *Federal Register* 8377 45 CFR 164.308 (a)(5)(ii)(D)	Addressable

Requirement: Protect our assets and confidential health information by creating, changing, and safeguarding passwords.

Sample policy: Our practice will create, change, and safeguard user IDs and passwords. We will manage those passwords according to the recommendations of our electronic health records (EHR) vendor, based on the capabilities and options embedded in or added to our practice's system access software.

Sample procedures: Our alpha-numeric passwords will be compatible with those designed by our practice management and EHR systems. Passwords will not relate to the user's personal identity, nor will two members of our staff have the same password.

Our security official and workforce member (user) are the only persons who will have knowledge of the user's password. Each workforce member is responsible for providing protection against loss or disclosure of any passwords in his or her possession. For example, passwords may not be posted on monitors or under keyboards or disclosed to other workforce members except the security official.

Passwords that are forgotten will not be reissued, but rather replaced.

Accounts will be locked out after three failed attempts. The security official will be required to unlock the account.

Passwords will be revoked immediately when a workforce member leaves employment with the practice.

Users are required to report any compromise of their password to the security official.

Security Incident Reporting		
Safeguard: Administrative	*Federal Register*	**Required/Addressable**
Security awareness and training	68 *Federal Register* 8377 45 CFR 164.308 (a)(6)(ii)	Required

Requirement: Implement policies and procedures to address security incidents.

Sample policy: Our practice will manage and mitigate the effects of suspected and known security incidents in the practice.

Sample procedures: Our workforce members are responsible for reporting security incidents to the security official as soon as they are recognized. Failure to report such incidents may result in sanctions, as appropriate.

Upon notification of a security incident, the security official will attempt to contain the incident and minimize damage to the practice's systems and data.

The security official shall document in a security incident report the security incident and actions taken to minimize damage to the practice's systems and data.

The security official shall maintain a current written security incident log.

The security official shall determine the extent of reporting, including to outside authorities as appropriate, based on business and legal considerations, and in response to HITECH Act breach notification requirements that are available in Appendix B. These considerations are to be determined with consultation from the practice's legal and IT advisors.

The security official will review security safeguard procedures following any security incident, make appropriate changes to minimize recurrence of such incidents, discuss changes with workforce members, and include these actions in the security incident report.

Use the sample Security Incident Report and sample Security Incident Log as part of your internal incident mitigation strategies. Most likely, you will see a trend and will be better able to manage future incidents.

Security Incident Log

Description of Attempted or Actual Security Incident:

_____

_____

_____

Date: _____   Time: _____   Location: _____

Who discovered the security incident: _____

How was it discovered?

_____

_____

Evidence of incident:

_____

_____

Actions taken to minimize damages to practice's systems and electronic data:

_____

_____

_____

Policy and Procedural changes implemented to avoid recurrence:

_____

_____

_____

_____

Security Official Name   Signature   Date

Security Incident Report

Description of Attempted or Actual Security Incident:

_____

_____

_____

Date: _____ Time: _____ Location: _____

Who discovered the security incident: _____

How was it discovered?

_____

_____

Evidence of incident:

_____

_____

Actions taken to minimize damages to practice's systems and electronic data:

_____

_____

_____

Policy and Procedural changes implemented to avoid recurrence:

_____

_____

_____

| Security Official Name | Signature | Date |

Anticipating and Managing Security Breaches

Reasonable and *appropriate* are key words used throughout HIPAA's Security Rule. So, use common sense when maintaining a security log. For example, it's unlikely you'll document every time a workstation is left unattended. Carefully consider consequences built into your sanctions policy so that you consistently apply these sanctions. All too often, one person will consider himself or herself to be immune to sanctions; and that can put your organization in an unsecured position.

Directions Consider the following security breaches that appear and need to be addressed and managed. Using a scale of 1 to 5, identify whether you believe this is likely to happen in your practice.

1= Never Happens; 2 = Pretty Unlikely; 3 = Likely; 4=Very Likely; 5 = Needs Extra Training

Security Breach Incident	Occurrence
Unsupervised visitors appear to be a little too curious about other patient's health information.	
Software download results in virus attack	
Patient identity doesn't match records	
Information system crashes	
Email sent to wrong person	
Faxes sent to wrong organization	
Backup tapes corrupted	
Portable computer lost or stolen	

continued next page

Security Breach Incident	Occurrence
Terminated employee keeps copies of patient records	
PHI improperly disposed of (paper or electronic media)	
Workstation monitors left logged on when not in use	
Someone impersonating an IT technician asks for passwords (either on phone or in person)	
Changes are made to workstation features without your knowledge	
Portable computers, including handhelds and smart phones are not encrypted	
Audit trails indicate same person is signed on at too many locations.	
Unauthorized person has accessed records	
Security controls are not applied according to access privileges	

Security Awareness and Training

Guidance

1. Set aside time each month at staff meetings to discuss the following:

   a. your practice's policies on logging-in to multiple computers

   b. system's capabilities to audit user access to the system

   c. patient's role in identity theft prevention

   d. alerts that indicate the patient may be a victim of identity theft or a security breach

   e. access to the server room

   f. your practice's policies on password sharing

   g. how to store multiple passwords and what to do when users can't remember a password.

2. When to train:

   a. at least every six months

   b. within 30 days following a new hire

   c. when a workforce member takes on new responsibilities.

3. HIPAA Certification is not a requirement. Awareness training is a requirement.

4. Online training supports your training program and it can be used to verify whether workforce members understood the content.

5. Create a security team name.

6. Post reminder signs near workstations.

7. Ask for help if uncertain of the policy or procedure.

Contingency Plan		
Safeguard: Administrative	*Federal Register*	**Required/Addressable**
Contingency plan	68 *Federal Register* 8377 45 CFR 164.308 (a)(7)(i)	Required

Requirement: Establish (and implement as needed) policies and procedures for responding to an emergency or other occurrence, such as fire, vandalism, system failure, or natural disaster, that damage systems containing electronic protected health information.

Sample policy: Our practice will respond to emergencies that may impair the practice's computer systems and electronic protected health information. This is a level 3 risk for us. <Name> is the owner of this risk.

Sample procedures: Our security official brought together members of our workforce to serve on the Contingency Planning Group.

Contingency Planning Group

Evaluate vulnerabilities, threats, such as fire, theft, floods, and add new possible threats that come from an electronic office, such as hackers, software viruses, or a sustained power outage.

See an example of a practice's contingency planning report in the following box.

Contingency Planning Group Risk Mitigation for (Name of Practice)

Workforce members involved in helping to develop our contingency plan include the following:

_____

_____

_____   (add names as appropriate)

This group analyzed the following key questions.

- How will the practice's patients be affected?
- What practice resources could be lost?
- What costs are associated with any loss?
- What efforts, costs, and time would be needed to recover?
- What would be the overall business impact to the practice?
- What backup systems do our vendors provide?
- What should be included in our "Downtime box"?

Our report, which is filed with our security official, includes the following:

We assessed the following vulnerabilities and threats as part of our risk analysis, and assigned numbers to each vulnerability and threat, with 1 being a low probability and 5 a high likelihood.

Vulnerabilities and Threats	Likelihood: 1 = not likely, 5 = highly likely or has occurred before
Fire at our building location or at storage facility	3
Theft, especially of new computers	4
Natural disaster, including weather related	2
Disgruntled employee	3
Terrorism or aggressive act from nonemployee or disgruntled former employee	2

With assistance from the security official, we assigned tasks and responsibilities that outline how we would respond to an emergency.

Operating Environment and Core Applications

As part of its risk analysis, the practice has identified the following as being potentially at risk: electronic medical records; practice software applications; practice management and database systems; servers; Internet applications; exchange server for e-mail; desktop applications; workstations, laptops, tablet PCs, and portable devices such as PDAs that contain electronic protected health information; and network printers, scanners, and copiers that receive electronic data.

Facility Locations

Street

City, State, <zip>

Contingency recovery site (also called hot site) that contains backups of computer systems and applications, where the practice can access electronic protected health information.

Key practice personnel responsible for achieving recovery

Name	Contact Information	Responsibility
<Name>	<xxx-xxx-xxxx>	Identify party who can declare a contingency
<Name>	<xxx-xxx-xxxx>	Invoke the recovery plan
<Name>	<xxx-xxx-xxxx>	Itemize tasks to accomplish recovery, which may include the following:

Data Backup Plan		
Safeguard: Administrative	*Federal Register*	Required/Addressable
Contingency plan	68 *Federal Register* 8378 45 CFR 164.308 (a)(7)(ii)(A)	Required

Requirement: Establish and implement procedures to create and maintain retrievable exact copies of electronic protected health information.

Sample policy: Our practice will back up its system applications and electronic protected health information according to the instructions and capabilities provided to us through our practice management and electronic health record systems.

Sample procedures: Our security official, working with the office manager, backs up data from the practice management, lab, pharmacy, and electronic health record systems on a daily basis and stores the data in secure off-site and on-site locations.

Our practice also maintains secure off-site daily, weekly, monthly, and quarterly backups of electronic protected health information on its patients.

Our practice continuously monitors backup system performance and tests its backup systems at least quarterly to determine that the integrity of the stored electronic protected health information is safeguarded.

Emergency Mode Operation Plan

Safeguard: Administrative	*Federal Register*	Required/Addressable
Contingency plan	68 *Federal Register* 8378 45 CFR 164.308 (a)(7)(ii)(C)	Required

Requirement: Establish (and implement as needed) procedures to enable continuation of critical business processes for protection of the security of electronic protected health information while operating in the emergency mode.

Sample policy: Our practice built and uses, as needed, an emergency mode operation plan.

Sample procedures: The practice's security official, working with the office administrator and practice management system vendor, is responsible for the following tasks:

- selecting and maintaining an alternate site to perform the practice's data processing and ensure that the back-up location is also secure;
- ensuring hardware and software compatibility at primary and backup sites;
- providing backup power and communications in the event of an emergency;
- appointing personnel to the emergency mode operations team;
- training all personnel in the emergency mode operation plan;
- testing the emergency mode operation plan and making modifications, as necessary; and
- ensuring that all actions are documented in writing.

The practice's security official, working with the emergency mode operation plan leader, if different from the security official, will ensure performance of the following tasks during execution of the plan:

- determine extent and seriousness of emergency.
- appropriate practice official <Name> declares emergency, given emergency plan criteria are met.

- invoke emergency mode operation plan, notify emergency recovery team, and set up meeting at emergency facility if practice facility is inaccessible or inoperable, or both.
- inform patients who may be affected by emergency during the time period that will be required to initiate and remediate emergency operations (eg, 24 to 48 hours, or less).
- determine additional equipment and supply requirements and order.
- notify system and practice management system vendors, explain emergency, and secure cooperation and assistance for recovery from emergency.[22]
- coordinate moving from practice to emergency facility site (if possible) or activate at emergency facility site appropriate telecommunications and systems equipment, with designated practice support personnel performing assigned responsibilities.
- as soon as practicable, run necessary tests on systems and software applications and verify integrity of backed-up electronic protected health information.
- following successful tests and verification, initiate emergency operations at emergency facility site.
- provide for reasonable and appropriate safeguarding of systems and electronic protected health information, given emergency.
- outline and execute plan for restoration of normal operations, including keeping patients informed of situation and progress toward recovery.

---

[22] If the practice's vendors cannot respond in a timely manner, we will consider alternative vendors that we identified in our risk and mitigation analysis.

Testing and Revision		
Safeguard: Administrative	*Federal Register*	**Required/Addressable**
Contingency plan	68 *Federal Register* 8378 45 CFR 164.308 (a)(7)(ii)(D)	Addressable

Requirement: Implement procedures for periodic testing and revision of contingency plans.

Sample policy: Our practice identified this as a level 3 risk for a period of <x> months between <date> and <date>, while we migrate from paper to electronic medical record software and build interfaces with labs, pharmacy, and imaging centers. Following this period, we will identify this as a level 2 risk. <Name> is assigned the manager of this risk.

Sample procedures: Our security official will be responsible for establishing a testing schedule for the practice's data backup, disaster recovery, and emergency mode operation plans. Each plan will be tested no less frequently than annually, based on considerations and outcomes of the risk analysis. Our security official will

- document actions observed during testing, especially successes, response times, and failures.
- evaluate the effectiveness of the practice's data backup, disaster recovery, and emergency mode operation plans.
- make modifications to relevant contingency plans following testing in order to correct deficiencies that resulted in test failures.
- inform workforce members of any plan modifications and conduct retraining of workforce members, as necessary.

Applications, Data Criticality Analysis

Safeguard: Administrative	*Federal Register*	Required/Addressable
Contingency plan	68 *Federal Register* 8378 45 CFR 164.308 (a)(7)(ii)(E)	Addressable

Requirements: Assess relative criticality of specific applications and data in support of other contingency plan components.

Sample policy: To assist in helping us develop new security habits, our practice identified this as a level 3 risk for a period of <x> months, from <date> to <date>. Near the end of that period, the practice will evaluate whether this should remain at level 3 or be reduced to a level 2 risk. <Name>, in collaboration with our information systems contractor, are the managers of this risk.

Sample procedures: Our security official will assign priorities to its contingency plan, including what is most important in safeguarding our systems and electronic protected health information, where the practice is most vulnerable, what are the practice's biggest threats, and what needs to happen to recover business operations following a disaster or emergency.

Evaluation		
Safeguard: Administrative	*Federal Register*	**Required/Addressable**
Evaluation	68 *Federal Register* 8378 45 CFR 164.308 (a)(8)	Required

Requirement: Perform a periodic technical and nontechnical evaluation, based initially upon the standards implemented under this rule and subsequently in response to environmental or operational changes affecting the security of electronic protected health information that establishes the extent to which an entity's security policies and procedures meet the requirements of security standards for the protection of electronic protected health information.

Sample policy: We will re-evaluate all of our security policies and procedures at least annually to determine whether the risks can be reduced or efforts should be increased and new tasks assigned to a workforce member to manage.

Sample Procedures: Our security official will

- design the evaluation process for the practice, referencing the risk analysis we used to build our policies and procedures.

- establish an evaluation committee comprised of the practice's workforce members. The committee, under the guidance of the security official, will delegate duties and functions, manage workflow, and prepare written reports of findings.

- develop criteria for determining what are acceptable levels of risk for vulnerabilities and potential threats that the practice identifies in its business operations, and mitigation strategies and procedures to maintain risks at acceptable levels to the practice.

- evaluate risks at least annually and whenever the practice determines that risks or changes in its operating environment warrant review.

Business Associate Agreements[23]

Safeguard: Administrative	*Federal Register*	Required/Addressable
Evaluation	68 *Federal Register* 8378 45 CFR 164.308 (b)(1)	Required

Requirement: In accordance with general rules of the security standards, a covered entity may permit a business associate to create, receive, maintain, or transmit electronic protected health information on the covered entity's behalf. This is permissible only if the covered entity obtains satisfactory assurances that the business associate will appropriately safeguard such information in accordance with the standard for business associate contracts or other arrangements under organizational requirements.

Sample policy: Our business associates may create, receive, maintain, or transmit electronic protected health information on our behalf only if the practice obtains satisfactory assurances that the business associate will appropriately safeguard protected health information in accordance with the standard for business associate contracts.

Sample procedures: In accordance with our privacy policies and procedures, we will make our business associates aware of security policies and procedures, either through contract language or a separate business associate agreement, and through direct communication or awareness when they enter our physical location.

We will either submit our business associate agreement to our health information exchange partners or review their existing contract if it provides, at a minimum, the following business associate agreement provisions:

- "implement administrative, physical, and technical safeguards that reasonably and appropriately protect the confidentiality, integrity, and availability of the electronic protected health information that it creates, receives, maintains, or transmits on behalf of the covered entity.

---

[23] Discussion of HITECH Act provisions in the American Recovery and Reinvestment Act of 2009 that modify requirements relating to a covered entity's business associates are discussed in the next chapter and Appendix B.

- "ensure that any agent, including a subcontractor, to whom it provides this information, agrees to implement reasonable and appropriate safeguards to protect it.
- "report to the covered entity any security incident of which it becomes aware.
- "authorize termination of the contract by the covered entity, if the covered entity determines that the business associate has violated a material term of the contract."[24]

KEY POINTS

- Workforce members will develop their own policies and procedures every day unless guidance is provided
- Computer usage at home is likely to be much less secure than computer usage in a healthcare setting
- A risk analysis is at the heart of policies and procedures. Build policies and procedures after completing a risk analysis. A sample risk analysis is provided in the Appendices
- Assign a risk manager to oversee and manage risks that have been identified as a risk for the practice
- Policies and procedures will be tested; they are equalizers. They apply to everyone in the workforce, including volunteers and physicians.

---

[24] 68 *Federal Register* 8379.

CHAPTER 2

Your Roadmap through the Decade of Health Information Technology

Roadmap n (1883) 2a: a detailed plan to guide progress toward a goal.[1]

IN THIS CHAPTER, YOU WILL LEARN

- How the Decade of Health Information Technology will affect your policies and procedures
- How the January 16, 2009, final rules for transaction and code set standards will affect your practice and software vendor
- How federal regulatory identity protection initiatives and market payment rules will affect your practice's policies and procedures.
- *How the Health Information Technology for Economic and Clinical Health Act (HITECH Act) provisions of the American Recovery and Reinvestment Act of 2009 (ARRA), signed into law

---

[1] *Merriam-Webster's Collegiate Dictionary,* Eleventh Edition. Springfield, MA: Merriam Webster, Incorporated, 2003, p.1077.

*See Appendix B for more information on HITECH Act.

by President Obama on February 17, 2009, will affect the way
your practice conducts business, especially with business
associates.

■ How the HITECH Act creates incentives for physician practices to
adopt certified electronic health record systems

Key Terms

Compliance date: The date covered entities are required to have
implemented policies in a final rule that are considered officially
adopted on the effective date.

Decade of Health Information Technology: a 2004 federal initiative of the US Department of Health and Human Services (HHS)
promoting countrywide adoption of electronic health record systems that are interoperable by 2014.

Effective date: The date that policies set forth in a final rule take
effect and are considered officially adopted.

Health information technology (Health IT or HIT): As defined
by US Department of Health and Human Services (HHS), HIT
"allows comprehensive management of medical information and
its secure exchange between health care consumers and providers."[2]

Roadmap to the Future: Where You've Been and Where You're Going

The roadmap to the future does lead to a destination: the year 2014,
which is the end of the Decade of Health Information Technology that
began in Summer 2004. We are just about halfway there in 2009. In

---

[2] See www.hhs.gov/healthit. Health information technology also is abbreviated as
"HIT," as in *Decade of HIT*, discussed online at www.hhs.gov/news/press/2004pres/
20040721.html.

2008, US national health care expenditure was projected to be just under $2.4 trillion; in 2014, it is projected to be around $3.5 trillion.[3] During that period, combined US total health care expenditures will be about 125% of today's annual gross domestic product.

It is hard to prognosticate 5 years into the future. After all, 5 years ago, YouTube did not exist.[4] In the next five years, we anticipate further mobile, wireless, and interoperability technology innovations and significantly greater attention paid to safeguarding growing creation, use, and transport via the Internet of electronic information, particularly in health care. In 2008, President-Elect Obama addressed in a *white paper* the importance of investing in electronic health information technology as a way to lower health care costs:[5]

(1) Invest in Electronic Health Information Technology Systems. Most medical records are still stored on paper, which makes them difficult to use to coordinate care, measure quality, or reduce medical errors. Processing paper claims also costs twice as much as processing electronic claims.[6] Barack Obama and Joe Biden will invest $10 billion a year over the next five years to move the US health care system to broad adoption of standards-based electronic health information systems, including electronic health records. They will also phase in requirements for full implementation of health IT and commit the

---

[3] Keehan, Sean, et al. "Health Spending Projections Through 2017: The Baby-Boom Generation Is Coming to Healthcare," *Health Affairs-Web Exclusive,* pp. w145–w155, Feb. 26, 2008. The figure for 2014 is based on growth at a projected 6.7 percent annual increase from the projected 2008 figure (see pp. w146–w147). Available online at: http://content.healthaffairs.org/cgi/reprint/27/2/w145.

[4] Signed, sealed, delivered. *The Economist,* Nov. 8, 2008, p. 42. Also, see The Origin of YouTube, at www.worldhistorysite.com/YouTube.html, which discusses YouTube's launch in April 2005.

[5] Barack Obama and Joe Biden's Plan to Lower Health Care Costs and Ensure Affordable, Accessible Health Coverage for All. Available online at: www.barackobama.com/pdf/issues/HealthCareFullPlan.pdf

[6] Girosi F, Meili R, Scoville R. *Extrapolating Evidence of Health Information Technology Savings and Costs.* Rand, p. 79. 2005.

necessary federal resources to make it happen. Barack Obama and Joe Biden will ensure that these systems are developed in coordination with providers and frontline workers, including those in rural and underserved areas. Barack Obama and Joe Biden will ensure that patients' safety is protected. A study by the Rand Corporation found that if most hospitals and doctors' offices adopted electronic health records, up to $77 billion of savings would be realized each year through improvements such as reduced hospital stays, avoidance of duplicative and unnecessary testing, more appropriate drug utilization, and other efficiencies.[7]

Many of the electronic information technology initiatives that President Obama espoused in this white paper were enacted as provisions in The Health Information Technology for Economic and Clinical Health Act (HITECH Act), which was part of the so-called stimulus bill, The American Recovery and Reinvestment Act of 2009 (ARRA) that President Obama signed into law on February 17, 2009. [8]

The HITECH Act focuses on incentives for physicians who adopt and meaningfully use certified electronic health records, new privacy breach notification rules and penalties, and the requirement that business associates of covered entities comply with the HIPAA Security Rule.

Many of the HITECH Act's provisions will be realized during the five-year period 2009–2014. For example, the HITECH Act provides

---

[7] Girosi F, Meili R, Scoville R. Extrapolating Evidence of Health Information Technology Savings and Costs. Rand, p. 36. 2005.

[8] The American Recovery and Reinvestment Act of 2009 (ARRA) is available online at http://frwebgate.access.gpo.gov/cgi-bin/getdoc.cgi?dbname=111_cong_bills&docid=f: h1enr.pdf. The Health Information Technology for Economic and Clinical Health Act– HITECH Act–comprises Title XIII of Division A (Appropriations Provisions): Health Information Technology (pp.112-165) and Title IV of Division B (Tax, Unemployment, Health, State Fiscal Relief, and Other Provisions): Medicare and Medicaid Health Information Technology; Miscellaneous Medicare Provisions (pp.353-382). Further references to this document in this chapter and in Appendix B will be cited in the reference format: section number *HITECH Act*, page number(s).

for new privacy notification requirements for breaches of unsecured protected health information in late 2009,[9] compliance of each covered entity's business associates with the HIPAA Security Rule on February 17, 2010[10], and financial incentives for certified EHR adoption by healthcare providers from 2011–2014.[11] These provisions of the HITECH Act are discussed in Appendix B.

During that period of 2009–2014, physician practices also will be complying with other electronic information initiatives. As discussed elsewhere in this book, ePrescribing will become the norm. A new 5010/D.0 version of the Health Insurance Portability and Accountability Act (HIPAA) administrative simplification transaction standards will modify the current 4010/4010A/5.1 version;[12] and ICD-10 will replace ICD-9.[13] Although there is a proposed HIPAA health

---

[9] 13402 *HITECH Act*, 146-149.

[10] 13401 *HITECH Act* 146.

[11] 3011 *HITECH Act* 132-133, and 4101 *HITECH Act* 353-363.

[12] On Jan. 1, 2012, the health care industry will undergo a significant modification of the federal HIPAA administrative simplification transaction standards, moving to Accredited Standards Committee (ASC) X12 Version 5010 from ASC X12 Version 4010/4010A and from National Council for Prescription Drug Programs (NCPDP) Version 5.1 to NCPDP Version D.0. Department of Health and Human Services, Office of the Secretary, 45 CFR Part 162: Health Insurance Reform; Modifications to the Health Insurance Portability and Accountability Act (HIPAA) Electronic Transaction Standards; Final Rules, *Federal Register,* v. 74, n. 11, Jan. 16, 2009, pp. 3295-3328. This document is available for online access at www.hipaa.com. CFR refers to the Code of Federal Regulations and "45," Title 45. Further references to this document in this chapter will be cited in the standard reference format, eg, 74 *Federal Register* 3295.

[13] On Oct. 1, 2013, the health care industry will undergo a significant modification of the federal HIPAA Administrative Simplification code set standards, moving from ICD-9 to ICD-10. Physician practices will be affected by a switch only to ICD-10 diagnosis codes and not to ICD-10 procedure codes. US Department of Health and Human Services, Office of the Secretary, 45 CFR Part 162: Health Administrative Simplification: Modifications to Medical Data Code Set Standards to Adopt ICD-10-CM and ICD-10-PCS; Final Rule, v. 74, n. 11, Jan. 16, 2009, 74 *Federal Register* 3328-3362. Available online at: www.hipaa.com. Further references to this document in this chapter will be cited in the standard reference format, eg, 74 *Federal Register* 3328.

care claim attachment standard,[14] the US Department of Health and Human Services (HHS) has indicated that it would take into consideration the health care industry's concern that the standard not "coincide with Level 1 implementation activities related to either Versions 5010 or ICD-10."[15] Accordingly, a final claim attachment rule may not be promulgated until the middle of or late in the five year period. Finally, there are other initiatives, such as the Federal Trade Commission's *Red Flags Rule* designed to protect against identity theft, scheduled for enforcement on November 1, 2009 after three delays,[16] and the Payment Card Industry (PCI) Data Security Standard (DSS) version 1.2, in effect now, and designed to protect against theft of cardholder data.[17]

Each of these initiatives will be analyzed in the pages and tables that follow. We start with the HIPAA administrative simplification transaction and code set modifications. Finally, we close with a discussion of new identity protection rules related with payment practices by physicians.

---

[14] Department of Health and Human Services, Office of the Secretary, 45 CFR 162: HIPAA Administrative Simplification: Standards for Electronic Health Claims Attachments; Proposed Rule, *Federal Register,* v. 70, n. 184, Sep. 23, 2005, pp. 55989-56025. Available online at: www.hipaa.com. Further references to this document in this chapter will be cited in the standard reference format, eg, 70 *Federal Register* 55989.

[15] 74 *Federal Register* 3335.

[16] See Federal Trade Commission (FTC) press release entitled: FTC Announces Expanded Business Education Campaign on 'Red Flags' Rule, July 29, 2009, which is available online at www.ftc.gov/opa/2009/07/redflags.shtm.

[17] "The standards apply to all organizations that store, process or transmit cardholder data." See PCI Security Standards Council's *PCI Quick Reference Guide: Understanding the Payment Card Industry Data Security Standard Version 1.2,* p.6. Available online at: www.pcisecuritystandards.org/pdfs/pci_ssc_quick_guide.pdf.

Health Insurance Portability and Accountability Act of 1996 Administrative Simplification

HIPAA Administrative Simplification was enacted in August 1996. In the years that followed, the federal government promulgated transaction and code set, privacy, security, identifier, claim attachment, and enforcement standards, as outlined in Table 2-1.

These standards have been discussed in the following publications: *HIPAA Plain and Simple: A Compliance Guide for Health Care Professionals*[18] and *HIPAA Transactions: A Nontechnical Business Guide for Health Care.*[19] The January 16, 2009, final rule modifications to the transaction and codes set standards are covered later in this chapter.

Need for Transaction and Code Set Modifications

On September 26, 2007, the National Committee on Vital and Health Statistics (NCVHS) made the following recommendation to HHS Secretary Leavitt: "The Secretary should **expedite** the development and issuance of a Notice of Proposed Rule Making (NPRM) to adopt the ASC X12N Version 5010 suite of transactions."[20] The NPRM was published in the *Federal Register* on August 22, 2008, allowing 60 days for

---

[18] Hartley CP, Jones ED. Chicago, IL: American Medical Association, 2004.

[19] Jones ED, Hartley, CP. Chicago, IL: American Medical Association, 2004.

[20] Letter from Simon P. Cohn, MD, MPH, Chair, NCVHS, to Michael O. Leavitt, Secretary, US Department of Health and Human Services, Revisions to HIPAA transaction standards urgently needed. Sept. 26, 2007. Available online at www.ncvhs.hhs.gov/070926lt.pdf.

TABLE 2-1	Status of HIPAA Administrative Simplification Rules (Jan. 2009)

HIPAA Administrative Simplification Rule	Status	Federal Register Publication Date	Compliance Date for Covered Entities	Compliance Date: Small Health Plans, if Applicable
Transactions and Code Sets	Final	Aug. 17, 2000	Oct. 16, 2003[21]	N/A
Modification to Transactions and Code Sets: Version 5010	Final	Jan. 16, 2009	Jan. 1, 2012	Jan. 1, 2013, only for new Medicaid Pharmacy Subrogation Standard Transaction
Modification to Transactions and Code Sets: ICD-10	Final	Jan. 16, 2009	Oct. 1, 2013	N/A
Privacy	Final	Dec. 28, 2000; Aug. 14, 2002 (modifications)	April 14, 2003	April 14, 2004
Security	Final	Feb. 20, 2003	April 20, 2005	April 20, 2006
National Provider Identifier	Final	Jan. 23, 2004	May 23, 2007	May 23, 2008

[21] In July 2003, the Centers for Medicare and Medicaid Services (CMS) determined that covered entities likely would not be compliant by the Oct. 16, 2003, date. See www.cms. hhs.gov/hipaa/hipaa2/general/default.asp#contingency_guide. On Aug. 4, 2005, CMS announced that it "will not process incoming non-HIPAA-compliant electronic Medicare claims" after Oct. 1, 2005. In its announcement, it reported: "As of June 2005 only about 0.5% of Medicare fee-for-service providers submitted non-HIPAA-compliant electronic claims. The highest rate of non-compliance as of May was from clinical laboratories, 1.72%. Only 1.45% of claims from hospitals were non-compliant and 0.45% from physicians. The high percentage among all provider types shows that everyone can become compliant. The law required all payers to conduct HIPAA-compliant transactions no later than Oct. 16, 2003. However, only about 31% of Medicare claims were compliant at that time. Other payers had even lower numbers of complaint claims." See 2005.08.04: CMS Ending Contingency for Non-HIPAA-Compliant Medicare Claims, CMS Press Release, Aug. 4, 2005, available online at www.cms.hhs.gov/media/press/release.asp?Counter=1528.

HIPAA Administrative Simplification Rule	Status	Federal Register Publication Date	Compliance Date for Covered Entities	Compliance Date: Small Health Plans, if Applicable
National Employer Identifier	Final	May 31, 2002	July 30, 2004	Aug. 1, 2005
National Plan Identifier	Under development			
National Individual Identifier	Congressional hold on development			
Claim Attachment	Notice of Proposed Rule Making	Sept. 23, 2005[22]		
Enforcement	Final	Feb. 16, 2006[23]	March 16, 2006	N/A

[22] "This rule proposes standards for electronically requesting and supplying particular types of additional health care information in the form of an electronic attachment to support submitted health care claims data." 70 *Federal Register* 55990. This NPRM originally allowed 60 days for public comment. On Nov. 21, 2005, HHS announced in the *Federal Register* an additional 60 days for public comment, which ended on Jan. 23, 2006. The final rule may be delayed as a result of the timeframes for the healthcare industry to begin complying with the final rules for modification of transactions and code set standards: Version 5010 and ICD-10. In the preamble to the ICD-10 final rule, HHS reported the following: "*Comment:* A number of commenters urged that the compliance date for the HIPAA health care claims attachment standard not coincide with the Level 1 implementation activities related to either Version 5010 or ICD-10. *Response:* We will take this into consideration in establishing a compliance date in the health care claims attachment standard final rule." 74 *Federal Register* 3335.

[23] "The Secretary of Health and Human Services is adopting rules for the imposition of civil money penalties on entities that violate rules adopted by the Secretary to implement the Administrative Simplification provisions of the Health Insurance Portability and Accountability Act of 1996, Public Law (104-191)(HIPAA). The final rule amends the existing rules relating to the investigation of noncompliance to make them apply to all of the HIPAA Administrative Simplification rules, rather than exclusively to the privacy standards. It also amends the existing rules relating to the process for imposition of civil money penalties. Among other matters, the final rule clarifies and elaborates upon the investigation process, bases for liability, determination of the penalty among, grounds for waiver, conduct of the hearing, and the appeal process." See Department of Health and Human Services, Office of the Secretary, "45 CFR parts 160 and 164, HIPAA Administrative Simplification: Enforcement; Final Rule," Feb. 16, 2006, 71 *Federal Register* 8389-8433 [quotation: 71 *Federal Register* 8390].

public comment to October 21, 2008.[24] The NPRM required all covered entities to use the new X12 5010 Version standards:

> Except as otherwise provided in this part, if a covered entity conducts with another covered entity that is required to comply with a transaction standard adopted under this part (or within the same covered entity), using electronic media, a transaction for which the Secretary has adopted a standard under this part, the covered entity must conduct the transaction as a standard transaction.[25]

For physician practices, these six typical electronic transactions standards are covered:

- Health Care Claims or Equivalent Encounter Information (Professional)[26]
- Eligibility for a Health Plan[27]
- Referral Certification and Authorization[28]

---

[24] 73 *Federal Register* 49741–49742.

[25] 73 *Federal Register* 49791.

[26] The [Accredited Standards Committee]ASC X12 Standards for Electronic Data Interchange Technical Report Type 3–Health Care Claim: Professional (837), May 2006. Washington Publishing Company, 005010X222. www.wpc-edi.com.

[27] The ASC Standards for Electronic Data Interchange Technical Report Type 3–Health Care Eligibility Benefit Inquiry and Response (270/271), April 2008. Washington Publishing Company 005010X279. www.wpc-edi.com.

[28] This covers three types of transactions: "(a) A request from a health care provider to a health plan for the review of health care to obtain an authorization for the health care. (b) A request from a health care provider to a health plan to obtain authorization for referring an individual to another health care provider. (c) A response from a health plan to a health care provider to a request described in paragraph (a) or (b) of this section." 73 *Federal Register* 49791. The ASC X12 Standards for Electronic Data Interchange Technical Report Type 3–Health Care Services Review–Request for Review and Response (278), May 2006, Washington Publishing Company 005010X217, and Type 1 Errata to Health Care Services Review–Request for Review and Response (278), ASC X12 Standards for Electronic Data Interchange Technical Report Type 3, April 2008, Washington Publishing Company 005010X217E1. www.wpc-edi.com.

- Health Care Claim Status[29]
- Health Care Payment and Remittance Advice[30]
- Coordination of Benefits Information.[31]

The NPRM explained why the transaction standards that were in place since October 2003 were being modified:

> In addition to technical issues and business developments necessitating consideration of the new versions of the standards, there remain a number of unresolved issues that had been identified by the industry early in the implementation period for the first set of standards, and those issues were never addressed through regulation. . . .[32]

The focus here is on the effect of two of these proposed modified standards: Health Care Payment and Remittance Advice Transaction (835) and Health Care Claim Status (276/277), because they have

---

[29] The ASC X12 Standards for Electronic Data Interchange Technical Report Type 3—Health Care Claim Status Request and Response (276/277), August 2006, Washington Publishing Company 005010X212, and Type 1 Errata to Health Care Claim Status Request and Response (276.277), ASC X12 Standards for Electronic Data Interchange Technical Report Type 3, April 2008, Washington Publishing Company 005010X212E1. www.wpc-edi.com.

[30] The ASC X12 Standards for Electronic Data Interchange Technical Report Type 3—Health Care Claim Payment/Advice (835), April 2006, Washington Publishing Company 005010X221. www.wpc-edi.com.

[31] The ASC X12 Standards for Electronic Data Interchange Technical Report Type 3—Health Care Claim: Professional (837), May 2006, Washington Publishing Company 005010X222. www.wpc-edi.com. Note that the ASC X12 transaction standard for the claim and for coordination of benefits is the same 837.

[32] 73 *Federal Register* 49743.

implications for policies and procedures in your practice that, over the next 5 years, may substantially enhance cash flow and reduce cost.[33]

Think about the effect on your practice of receiving your remittances and payments more quickly in electronic formats and having them automatically posted to your practice management system without human intervention. Also, think about making automated claim status inquiries without human intervention based on rules embedded in your software, thus eliminating the need for your staff to spend time on the telephone with health plans. (How much time does your practice currently spend on the telephone handling remittance, payment, and claim status issues with health plans?) The regulatory impact analysis that is part of the NPRM for Version 5010 indicates that both health care providers and health plans receive a net gain in implementing electronic payments and remittance and claim status standards capabilities.[34]

What does the NPRM suggest as specific improvements underlying the modifications of the payments and remittance and claim status standards? Remember, unlike the policies and procedures required by, for example, the Security Rule, policies and procedures would be business-driven by changes in how the practice processed remittances and payments from and made claim status inquiries to health plan payers. Your software vendor will play a key role in helping your practice address these policy and procedures issues. Be sure to ask your software vendor how the practice can prepare information to make its job easier. Also,

---

[33] In *HIPAA Plain & Simple: A Compliance Guide for Health Care Professionals,* the concepts of raising the bridge and lowering the river was discussed. *"Raising the bridge* means generating more revenue per unit of service. *Lowering the river* means lowering costs per unit of service. Either, controlling for the other, will increase net revenue. Both will increase it even more." See Hartley CP, Jones ED, *HIPAA Plain & Simple: A Compliance Guide for Health Care Professionals.* Foreword by Louis W. Sullivan, MD. Chicago, IL: AMA Press, 2004, pp. 193–194.

[34] 73 *Federal Register* 49757-49768, especially 49767-49768.

consider any expenditure of preparation time or money as an investment in your practice's business future.

Health Care Payment and Remittance Advice Transaction (835)[35]

According to the NPRM, "[m]any of the enhancements in Version 5010 involve the Front Matter section of the Technical Report Type 3, which contains expanded instructions for accurately processing a compliant 835 transaction. Version 5010 provides refined terminology for using a standard, and enhances the data content to promote clarity." The NPRM highlights the following potential benefits of the refinements:

- more accurate use of this standard,
- reduction of manual intervention, and
- motivation to vendors and billing services to provide more cost-effective solutions for electronic remittance advice transactions.

The NPRM goes on to highlight other changes:

- tightened business rules and fewer code value options in Version 5010:
  - The current version "lacks standard definitions and procedures for translating remittance information and payments from various health plans to a provider, which makes automatic remittance posting difficult."
- new instructions for handling certain business situations in Version 5010:
  - "Version 5010 instructs providers on how to negate a payment that may be incorrect and post a correction."

---

[35] The NPRM discussion of this transaction standard is at 73 *Federal Register* 49748.

- flexibility to test Version 5010 835 remittance transaction with existing Version 4010/4010A claim transaction:

  - This compatibility facilitates testing of the modified remittance standard with existing claims prior to the compliance date of January 1, 2012, for Version 5010, as "there may be a transition period with claims for services rendered before the compliance date that will be in the older version of the standard because data elements required in Version 5010 might not have been captured at the time services were rendered."

- inclusion of a new Medical Policy segment in Version 5010:

  - This segment "provides more up-to-date information on payer policies and helps in detail management, appeals, and reduces telephone and written inquiries to payers."

  - This segment also "helps providers locate related published medical policies that are used to determine benefits by virtue of the addition of a segment for a payer's [Uniform Resource Locator] URL for easy access to a plan's medical policies."

- elimination of Not Advised codes in Version 5010:

  - In Version 4010/4010A, there was confusion in a payment context on the use of the code "debit," which was marked "Not Advised." In Version 5010, it is treated "as situational, with instructions on how and when to use the code."

- clarification for use of claim status indicator codes in the Version 5010 835 transaction standard:

  - In Version 4010/4010A, there are "status codes that indicate a primary, secondary, or tertiary claim, but no instructions for the use of these codes," which "creates confusion when a claim is partially processed, or when a claim is processed but there is no payment."[36]

---

[36] This and preceding quotations in this section are from 73 *Federal Register* 49748.

In general, these changes provide a practice more convenient access to health plan information that will facilitate submission of claims, thereby expediting remittance processing and payment. The NPRM estimates that costs savings for claim and remittance processing with the modification to standards for the claim (837) and remittance (835) components will amount to $0.55 per claim for providers and $0.18 for health plans, for a total of $0.73 per claim.[37]

Health Care Claim Status (276/277)[38]

Unlike the 835 remittance advice, which is estimated to be currently accepted by about 60 percent of all covered entities, the 276/277 claims status request and response is estimated to be currently accepted by only about 10 percent of all covered entities.[39] Version 5010 addresses the following issues in order to increase the percentage of acceptance:

- Identification of prescription numbers to determine which "prescription numbers are paid or not paid at the claim level" of the transaction.
  - "The ability to identify a prescription by the prescription number is important for pharmacy providers when identifying claims data in their systems."
- Elimination of some sensitive personal information that is extraneous to the purpose of checking claim status and that raises privacy and minimum necessary data issues under HIPAA Administrative Simplification.
  - For example, the existing standard "requires the subscriber's date of birth and insurance policy number, which often is a

---

[37] 73 *Federal Register* 49765.

[38] The NPRM discussion of this transaction standard is at 73 *Federal Register* 49750.

[39] 73 *Federal Register* 49763.

Social Security number," which "is not needed to identify the subscriber because the policy number recorded for the patient already uniquely identifies the subscriber."

■ Clarification of *situational data element* rules in Version 5010 in order to "reduce reliance on *companion guides*[40] and ensure consistency in the use of Implementation Guides," and to "reduce multiple interpretations."

   ■ Physician practice reliance on identifying different interpretations of situational fields and data elements for properly submitting claims to their patients' multiple health plans is time consuming and costly.

   "For example, Version 5010 clarifies the relationships between dependents and subscribers, and makes a clear distinction between the term 'covered status' (whether the particular service is covered under the benefit package) and 'covered beneficiary' (the individual who is eligible for services)."

■ Implementation of consistent rules across all standards "regarding the requirement to include both patient and subscriber information in the transaction."

   ■ If the dependent patient can be uniquely identified with an "individual identification number," then the subscriber identification is not necessary in the transaction: "to include the subscriber information with the dependent member information for a uniquely identifiable dependent is an administrative burden for the provider."

---

[40] "These deficiencies in the current implementation specifications have caused much of the industry to rely on 'companion guides' created by health plans to address areas of Version 4010/4010A that are not specific enough or require work-around solutions to address business needs. These companion guides are unique, plan-specific implementation instructions for the situational use of certain fields and/or data elements that are needed to support current business operations." 73 *Federal Register* 49746.

Version 5010 Payment and Remittance Advice and Claim Status transactions standards have been singled out for implementation by the
physician practice because improvements in the implementation specifications have the promise to reduce time and cost regarding the
receipt of payment for services rendered by health plans. In 2005, the
Medical Group Management Association indicated that "it takes
45 days for a doctor to get an average payment."[41] With patient co-
insurance at the front end of an encounter and health plan processing
of a claim and a final payment from the patient, if any, after the delivery of service, it may actually take considerably longer for an account
receivable to be reconciled and for a claim to be paid in full and
closed. Improvements to the Version 5010 Payment and Remittance
Advice and Claim Status transactions standards have the potential to
markedly speed up payment, which could favorably affect practice cash
flow and claim and remittance processing costs.

Finally, for your reference online, the Centers for Medicare and
Medicaid Services (CMS) has made available comparisons of the
Version 4010/4010A with Version 5010, element by element.[42] The
site for payment and remittance advice, from which page one is illustrated as Figure 2-1, is: www.cms.hhs.gov/ElectronicBillingEDITrans/
Downloads/Remittance4010A1to5010.pdf. The similar comparison
site for claim status is shown in Figure 2-2 (www.cms.hhs.gov/
ElectronicBillingEDITrans/Downloads/ClaimStatus4010A1to5010.pdf).
Also, see ww.cms.hhs.gov/ElectronicBillingEDITrans/18_5010D0.asp
for other standards comparisons of interest to physician practices,
including Professional Claim 837 and Eligibility 270/271.

---

[41] Lieber R. Asking your doc for discounts: New health plans mean it's not as far-
fetched as it sounds. *The Wall Street Journal,* October 29–30, 2005, p. B1.

[42] 73 *Federal Register* 49746.

4010A1							
Element Identifier	Description	ID	Min. Max.	Usage Reg.	Loop	Loop Repeat	Values
	835 4010A1						
ISA	INTERCHANGE CONTROL HEADER			1 R		1	
ISA01	Authorization Information Qualifier	ID	2–2	R			00,03
ISA02	Authorization Information	AN	10–10	R			
ISA03	Security Information Qualifier	ID	2–2	R			00,01
ISA04	Security Information	AN	10–10	R			
ISA05	Interchange ID Qualifier	ID	2–2	R			01,14,20,27, 28, 29, 30, 33, ZZ
ISA06	Interchange Sender ID	AN	15–15	R			
ISA07	Interchange ID Qualifier	ID	2–2	R			01,14,20,27, 28, 29, 30, 33, ZZ
ISA08	Interchange Receiver ID	AN	15–15	R			
ISA09	Interchange Date	DT	6–6	R			YYMMDD
ISA10	Interchange Time	TM	4–4	R			HHMM
ISA11	Interchange Control Standards ID	ID	1–1	R			U
ISA12	Interchange Control Version Number	ID	5–5	R			00401
ISA13	Interchange Control Number	N0	9–9	R			=IEA02
ISA14	Acknowledgement Requested	ID	1–1	R			0
ISA15	Usage Indicator	ID	1–1	R			P,T
ISA16	Component Element Separator		1–1	R			
GS	Functional Group Header			1 R	———	1	
GS01	Functional Identifier Code	ID	2–2	R			HP
GS02	Application Sender's Code	AN	2–15	R			
GS03	Application Receiver's Code	AN	2–15	R			
GS04	Date	DT	8–8	R			CCYYMMDD
GS05	Time	TM	4–8	R			HHMM
GS06	Group Control Number	N0	1–9	R			=GE02
GS07	Responsible Agency Code	ID	1–2	R			X
GS08 GS08	Version/Release/Industry Id code Version/Release/Industry Id Code	AN	1–12	R			004010X091 004010X091A1

5010							
Element Identifier	Description	ID	Min. Max.	Usage Reg.	Loop	Loop Repeat	Values
	835 5010						
ISA	INTERCHANGE CONTROL HEADER			1 R		1	
ISA01	Authorization Information Qualifier	ID	2–2	R			00,03
ISA02	Authorization Information	AN	10–10	R			
ISA03	Security Information Qualifier	ID	2–2	R			00,01
ISA04	Security Information	AN	10–10	R			
ISA05	Interchange ID Qualifier	ID	2–2	R			01,14,20,27, 28, 29, 30, 33, ZZ
ISA06	Interchange Sender ID	AN	15–15	R			
ISA07	Interchange ID Qualifier	ID	2–2	R			01,14,20,27, 28, 29, 30, 33, ZZ
ISA08	Interchange Receiver ID	AN	15–15	R			
ISA09	Interchange Date	DT	6–6	R			YYMMDD
ISA10	Interchange Time	TM	4–4	R			HHMM
ISA11	Interchange Control Standards ID	ID	1–1	R			U
ISA12	Interchange Control Version Number	ID	5–5	R			00401
ISA13	Interchange Control Number	N0	9–9	R			=IEA02
ISA14	Acknowledgement Requested	ID	1–1	R			0
ISA15	Usage Indicator	ID	1–1	R			P,T
ISA16	Component Element Separator		1–1	R			
GS	Functional Group Header			1 R	———	1	
GS01	Functional Identifier Code	ID	2–2	R			HP
GS02	Application Sender's Code	AN	2–15	R			
GS03	Application Receiver's Code	AN	2–15	R			
GS04	Date	DT	8–8	R			CCYYMMDD
GS05	Time	TM	4–8	R			HHMM
GS06	Group Control Number	N0	1–9	R			=GE02
GS07	Responsible Agency Code	ID	1–2	R			X
GS08	Version Identifier Code	AN	1–12	R			005010X221

Figure 2-1 Comparison Site for Payment and Remittance Advice

What This Means for Your Practice

Modifications to the transactions standards will affect your practice's policies and procedures for following up with health plans about payment status. For example, workflow procedures may change if you conduct fewer follow-ups over the telephone and more by computer. Your practice, with help from your IT vendor, may be able to fashion rules to prioritize workforce action when remittance advice is not received by a certain time after delivery of service or date of submission of claim. The claim status transaction standard will minimize the amount of time that your practice's workforce spends on the telephone with health plans—a benefit that accrues to your practice and the health plan as well! Similarly, the new remittance advice standard makes it easier to tie time of recognition of payment to remittance advice. In turn, your practice's accounts receivable position and cash flow will improve.

4010A1

Element Identifier	Description	ID	Min. Max.	Usage Reg.	Loop	Loop Repeat	Values
	276 4010A1						
ISA	INTERCHANGE CONTROL HEADER			1	R		1
ISA01	Authorization Information Qualifier	ID	2-2	R			00, 03
ISA02	Authorization Information	AN	10-10	R			
ISA03	Security Information Qualifier	ID	2-2	R			00, 01
ISA04	Security Information	AN	10-10	R			
ISA05	Interchange ID Qualifier	ID	2-2	R			01, 14, 20, 27, 28, 29, 30, 33, ZZ
ISA06	Interchange Sender ID	AN	15-15	R			
ISA07	Interchange ID Qualifier	ID	2-2	R			01, 14, 20, 27, 28, 29, 30, 33, ZZ
ISA08	Interchange Receiver ID	AN	15-15	R			
ISA09	Interchange Date	DT	6-6	R			YYMMDD
ISA10	Interchange Time	TM	4-4	R			HHMM
ISA11	Interchange Control Standards ID	ID	1-1	R			U
ISA12	Interchange Control Version Number	ID	5-5	R			00401
ISA13	Interchange Control Number	N0	9-9	R			
ISA14	Acknowledgement Requested	ID	1-1	R			0, 1
ISA15	Usage Indicator	ID	1-1	R			P, T
ISA16	Component Element Separator	AN	1-1	R			
GS	FUNCTIONAL GROUP HEADER			1	R		>1
GS01	Functional Identifier Code	ID	2-2	R			HR
GS02	Application Sender Code	AN	2-15	R			
GS03	Application Receiver Code	AN	2-15	R			
GS04	Date	DT	8-8	R			CCYYMMDD
GS05	Time	TM	4-8	R			HHMMSSDD
GS06	Group Control Number	N0	1-9	R			
GS07	Responsible Agency Code	ID	1-2	R			X
GS08	Version Identifier Code	AN	1-12	R			004010X093

5010

Element Identifier	Description	ID	Min. Max.	Usage Reg.	Loop	Loop Repeat	Values
	276 5010						
ISA	INTERCHANGE CONTROL HEADER			1	R		1
ISA01	Authorization Information Qualifier	ID	2-2	R			00, 03
ISA02	Authorization Information	AN	10-10	R			
ISA03	Security Information Qualifier	ID	2-2	R			00, 01
ISA04	Security Information	AN	10-10	R			
ISA05	Interchange ID Qualifier	ID	2-2	R			01, 14, 20, 27, 28, 29, 30, 33, ZZ
ISA06	Interchange Sender ID	AN	15-15	R			
ISA07	Interchange ID Qualifier	ID	2-2	R			01, 14, 20, 27, 28, 29, 30, 33, ZZ
ISA08	Interchange Receiver ID	AN	15-15	R			
ISA09	Interchange Date	DT	6-6	R			YYMMDD
ISA10	Interchange Time	TM	4-4	R			HHMM
ISA11	Repetition Seperator	AN	1-1	R			
ISA12	Interchange Control Version Number	ID	5-5	R			00501
ISA13	Interchange Control Number	N0	9-9	R			
ISA14	Acknowledgement Requested	ID	1-1	R			0, 1
ISA15	Usage Indicator	ID	1-1	R			P, T
ISA16	Component Element Separator	AN	1-1	R			
GS	FUNCTIONAL GROUP HEADER			1	R		>1
GS01	Functional Identifier Code	ID	2-2	R			HR
GS02	Application Sender Code	AN	2-15	R			
GS03	Application Receiver Code	AN	2-15	R			
GS04	Date	DT	8-8	R			CCYYMMDD
GS05	Time	TM	4-8	R			HHMMSSDD
GS06	Group Control Number	N0	1-9	R			
GS07	Responsible Agency Code	ID	1-2	R			X
GS08	Version Identifier Code	AN	1-12	R			005010X212

Figure 2-2 Comparison Site for Claim Status

HIPAA Standard Transaction and Code Set Modifications: Final Rules

On January 16, 2009, less than 5 months after publication of the NPRM, considered a quick period if calculated in "HIPAA-time," the office of the secretary of HHS published in the *Federal Register* final rules pertaining to Health Insurance Reform: Modifications to the Health Insurance Portability and Accountability Act (HIPAA) Electronic Transaction Standards[43] and HIPAA Administrative Simplification: Modifications to Medical Data Code Set Standards to Adopt ICD-10-CM and ICD-10-PCS.[44]

---

[43] 74 *Federal Register* 3295-3328.

[44] 74 *Federal Register* 3328-3362.

Each rule is discussed below.[45] Note that the discussion pertaining to the Version 5010/D.0 and ICD-10 NPRMs, except where noted, is unaffected by changes in the final rules.

Transaction Standards Modifications

This final rule adopts Accredited Standards Committee (ASC) X12 Version 5010 and National Council for Prescription Drug Programs (NCPDP) Versions D.0, 3.0, and 5.1 standards for electronic transactions, as shown in Table 2-2 (reproduced here from Table 1 in the final rule).[46]

Most of the standards reflect updates. The Medicaid pharmacy subrogation standard is newly adopted, and two standards are adopted for retail pharmacy supplies and professional services. Table 2-3 compares current transaction standards and modified transactions standards that will require compliance beginning January 1, 2012.

Effective dates. There are two effective dates for this final rule. For all standards except the Medicaid Pharmacy Subrogation Transaction, the effective date is March 17, 2009. For the Medicaid Pharmacy Subrogation Transaction standard, the effective date is January 1, 2010. "[T]he effective date is the date that the policies set forth in this final rule take effect, and new policies are considered to be officially adopted."[47]

---

[45] These documents can be accessed at www.hipaa.com and downloaded in portable document format (pdf).

[46] 74 *Federal Register* 3296-3297.

[47] 74 *Federal Register* 3302.

text continues on page 93

TABLE 2-2 | HIPAA Standard and Transaction

Standard	Transaction
ASC X12 837D	Health care claims—Dental
ASC X12 837P	Health care claims—Professional
ASC X12 837I	Health care claims—Institutional
NCPDP D.0	Health care claims—Retail pharmacy drug
ASC X12 837P and NCPDP D.0	Health care claims—Retail pharmacy supplies and professional services
NCPDP D.0	Coordination of benefits—Retail pharmacy drug
ASC X12 837D	Coordination of benefits—Dental
ASC X12 837P	Coordination of benefits—Professional
ASC X12 837I	Coordination of benefits—Institutional
ASC X12 270/271	Eligibility for a health plan (request and response)—Dental, professional, and institutional
NCPDP D.0	Eligibility for a health plan (request and response)—Retail pharmacy drugs
ASC X12 276/277	Health care claim status (request and response)
ASC X12 834	Enrollment and disenrollment in a health plan
ASC X12 835	Health care payment and remittance advice
ASC X12 820	Health plan premium payment
ASC X12 278	Referral certification and authorization (request and response)—Dental, professional, and institutional
NCPDP D.0	Referral certification and authorization (request and response)—Retail pharmacy drugs
NCPDP 5.1 and NCPDP D.0	Retail pharmacy drug claims (telecommunication and batch standards)
NCPDP 3.0	Medicaid pharmacy subrogation (batch standard)

TABLE 2-3	Comparison of ASC X12 Version 4010/4010A1 and Version 5010 Standards		
Standard	**Transaction**	**Version 4010/4010A1**	**Version 5010**
Health Care Claims or Equivalent Encounter Information Transaction	Retail pharmacy drug claims	NCPDP Telecommunication Standard Implementation Guide, Version 5, Release 1 (Version 5.1), Sept. 1999, and equivalent NCPDP Batch Implementation Guide, Version 1, Release 1 (Version 1.1), Jan. 2000, in support of Telecommunication Standard Implementation Guide, Version 5.1, for the NCPDP Data Record in the Detail Data Record	Telecommunication Standard Implementation Guide Version D, Release 0 (Version D.0), Aug. 2007 and equivalent Batch Standard Implementation Guide, Version 1, Release 2 (Version 1.2), NCPDP
	Dental health care claims	Accredited Standards Committee (ASC) X12N 837-Healthcare Claim: Dental, Version 4010, May 2000, WPC2, 004010X097, and Addenda to Healthcare Claim: Dental, Version 4010, Oct. 2002, WPC, 004010X097A1	ASC X12 Standards for Electronic Data Interchange Technical Report Type 3-Health Care Claim: Dental (837), May 2006, WPCxxx, 005010X224, and Type 1 Errata to Health Care Claim: Dental (837), ASC X12 Standards for Electronic Data Interchange Technical Report Type 3, Oct. 2007, WPC, 005010X224A1

Standard	Transaction	Version 4010/4010A1	Version 5010
	Professional health care claims	ASC X12N 837-Healthcare Claim: Professional, Volumes 1 and 2, Version 4010, May 2000, WPC, 004010X098, and Addenda to Healthcare Claim: Professional, Volumes 1 and 2, Version 4010, Oct. 2002, WPC, 004010X098A1	ASC X12 Standards for Electronic Data Interchange Technical Report Type 3-Health Care Claim: Professional (837), May 2006, WPC, 005010X222
	Institutional health care claims	ASC X12N 837-Healthcare Claim: Institutional, Volumes 1 and 2, Version 4010, May 2000, WPC, 004010X096, and Addenda to Healthcare Claim: Institutional, Volumes 1 and 2, Version 4010, Oct. 2002, WPC, 004010X096A1	ASC X12 Standards for Electronic Data Interchange Technical Report Type 3-Health Care Claim: Institutional (837), May 2006, WPC, 005010X223, and Type 1 Errata to Health Care Claim: Institutional (837), ASC X12 Standards for Electronic Data Interchange Technical Report Type 3, Oct. 2007, WPC,

continued next page

TABLE 2-3	Comparison of ASC X12 Version 4010/4010A1 and Version 5010 Standards—continued		

Standard	Transaction	Version 4010/4010A1	Version 5010
	Retail pharmacy supplies and professional services claims		Telecommunication Standard Implementation Guide Version D, Release 0 (Version D.0), Aug. 2007, and equivalent Batch Standard Implementation Guide, Version 1, Release 2 (Version 1.2), NCPDP; and ASC X12 Standards for Electronic Data Interchange Technical Report Type 3-Health Care Claim: Professional (837), May 2006, WPC, 005010X222
Eligibility for a Health Plan	Retail pharmacy drugs	NCPDP Telecommunication Standard Implementation Guide, Version 5, Release 1 (Version 5.1), Sept. 1999, and equivalent NCPDP Batch Implementation Guide, Version 1, Release 1 (Version 1.1), Jan. 2000, in support of Telecommunication Standard Implementation Guide, Version 5.1, for the NCPDP Data Record in the Detail Data Record	Telecommunication Standard Implementation Guide Version D, Release 0 (Version D.0), Aug. 2007, and equivalent Batch Standard Implementation Guide, Version 1, Release 2 (Version 1.2), NCPDP

Standard	Transaction	Version 4010/4010A1	Version 5010
	Dental, professional, and institutional health care eligibility benefit inquiry and response	ASC X12N 270/271-Healthcare Eligibility Benefit Inquiry and Response, Version 4010, May 2000, WPC, 004010X092, and Addenda to Healthcare Eligibility Benefit Inquiry and Response, Version 4010, Oct. 2002, WPC, 004010X092A1	ASC X12 Standards for Electronic Data Interchange Technical Report Type 3-Health Care Eligibility Benefit Inquiry and Response (270/271), April 2008, WPC, 005010X279
Referral Certification and Authorization	Retail pharmacy drugs	NCPDP Telecommunication Standard Implementation Guide, Version 5, Release 1 (Version 5.1), Sept. 1999, and equivalent NCPDP Batch Implementation Guide, Version 1, Release 1 (Version 1.1), Jan. 2000, in support of Telecommunication Standard Implementation Guide, Version 5.1, for the NCPDP Data Record in the Detail Data Record	Telecommunication Standard Implementation Guide Version D, Release 0 (Version D.0), Aug. 2007, and equivalent Batch Standard Implementation Guide, Version 1, Release 2 (Version 1.2), NCPDP

continued next page

TABLE 2-3	Comparison of ASC X12 Version 4010/4010A1 and Version 5010 Standards—continued		
Standard	**Transaction**	**Version 4010/4010A1**	**Version 5010**
	Dental, profes- sional, and institutional request for review and response	ASC X12N 278-Healthcare Services Review: Request for Review and Response, Version 4010, May 2000, WPC, 004010X094, and Addenda to Healthcare Services Review: Request for Review and Response, Version 4010, Oct. 2002, WPC, 004010X094A1	ASC X12 Standards for Electronic Data Interchange Technical Report Type 3-Health Care Services Review- Request for Review and Response (278), May 2006, WPC, 005010X217, and Type 1 Errata to Health Care Services Review- Request for Review and Response (278), ASC X12 Standards for Electronic Data Interchange Technical Report Type 3, April 2008, WPC, 005010X217E1

Standard	Transaction	Version 4010/4010A1	Version 5010
Health Care Claim Status	Dental, professional, institutional, and pharmacy	ASC X12N 276/277-Healthcare Claim Status Request and Response, Version 4010, May 2000, WPC, 004010X093, and Addenda to Healthcare Claim Status Request and Response, Version 4010, Oct. 2002, WPC, 004010X093A1	ASC X12 Standards for Electronic Data Interchange Technical Report Type 3-Health Care Claim Status Request and Response (276/277), Aug. 2006, WPC, 005010X212, and Type 1 Errata to Health Care Claim Status Request and Response (276/277), ASC X12 Standards for Electronic Data Interchange Technical Report Type 3, April 2008, WPC, 005010X212E1
Enrollment and Disenrollment in a Health Plan		ASC X12N 834-Benefit Enrollment and Maintenance, Version 4010, May 2000, WPC, 004010X095, and Addenda to Benefit Enrollment and Maintenance, Version 4010, Oct. 2002, WPC, 004010X095A1	ASC X12 Standards for Electronic Data Interchange Technical Report Type 3-Benefit Enrollment and Maintenance (834), Aug. 2006, WPC, 005010X220

continued next page

TABLE 2-3 | Comparison of ASC X12 Version 4010/4010A1 and Version 5010 Standards—continued

Standard	Transaction	Version 4010/4010A1	Version 5010
Health Care Payment and Remittance Advice	Dental, professional, institutional, and pharmacy	ASC X12N 835-Healthcare Claim Payment/Advice, Version 4010, May 2000, WPC, 004010X091, and Addenda to Healthcare Claim Payment/Advice, Version 4010, Oct. 2002, WPC, 004010X091A1	ASC X12 Standards for Electronic Data Interchange Technical Report Type 3-Health Care Claim Payment/Advice (835), April 2006, WPC, 005010X221
Health Plan Premium Payments		ASC X12N 820-Payroll Deducted and Other Group Premium Payment for Insurance Products, Version 4010, May 2000, WPC, 004010X061, and Addenda to Payroll Deducted and Other Group Premium Payment for Insurance Products, Version 4010, Oct. 2002, WPC, 004010X061A1	ASC X12 Standards for Electronic Data Interchange Technical Report Type 3-Payroll Deducted and Other Group Premium Payment for Insurance Products (820), Feb. 2007, WPC, 005010X218

Standard	Transaction	Version 4010/4010A1	Version 5010
Coordination of Benefits Information	Retail pharmacy drug claims	NCPDP Telecommunication Standard Implementation Guide, Version 5, Release 1 (Version 5.1), Sept. 1999, and equivalent NCPDP Batch Implementation Guide, Version 1, Release 1 (Version 1.1), Jan. 2000, in support of Telecommunication Standard Implementation Guide, Version 5.1, for the NCPDP Data Record in the Detail Data Record	Telecommunication Standard Implementation Guide Version D, Release 0 (Version D.0), Aug. 2007 and equivalent Batch Standard Implementation Guide, Version 1, Release 2 (Version 1.2), NCPDP
	Dental health care claims	Accredited Standards Committee (ASC) X12N 837-Healthcare Claim: Dental, Version 4010, May 2000, WPC, 004010X097, and Addenda to Healthcare Claim: Dental, Version 4010, Oct. 2002, WPC, 004010X097A1	ASC X12 Standards for Electronic Data Interchange Technical Report Type 3-Health Care Claim: Dental (837), May 2006, WPC, 005010X224, and Type 1 Errata to Health Care Claim: Dental (837) ASC X12 Standards for Electronic Data Interchange Technical Report Type 3, Oct. 2007, WPC, 005010X224A1

continued next page

TABLE 2-3	Comparison of ASC X12 Version 4010/4010A1 and Version 5010 Standards—continued

Standard	Transaction	Version 4010/4010A1	Version 5010
	Professional health care claims	ASC X12N 837-Healthcare Claim: Professional, Volumes 1 and 2, Version 4010, May 2000, WPC, 004010X098, and Addenda to Healthcare Claim: Professional, Volumes 1 and 2, Version 4010, Oct. 2002, WPC, 004010X098A1	ASC X12 Standards for Electronic Data Interchange Technical Report Type 3-Health Care Claim: Professional (837), May 2006, WPC, 005010X222
	Institutional health care claims	ASC X12N 837-Healthcare Claim: Institutional, Volumes 1 and 2, Version 4010, May 2000, WPC, 004010X096, and Addenda to Healthcare Claim: Institutional, Volumes 1 and 2, Version 4010, Oct. 2002, WPC, 004010X096A1	ASC X12 Standards for Electronic Data Interchange Technical Report Type 3-Health Care Claim: Institutional (837), May 2006, WPC, 005010X223, and Type 1 Errata to Health Care Claim: Institutional (837), ASC X12 Standards for Electronic Data Interchange Technical Report Type 3, Oct. 2007, WPC, 005010X223A1

Compliance dates. With one exception, all covered entities must comply with the standards in the final rule by January 1, 2012, less than 3 years from the date that this was written. The exception is that small health plans have an additional year, to January 1, 2013, to comply with the Medicaid Pharmacy Subrogation standard. Note the following discussion in the preamble to the final rule:

> Covered entities are urged to begin preparations *now*, to incorporate effective planning, collaboration and testing in their implementation strategies, and to identity and mitigate any barriers long before the deadline. *While we have authorized contingency plans in the past, we do not intend to do so in this case, as such an action would likely adversely impact ICD-10 implementation activities. HIPAA gives us* [HHS] *authority to invoke civil money penalties against covered entities who do not comply with the standards, and we have been encouraged by industry to use our authority on a wider scale.*[48] [emphasis added]

As mentioned in Appendix B, the HITECH Act, enacted on February 17, 2009, as part of the American Recovery and Reinvestment Act, provides for increased civil penalties for noncompliance. Accordingly, your practice should discuss with your software vendor and other related business associates, such as your clearinghouse, how this federal policy change will affect your practice's policies and procedures and testing of transactions.

Testing dates. Again, referring to the preamble of this final rule, HHS outlines *expectations* for covered entities to conduct two levels of testing of the standard transactions.[49] To facilitate testing from the effective date of the final rule (March 17, 2009) until the compliance date (January 1, 2012), HHS permits, subject to trading partner agreement, "dual use of standards during that timeframe, so that either Version 4010/4010A1 or Version 5010, and either Version 5.1 or D.0, may be used."

---

[48] 74 *Federal Register* 3303.

[49] 74 *Federal Register* 3302–3303.

Level 1 testing: "The level 1 testing period is the period during which covered entities perform all of their internal readiness activities in preparation for testing the new versions of the standards with their trading partners. When we refer to compliance with Level 1, we mean that a covered entity can demonstrably create and receive compliant transactions, resulting from the completion of all design/build activities and internal testing."

- January 2009: Begin Level 1 testing period activities (gap analysis, design, development, internal testing) for Versions 5010 and D.0.

- January 2010: Begin internal testing for Versions 5010 and D.0.

- December 31, 2010: Achieve Level 1 compliance (covered entities have completed internal testing and can send and receive compliant transactions) for Versions 5010 and D.0.

Level 2 Testing: "The Level 2 testing period is the period during which covered entities are preparing to reach full production readiness with all trading partners. When a covered entity is in compliance with Level 2, it has completed end-to-end testing with each of its trading partners, and is able to operate in production mode with the new versions of the standards by the end of that period. By 'production mode,' we mean that covered entities can successfully exchange (accept and/or send) standard transactions and, as appropriate, be able to process them successfully."

- January 2011: Begin Level 2 testing period activities (end-to-end testing with trading partners, achieve production mode exchange of appropriate standard transactions with trading partners).

- January 1, 2012: "[A]ll covered entities will have reached Level 2 compliance, and must be fully compliant in using Versions 5010 and D.0 exclusively."

ICD-10: Code Set Standards Modification

The Notice of Proposed Rulemaking (NPRM) for ICD-10 was published in the *Federal Register* on August 22, 2008,[50] the same day that the NPRM for Version 5010/D.0 was published. As with the NPRM for Version 5010, the public had 60 days (until October 21, 2008) to comment on the NPRM for ICD-10. Similarly, the final rules for both ICD-10 and Version 5010/D.0 were published on January 16, 2009, in the *Federal Register,* as referenced at the beginning of this chapter.[51] The 5010/D.0 and ICD-10 rules go together: ICD-10 cannot work with the current 4010/4010A transaction standards, and 5010/D.0 needs to be in place in order to accommodate a different ICD-10 data element character length, as indicated below. In the discussion that follows, we reference both proposed and final ICD-10 rules as "for the most part, the final rule incorporates the provisions of the August 22, 2008 proposed rule,"[52] except for compliance date change.

ICD-10 final rule. The final rule adopts modifications to two code set standards in the Transactions and Code Sets Final Rule that required

---

[50] Department of Health and Human Services, Office of the Secretary, 45 CFR Parts 160 and 162: HIPAA Administrative Simplification: Modification to Medical Data Code Set Standards to Adopt ICD-10-CM and ICD-10-PCS; Proposed Rule, *Federal Register,* v. 73, n. 164, Aug. 22, 2008, pp. 49795–49832. This document is available for online access at www. hipaa.com. CFR refers to a specific Part of Title 45 of the Code of Federal Regulations. Further references to this document in this chapter will be cited in the standard reference format, eg, 73 *Federal Register* 49795–49832.

[51] 74 *Federal Register* 3295-3328 for the 5010/D.0 final rule, and 74 *Federal Register* 3328-3362 for the ICD-10 final rule.

[52] 74 *Federal Register* 3341.

compliance by covered entities on or after October 16, 2003. The January 16, 2009, ICD-10 final rule comprises two parts:

- *International Classification of Diseases, Tenth Revision, Clinical Modification* (ICD-10-CM)[53]
- *International Classification of Diseases, Tenth Revision, Procedure Coding System* (ICD-10-PCS).[54]

The final rule modifies standard medical data code sets for coding diagnoses (ICD-10-CM) in inpatient and outpatient settings and inpatient hospital procedures (ICD-10-PCS). Non-inpatient (ambulatory) procedures continue to be coded under the existing and modified rules using Current Procedural Terminology, 4th Edition (CPT-4), and Healthcare Common Procedure Coding Systems (HCPCS). Table 2-4 compares code sets under existing and modified rules. Even though only ICD-10-CM is germane to transactions generated in the physician practice, physicians that practice in hospitals, on staff or privileged, must be familiar with the structure of the ICD-10-PCS procedural codes.

Effective date. The effective date of the ICD-10 Final Rule was March 17, 2009. "The effective date is the date that the policies herein take effect, and new policies are considered to be officially adopted."[55]

---

[53] ICD-10-CM means International Classification of Diseases, 10th Revision, Clinical modification for diagnosis coding, including the Official ICD-10-CM Guidelines for Coding and Reporting, as maintained and distributed by the US Department of Health and Human Services (HHS). The National Center for Health Statistics (NCHS), part of the Centers for Disease Control and Prevention, is responsible for implementing the ICD-CM codes. ICD-10-CM applies to inpatient and outpatient diagnoses.

[54] ICD-10-PCS means International Classification of Diseases, 10th Revision, Procedure coding system for inpatient hospital procedure coding, including the Official ICD-10-PCS Guidelines for Coding and Reporting, as maintained and distributed by HHS. The Centers for Medicare & Medicaid Services (CMS) maintains the ICD-10-PCS codes. ICD-10-PCS applies only to inpatient procedures; non-inpatient (ambulatory) providers will continue to use current procedure codes, as outlined in text.

[55] 74 *Federal Register* 3328.

TABLE 2-4	Modification of Transaction and Code Set Rule Diagnosis and Procedure Codes

	Current Code Set Rule	Modified Code Set Rule
All diagnoses	International Classification of Diseases, 9th Revision, Clinical Modification, Volumes 1 and 2, including the Official ICD-9-CM Guidelines for Coding and Reporting, known as ICD-9-CM Volumes 1 and 2	ICD-10-CM
Inpatient procedures	International Classification of Diseases, 9th Revision, Clinical Modification, Volume 3, including the Official ICD-9-CM Guidelines for Coding and Reporting, known as ICD-9-CM Volume 3	ICD-10-PCS
Non-inpatient (ambulatory) procedures	CPT-4 and HCPCS	CPT-4 and HCPCS

Compliance date. The compliance date for the modification of the diagnosis and procedure code rule from ICD-9 to ICD-10 is October 1, 2013. "The compliance date is the date on which entities are required to have implemented the policies adopted in this rule."[56]

October 1 was chosen to coincide with the effective date of the annual Medicare Inpatient Prospective Payment System. The ICD-10 compliance date is 21 months after the compliance date for the 5010/D.0 rule. Based on health care industry input, "it appears that 24 months

---

[56] 74 *Federal Register* 3328.

(2 years) is the minimum amount of time that the industry needs to achieve compliance with ICD-10 once Version 5010/D.0 has moved into external (Level 2) testing,"[57] which commences January 1, 2011 (33 months before the ICD-10 compliance date).

> HHS has concluded that it would be in the health care industry's best interests if *all entities* [emphasis added] were to comply with the ICD-10 code set standards at the same time to ensure the accuracy and timeliness of claims and transaction processing.... The availability and use of crosswalks, mappings and guidelines should assist entities in making the switchover from ICD-9 to ICD-10 code sets on October 1, 2013, without the need for the concurrent use of both code sets [ICD-9 and ICD-10] in claims processing, medical record and related systems with respect to claims for services provided on the same day .... HHS believes that different compliance dates based on the size of a health plan would also be problematic since a provider has no way of knowing if a health plan qualifies as a small health plan or not.[58]

As is presently the case, coding before, on, or after the compliance date is based on the *date of discharge.*

Testing. Compliance dates for completing levels 1 and 2 testing were not mandated by HHS: "HHS has not established dates for Level 1 and Level 2 testing compliance for ICD-10 implementation. We encourage all industry segments to be ready to test their systems with ICD-10 as soon as it is feasible."[59] Recalling definitions of Level 1 and 2 testing from the 5010 final rule:

> Level 1 testing: "The Level 1 testing period is the period during which covered entities perform all of their internal readiness activities in

---

[57] 74 *Federal Register* 3334.

[58] 74 *Federal Register* 3335.

[59] 74 *Federal Register* 3336.

preparation for testing the new versions of the standards with their trading partners. When we refer to compliance with Level 1, we mean that a covered entity can demonstrably create and receive compliant transactions, resulting from the completion of all design/build activities and internal testing."[60]

Level 2 testing: "The Level 2 testing period is the period during which covered entities are preparing to reach full production readiness with all trading partners. When a covered entity is in compliance with Level 2, it has completed end-to-end testing with each of its trading partners, and is able to operate in production mode with the new versions of the standards by the end of that period. By 'production mode,' we mean that covered entities can successfully exchange (accept and/or send) standard transactions and, as appropriate, be able to process them successfully."[61]

ICD-9 v. ICD-10

ICD-10-CM codes will replace the currently used ICD-9-CM diagnosis codes that were "adopted as a HIPAA [code set] standard in 2000 for reporting diagnoses, injuries, impairments, and other health problems and their manifestations, and causes of injury, disease, impairment or other health problems in standard transactions."[62] ICD-9-CM diagnoses codes, of which there are approximately 13,000,[63] are 3 to 5 digits long.

The ICD-9-CM code set functionality "has been exhausted" and "is nearing the end of its useful life."[64] In addition to concerns with space limitations, there are three other key reasons to replace this code set:[65]

---

[60] 74 *Federal Register* 3302.

[61] Ibid.

[62] 73 *Federal Register* 49798.

[63] 73 *Federal Register* 49799.

[64] Ibid.

[65] 73 *Federal Register* 49799–49800.

- Effects of workarounds on structural hierarchy
  - Because some parts of the ICD-9-CM are full, codes "must be assigned to other topically unrelated chapters," making the codes sometimes difficult to find.
- Lack of detail
  - "[I]n an age of electronic health records, it does not make sense to use a coding system that lacks specificity and does not lend itself well to updates.... Emerging health care technologies, new and advanced terminologies, and the need for interoperability amid the increase in electronic health records (EHRs) and personal health records (PHRs) require a standard code set that is expandable and sufficiently detailed to accurately capture current and future health care information."[66]
- Obsolescence
  - The ICD is developed and maintained by the World Health Organization (WHO). ICD-9-CM is no longer supported or maintained by the WHO: "As we [United States] become a global community, it is vital that our health care data represent current medical conditions and technologies, and that they are compatible with the international version of ICD-10."[67]

In contrast to the ICD-9-CM, "ICD-10-CM diagnosis codes are three (3) to seven (7) alphanumeric characters," and "the number of ICD-10-CM codes is approximately 68,000. The ICD-10-CM code set provides much more information and detail within the codes than ICD-9-CM, facilitating timely electronic processing of claims by reducing requests

---

[66] 73 *Federal Register* 49800.

[67] Ibid.

for additional information."[68] This last point is very important: in conjunction with Version 5010 transaction standards modifications, ICD-10-CM will facilitate better information exchange between health care stakeholders, thereby leading to more efficient processing of claims and payments. Looking to the future, the ICD-10 NPRM concludes that "ICD-10 code sets provide a standard coding convention that is flexible, providing unique codes for all substantially different procedures of health conditions and allowing new procedures and diagnoses to be easily incorporated as new codes for both existing and future clinical protocols."[69] The final rule concurs with this statement.[70]

The ICD-10 NPRM provided a compliance date of October 1, 2011, for use of ICD-10-CM in physician practices and by other covered entities. During the ICD-10 proposed rule public comment period, the Workgroup for Electronic Data Interchange (WEDI), in its advisory role to HHS under the HIPAA administrative simplification legislation and enabling regulations, submitted comments on the ICD-10 NPRM to HHS. These comments indicated that the compliance date offered insufficient time for a successful implementation in the health care industry.[71] Instead, WEDI "recommend[ed] that a minimum of four years [would] be needed after completion of transaction upgrades and a total of six years after publication of the final rules for upgrades of

---

[68] 73 *Federal Register* 49801.

[69] 73 *Federal Register* 49800.

[70] "The ICD-10 code sets provide a standard coding convention that is flexible, providing unique codes for all substantially different health conditions. It also allows new procedures and diagnoses to be easily incorporated as new codes for both existing and future clinical protocols. ICD-10-CMS and ICD-10-PCS provide specific diagnosis and treatment information that can improve quality measurements and patient safety, and the evaluation of medical processes and outcomes. ICD-10-PCS has the capability to readily expand and capture new procedures and technologies." 74 *Federal Register* 3330.

[71] Letter from Jim Whicker, Chair, WEDI, to Centers for Medicare & Medicaid Services, Oct. 20, 2008. See www.WEDI.org.

transactions and medical code sets (October 1 after the anniversary of the sixth year)."[72] The WEDI proposed compliance date for ICD-10 would make that date near or several years after the end of the Decade of Health Information Technology in 2014. By taking such a long period of time, the US health care industry would be unable to achieve the objectives of implementing electronic health records (EHRs) and interoperability in a timely manner—as reflected in the EHR-adoption incentive period as outlined in the HITECH Act[73]—and cost-effectively updating its code sets to comport with EHR clinical formats. The compliance date of October 1, 2013, just prior to completion of the Decade of Health Information Technology, reflects a compromise for health care stakeholders.[74]

In 2005, Linda Kloss, CEO of the Chicago-based American Health Information Management Association (AHIMA), made the following statement:

> The full benefits of an EHR can only be realized if we improve the quality of data that EHRs are designed to manage. The current classification coding system used in the US, ICD-9-CM, is a 30-year-old system and can no longer accurately describe today's practice of medicine. Continuing to use this system jeopardizes the ability to effectively collect and use accurate, detailed healthcare data and

---

[72] Ibid.

[73] 4101 *HITECH Act* 353–355.

[74] "In establishing the ICD-10 compliance date, we have sought to select a date that achieves a balance between the industry's need to implement ICD-10 with a feasible amount of time, and our need to begin reaping the benefits of the use of these code sets; stop the hierarchical deterioration and other problems associated with the continued use of the ICD-9-CM code sets; align ourselves with the rest of the world's use of ICD-10 to achieve global health care data compatibility; plan and budget for the transition to ICD-10 appropriately; and mitigate the cost of further delays. We [HHS] believe that an October 1, 2013 ICD-10 compliance date achieves that balance, being 2 years later than our proposed October 2011 ICD-10 compliance date and providing a total of nearly 5 years from the publication of the Version 5010 final rule through final compliance with ICD-10." 74 *Federal Register* 3334.

information for the betterment of domestic and global healthcare. By failing to upgrade, we could find ourselves building an infrastructure that does not provide the information necessary to meet the healthcare demands of the 21st century.[75]

On November 5, 2003, in a letter to then-secretary of HSS Tommy Thompson, the National Committee on Vital and Health Statistics (NCVHS) recommended that ICD-10-CM be adopted as a HIPAA Administrative Simplification Code Set Standard.[76] NCVHS made the following observation in its letter:

> Benefits are harder to quantify, but appear to outweigh the costs. They include facilitating improvements to the quality of care and patient safety, fewer rejected claims, improved information for disease management, and more accurate reimbursement rates for emerging technologies. These costs and benefits and related issues also have been substantially documented in testimony before the Subcommittee, as well as in a cost/benefit study by the RAND Corporation (RAND)[77] that was specially commissioned by NCVHS.

The ICD-10 NPRM highlights the following projected benefits for adopting ICD-10:[78]

- more accurate payments for new procedures,
- fewer rejected claims,
- fewer improper claims,
- better understanding of new procedures,

---

[75] Kloss L. The Promise of ICD-10-CM. *Health Management Technology,* July 2005, p. 48. Available online at: www.healthmgttech.com.

[76] Available online at: www.ncvhs.hhs.gov/031105lt.htm.

[77] The referenced RAND study is Libicki MC, Brahmakulam IT, *The Costs and Benefits of Moving to the ICD-10 Code Sets.* TR-132-DHS. Santa Monica, CA: RAND Corporation, March 2004. Available online in portable document format (pdf) at: www.rand.org/pubs/technical_reports/2004/RAND_TR132.sum.pdf.

[78] 73 *Federal Register* 49821.

- improved disease management, and

- better understanding of health conditions and health care outcomes.

For physician practices, the NPRM analysis estimates that practices, on average, will experience costs of 0.04 percent of revenue/receipts, which "include a portion of the coding training costs and productivity losses in addition to costs directly allocated to physicians and practice expenses."[79] In the final rule, this estimate is revised to 0.03 percent of revenue/receipts, "based on industry comments received during the proposed rule's comment period,"[80] and use of more recent industry cost information. Actual costs and benefits will have to be determined by each practice.

Crosswalks. HHS acknowledges that crosswalks, or mappings of data element code values, between ICD-9 and ICD-10 "will be critical" for making the transition from ICD-9 to ICD-10. Under section 1174(b)(2)(B)(ii) of the act, HIPAA administrative simplification requires that "if a code set is modified under this subsection, the modified code set shall include instructions on how data elements of health information that were encoded prior to the modification may be converted or translated so as to preserve the informational value of the data elements that existed before the modification . . . and in a manner that minimizes the disruption and cost of complying with such modification."[81] Bi-directional crosswalks that can translate from the old code to the new or from the new to the old are referred to as *general equivalency mappings*. The National Center for Health Statistics (NCHS) of the Centers for Disease Control and Prevention (CDC) has developed a bi-directional mapping between ICD-9-CM diagnosis codes and

---

[79] 73 *Federal Register* 49820.

[80] 74 *Federal Register* 3357.

[81] 74 *Federal Register* 3337.

ICD-10-CM, which is available online at www.cdc.gov/nchs/about/ otheract/icd9/icd10cm.htm. Once on the site, you can download Diagnosis Code Set General Equivalence Mappings [Zip, 1.2MB] and start with the Documentation and Users Guide (2007 Version).[82]

CMS has developed bi-directional mappings between ICD-9-CM, Volume 3, and ICD-10-PCS as well as a guide for using the mappings, which is available online at www.cms.hhs.gov/ICD10/01m_2009_ ICD10PCS.asp.

What This Means to Your Practice

The clock is ticking for Version 5010/D.0 and ICD-10! Each final rule proposed that health care–covered entities begin as soon as possible, and no later than the effective date of March 17, 2009, to begin test planning, starting with a gap analysis. If your practice hasn't started planning yet, you should begin thinking immediately about how these transaction version and code set changes will impact your practice, especially business-related policies and procedures. You will want help from your IT vendor, because the 5010/D.0 and ICD-10 modifications will have significant impacts on any software that is related to standard transactions and on how you identify diagnoses in your electronic health record and practice management systems.

The final 5010/D.0 and ICD-10 transaction and code set rule modifications will have a significant impact on your practice's administrative policies and procedures. Time will pass quickly from today to each rule's compliance date(s). Also, the federal HITECH Act electronic information technology and privacy initiatives will compound your workload, as clinical workflows, policies, and procedures change as you introduce new electronic tools and records for collecting, compiling, safeguarding, analyzing, and reporting data.

---

[82] The reader may access an updated version by the time this book is published. At the time of this writing, the filename is: *Dxgem_guide_2007.pdf* (26 pages).

The first step is to have an organizational meeting within your practice to develop a game plan. Have your software vendor attend and outline its plan for enabling the 5010/D.0 and ICD-10 standards in your software. Plan to meet monthly to check progress, and make sure that key workforce members are aware of and understand the final rules, and acknowledge same in writing. The processes of planning for these changes and assessing their impacts have been discussed in other chapters of this book, the books mentioned earlier in this chapter, and in *EHR Implementation: A Step-by-Step Guide for the Medical Practice*[83] and *Technical and Financial Guide to EHR Implementation.*[84]

It is important for your practice to follow developments related to these rules between effective and compliance dates. To keep your practice informed, consider subscribing—at no cost—to the California HealthCare Foundation's daily electronic newsletter, *iHealthBeat,* which is available online at www.ihealthbeat.org. As discussed elsewhere in this chapter, HITECH Act electronic information technology and privacy initiatives will affect how you conduct business in your practice. Periodically check the Library of Congress Web site, http://thomas.loc.gov, to keep abreast of further federal legislative initiatives.[85] You also can follow these developments, as well as enabling federal regulatory initiatives that will impact your practice, at www.cms.hhs.gov and www.hipaa.com.

Payment Processing

In the past, when a patient visited a physician's practice, he or she would present a benefit card, have the physician provide medical services, and either pay for the service by check or credit card at the point of service or mail in a check to the physician's practice after receiving a

---

[83] Hartley CP, Jones ED. Chicago, IL: American Medical Association, 2005.

[84] Hartley CP, Jones ED, Ens D, Whitt D. Chicago, IL: American Medical Association, 2007(R).

[85] See House Lawmaker's 2009 Health Care Agenda Includes Health IT. Nov. 11, 2008.

bill through the mail. Today, the process is quite different. First, patients have a variety of health care benefit programs—either group or individual—and generally make a co-insurance payment at the physician's practice prior to receiving service; a balance payment, if any, is made after the health plan or plans have adjudicated the claim. Today, and increasingly, those payments are made by credit or debit card.

Safeguarding protected health information in the practice and controlling access to protected health information by unauthorized users are paramount objectives of the HIPAA administrative simplification privacy and security rules. Relatively little attention was given to payments during the initial promulgation of those rules, as compared to protecting information contained in a patient's health care record. This is changing for the health care industry, and there are two rules that your practice must comply with: the Federal Trade Commision's Red Flags Rule and the Payment Card Industry Data Security Standard.

Red Flag Rules

The Federal Trade Commission (FTC) has issued the so-called Red Flags Rule that requires "financial institutions and creditors to develop and implement written identity theft prevention programs, as part of the Fair and Accurate Credit Transaction (FACT) Act of 2003."[86] These rules were supposed to go into effect November 1, 2008, but on October 22, 2008, the FTC extended that compliance date 6 months to May 1, 2009. Then, on April 30, 2009, the FTC extended the compliance date an additional three months to August 1, 2009.[87] More

---

[86] New "Red Flag" Requirements for Financial Institutions and Creditors Will Help Fight Identity Theft. *FTC Business Alert,* nd. Available online at: www.ftc.gov/bcp/edu/pubs/business/alerts/alt.shtm.

[87] "FTC Will Grant Three-Month Delay of Enforcement of 'Red Flags' Rule Requiring Creditors and Financial Institutions to Adopt Identity Theft Prevention Programs," News Release, April 30, 2009, available online at www.ftc.gov/opa/2009/04/redflagsrule.shtm.

recently, the FTC extended the compliance date for the third time by three months, to November 1, 2009.[88]

The FTC considers "most healthcare organizations to be creditors under the rule."[89] A creditor would be required to establish guidelines on identity theft, prevention, and mitigation—not unlike the risk analysis that a health care provider, as a covered entity, must perform as part of compliance with the HIPAA Administrative Simplification Security Rule. Categories of red flags include the following[90]:

- alerts, notifications, or other warnings received from consumer reporting agencies or service providers, such as fraud detection services;

- presentation of suspicious documents;

- presentation of suspicious personal identifying information, such as a suspicious address change;

- unusual use of, or other suspicious activity related to, a covered account; and

- notice from customers, victims of identity theft, law enforcement authorities, or other persons regarding possible identity theft in connection with covered accounts held by the creditor.

---

[88] "FTC Announces Expanded Business Education Campaign on 'Red Flag' Rules," July 29, 2009, which is available online at www.ftc.gov/opa/2009/07/redflag.shtm.

[89] Blesch G, Yellow flags on "red flags" rule. *Modern Healthcare,* Oct. 27, 2008, available online at www.modernhealthcare.com/article/20081027/SUB/810249985.

[90] See Bass, Berry & Sims, PLC. Red Flag for Healthcare Providers: The FTC's New Red Flag and Address Discrepancy Rules. *Health Law Update,* Oct. 8, 2008. Available online at: www.bassberry.com (go to Communications Center>Newsletters> October 8, 2008).

Red Flag Rules Policies and Procedures

Sample Policy: The Federal Trade Commission (FTC) has issued Red Flags Rules that require financial institutions and creditors, including healthcare practices such as ours, to develop and implement written identity theft prevention and detection program.

We may be subject to the Red Flag Rules for the following reasons:

- We accept credit and debit cards for payment.
- We coordinate payments through multiple health plans and require a balance payment to close out the claim.
- We extend credit to our patients.
- Invoices sent to our patients include information about an episode of care.

Our practice will follow all federal and state laws and reporting requirements regarding identity theft, and we will review this policy at least annually. Members of our workforce will be trained by November 1, 2009 and new members will trained within a reasonable time after they have joined the practice.

Sample Procedures: Our security official, <Name> and billing manager, _____ <Name> are the owners of this risk. This is a Level 4 risk for us.

1. Our practice has complied with HIPAA Security Rule's policies and procedures and implemented safeguards to protect confidential health information.
2. We identified the following Red Flags as events that have, or could occur, in our practice.
   - The photo offered from a patient does not look like the patient, or the photo-ID appears to be altered.

- A patient has changed his/her name and does not provide supporting documentation, such as a marriage certificate or new social security number.

- A patient has an insurance number but does not produce an insurance card or physical documentation of insurance.

- The patient's insurance card (Medicare, Medicaid, Private Payer) does not match the subscriber's or insured's name.

- Mail repeatedly sent to the address provided by the patient is returned and we cannot contact the patient to provide an updated address.

- Another provider, law enforcement agency, or insurer sends us an alert that the patient's identity may have been compromised.

- The photo provided in the patient record does not match the patient.

- Records showing medical treatment that is inconsistent with a physical examination or with a medical history as reported by the patient.

- A complaint or question from a patient about the receipt of a collection notice from a bill collector.

- A patient or health insurer report that coverage for legitimate hospital stays is denied because insurance benefits have been depleted or a lifetime cap has been reached.

- A complaint or question from a patient about information added to a credit report by a health care provider or health insurer.

- A dispute of a bill by a patient who claims to be the victim of any type of identity theft.

3. When patients call to schedule an appointment, they are asked to bring the following documentation:

    - Driver's license or other photo ID. If the photo ID does not show current residence, the patient may bring in a utility bill or other correspondence indicating current residence. If the

patient is a minor, the patient's parent or guardian will produce the documentation.

■ Current health insurance card.

■ We may choose to waive this documentation for patients
who are known to the workforce members and have visited
the practice in the last six months.

4. As we transition into electronic medical records, we will take a
photo of each patient and upload it into the patient's record so
that the practitioner can match the patient to the appropriate
episode of care. Our system also produces barcodes so that we
can match chemotherapy to the appropriate patient.

5. Credit card information may or may not be stored in our
e-commerce system, but we do not have access to that payment
information. Credits to an account are made through our
e-commerce partner who acts on our behalf as a business associate.

6. During routine system audits, we will immediately act on any
atypical reports that flag a possible identity theft through one or
more of the following actions:

■ Determine whether this is a system or hardware problem.

■ Validate the data by determining whether the patient inten-
tionally provided false information or if our workforce inac-
curately entered information into the system.

7. Mitigation:

■ Our Security Official or billing manager will be immediately
notified if any workforce member suspects identity theft.

■ According to the FTC's and State Identity Theft Laws, we will
contact the patient, submit required remediation validation
records, and direct the patient to immediately report the suspected identity theft to bank and credit card companies.

■ Our HIPAA security policies and procedures regarding
breach of confidential health information will be put
into effect.

- As appropriate, we will notify the following:
    i.   Affected patient
    ii. Law enforcement agencies
    iii. Referring physicians involved in the patient's care.
    iv. Business associates, including credit card companies, payers, and banks of a confirmed identity theft.

- As appropriate, we will determine whether to close out the patient's medical record.

Payment Card Industry Data Security Standard

As your practice prepares to comply with the Red Flags Rule, you also need to consider the payment card industry's new Data Security Standard (PCI DSS), version 1.2, released October 1, 2008, because you accept credit and debit cards at the point of sale and likely on invoices sent to patients to conclude an episode of care (claim).[91] PCI DSS applies "to all organizations that store, process or transmit cardholder data."[92] "If you are a merchant who accepts or processes payment cards, you must comply with the PCI DSS."[93]

PCI DSS outlines three steps for compliance, which would be part of your practice's risk analysis:

- Access—Identifying cardholder data, taking an inventory of your IT assets and business processes for payment card processing, and analyzing them for vulnerabilities that could expose cardholder data.

---

[91] Information on PCI DSS is taken from the PCI Security Standards Council's *PCI Quick Reference Guide: Understanding the Payment Card Industry Data Security Standard Version 1.2*. Available online at: www.pcisecuritystandards.org/pdfs/pci_ssc_quick_guide.pdf.

[92] Ibid., p. 6.

[93] Ibid., p. 7.

- Remediate—Fixing vulnerabilities and not storing cardholder data unless you need it.

- Report—Compiling and submitting required remediation validation records (if applicable), and submitting compliance reports to the acquiring bank and card brands you do business with.[94]

PCI DSS outlines 6 goals comprising 12 PCI DSS requirements that are part of version 1.2.[95] These are reproduced in Table 2-5 for the attention of your practice's security official.

Your security official will note that many of these requirements mirror risk analysis and the policies and procedures that your practice has in place for compliance with the HIPAA Administrative Simplification Security Rule. The types of questions that your practice needs to address, if it does not know the answers today, are:

- Does your practice store payment card numbers?
- Does your practice store payment card expiration dates?
- Does your practice store payment card verification codes?
- Does your practice store patient (or plan subscriber) data from the payment card magnetic stripe?
- Does your practice store other personal data?

The *PCI Quick Reference Guide* shows the results of a Forrester Consulting survey of businesses in the United States and Europe for each of these risky behavior categories (see p. 4 of the *Guide*). Check the *Guide* for those results after you determine your practice's activities within each category.

---

[94] Ibid., p. 5.

[95] Ibid., p. 8.

| TABLE 2-5 | Six Goals of PCI DSS Requirements |

Goals	PCI DSS Requirements
Build and maintain a secure network	1. Install and maintain a firewall configuration to protect cardholder data. 2. Do not use vendor-supplied defaults for system passwords and other security parameters.
Protect cardholder data	3. Protect stored cardholder data. 4. Encrypt transmission of cardholder data across open, public networks.
Maintain a vulnerability management program	5. Use and regularly update anti-virus software or programs. 6. Develop and maintain secure systems and applications.
Implement strong access control measures	7. Restrict access to cardholder data by business need-to-know. 8. Assign a unique ID to each person with computer access. 9. Restrict physical access to cardholder data.
Regularly monitor and test networks	10. Track and monitor access to network resources and cardholder data. 11. Regularly test security systems and processes.
Maintain an information security policy	12. Maintain a policy that addresses information security for employees and contractors.

What This Means for Your Practice

The FTC's Red Flags Rule and PCI DSS shift your practice's focus to include payment practices and identity protection of your patients (customers) as well as their electronic protected health information.[96] After three enforcement delays, the Red Flags Rule has to be in place by November 1, 2009. Check www.ftc.gov for further updates on compliance and enforcement. If your practice accepts payment cards, your practice needs to comply with PCI DSS version 1.2 today. These rules provide the opportunity for your practice to conduct your risk analysis, reevaluate how well your policies and procedures are working, and refine and introduce new policies and procedures as necessary to mitigate potential risks associated with identity protection.

Looking Ahead

The US economy is in a serious recession. With enactment of the HITECH Act provisions and the financial incentives of the American Recovery and Reinvestment Act on February 17, 2009, which are discussed in Appendix B, the Obama Administration dramatically increased the prospect of health care providers spending money on electronic health records and of converting their paper-based practices to electronic environments beginning in 2011 and continuing into the middle of the next decade.

The demand for health care services will continue to grow, especially after baby boomers begin moving into Medicare, also beginning in 2011. In order to contain rising health care costs for services, the federal government is focused on ways to control the administrative costs of health care processing. These costs continue to increase at a rate relatively higher than the overall rate of inflation.

---

[96] Although the focus here is on the electronic safeguards, do not forget that the HIPAA Administrative Simplification Privacy Rule covers your practice's responsibility to safeguard oral and written protected health information as well.

Increasingly, business is conducted on the Internet, including handling bank transactions, paying for air travel by credit or debit card, downloading boarding passes, and building information bases through search engines. Today, these activities are performed from desktops and laptops using Wi-Fi; tomorrow these tasks will be performed using smaller, more mobile instruments such as cell phones and personal data assistants (PDAs) connected to the Internet.

From the physician practice perspective, these factors and changes are of critical importance because they impact practice workflows, privacy and security, performance and efficiency, cash flow, and morale. When HIPAA administrative simplification was enacted in August 1996 and in the following years when the federal government was promulgating transaction and code set, privacy, and security, identifier, and enforcement standards regulations, little thought was given to the role of banks in the health care payments process, ie, the actual movement of money as opposed to the electronic remittance advice or paper explanation of benefits.

Clearly, posting and recognition of funds by a practice have a significant impact on cash flow. In addition, with denials and exceptions of claim payments as high as one in five (or 20 percent), some claims involving multiple health plan payers, and physicians experiencing the squeeze on allowable payment for service, it is no surprise that physicians are increasingly concerned about payment.[97]

---

[97] Another wrinkle and concern for physicians is the growth in health savings accounts (HSAs), where the patient as consumer is responsible for paying for health care expenditures below a high deductible threshold. In 2009, that threshold (minimum) is $1,150 for single persons and $2,300 for families. It may be easier for physician practices to determine benefit eligibility and seek payment from a health plan than from an HSA consumer, especially if it is early in the year and the patient's HSA account has not been funded. Contribution levels in 2009 are $3,000 for a single person and $5,950 for a family. Data for 2009 are available online at: http://bestquoteus.com/bestquotes/health-insurance/irs-hsa-health-savings-accounts-guidelines-for-2009/.

Banks are and will continue to be key players in the health care remittance and payment cycle. After all, at one time or another, and frequently more than once, each dollar of health care expenditure goes through the banking system. An electronic funds transfer is sent by health plan payers directly to health care providers' banks. Paper checks frequently are sent either directly from the health plan to the providers' bank lockbox or deposited by the practice in the provider's bank account if checks are sent via the practice.

The way in which the payment gets from the health plan payer to the health care provider for services rendered is important. However, there is an even more important issue to be resolved if health care is *ever* to achieve efficiency and benefit from electronic business systems. Health care is the only industry in which a provider sends out an invoice for services rendered–the claim–and has a very small likelihood of knowing what his or her payment will be.[98]

A patient coming into a practice may have an initial co-insurance (eg, co-payment or deductible), multiple coordinating health plans (eg, patient and spouse beneficiary plans), and a balance payment to close out the claim episode. These are complex transactions and quite a bit different than paying a monthly utility bill, where the utility knows exactly what it will receive back in payment from the customer.

Compounding the difficulty in payment processing, health care providers work with many health plan beneficiaries, and each health plan payer has specific business requirements outlined in a companion guide that tell the health care provider submitting the claim exactly what situational data element values the health plan will accept in an electronic claim submission. In the final 5010/D.0 rule, HHS reported that "the improvements to Version 5010 should minimize dependence

---

[98] This is a different situation than for a pharmacy as covered entity, which can connect in real time with a pharmacy benefit manager (PBM) of a patient's health plan and determine the patient's co-payment at point of sale and the amount that the PBM will eventually forward to the pharmacy to conclude the sale.

on companion guides."[99] Furthermore, HHS stated that "we strongly discourage health plans from having companion guides unless they are focused significantly on the basics for connectivity, trading partner arrangements, and use of situational data elements. . . . [I]f companion guides contradict the implementation guides, the transaction will not be compliant."[100]

Summary

The changes discussed in this chapter, at the midpoint of the Decade of Health Information Technology, are the beginning of an acceleration in administrative and clinical processing in the physician practice specifically and across the health care environment generally. Change now and in the future will encompass technology, legislation, and regulation in order to improve practice efficiency, improve the quality of delivery of health care to patients in terms of outcomes, and decrease the administrative costs of processing health care transactions. As the authors have discussed in other publications, the change in clinical processes (eg, EHRs and the drive toward certification of those EHR systems) has been greater than change in administrative processing in the past 5 years. Change is expected to accelerate with both clinical and administrative processing in the next 5 years, bringing us to the close of the Decade of Health Information Technology in 2014.

---

[99] 74 *Federal Register* 3307.

[100] 74 *Federal Register* 3308.

KEY POINTS

- The HITECH Act, included in the American Recovery and Reinvestment Act of 2009 (ARRA) provides incentive funding for electronic health record systems, implementation and training; and it also mandates stepped up privacy and security requirements.

- The Meaningful Use Matrix provides an excellent roadmap for 2011, 2013, and 2015 reporting requirements. The most current matrix is available at www.HHS.gov or at www.hipaa.com.

- Before 2014, transaction standards will transition from 4010/4010A/5.1 to 5010/D.0 and ICD-9-CM codes will be replaced with ICD-10-CM, which will impact your policies and procedures. Watch for updates.

- Breach Notification requirements are so substantial that the cost or inconvenience of loading encryption software to servers, portable computers, and handheld devices becomes well justified.

- Business Associates are now covered entities that are required to put policies and procedures in place, which in turn, requires practices to construct and made available, a new business associates' agreement.

Evaluating Safeguards for Technology Adoption, Updates, and Health Information Exchange (HIE)

IN THIS CHAPTER, YOU WILL LEARN

- How to develop new work processes that protect your systems, facility, and electronically protected health information
- How to customize physical and technical policies and procedures for your environment that also make sense to your workforce
- How to evaluate physical and technical safeguards of health exchange partners such as labs, pathology and imaging centers, hospitals, and patients.

Key Terms

Access control: Mechanisms for protecting sensitive communication transmissions over open or private networks so that the communication cannot easily be intercepted and interpreted by parties other than the intended recipient.

Audit controls: Mechanisms employed to record and examine system activity.

Audit trail: Information regarding activity on the network, which provides the basis for a security audit.

Authentication: Corroboration that a person is the person claimed to be.

Availability: The property that data or information are accessible and usable upon demand by an authorized person.

Confidentiality: Property that data or information are not made available or disclosed to unauthorized persons or processes.

Covered entity: Health plan, health care clearinghouse, or health care provider (eg, physician practice) that transmits any health information in electronic form under the Health Insurance Portability and Accountability Act Administrative Simplification Transaction Rule.

Data authentication: Corroboration that data have not been altered or destroyed in an unauthorized manner.

Decryption: Reverse of an encryption, which transforms data into a usable form.

Electronic storage media: Electronic storage media include memory devices in computers (hard drives) and any removable/transportable digital memory medium, such as magnetic tape or disk, optical disk, or digital memory card, or transmission media used to exchange information already in electronic storage media. Transmission media include the Internet (open), extranet (using Internet technology to link a business with information accessible only to collaborating parties), leased lines, dial-up lines, private networks, and the physical movement of removable/transportable electronic storage media. Certain transmissions, including of paper, via facsimile (fax), and of voice, via telephone, are not considered to be transmissions via electronic media because the information being exchanged did not exist in electronic form before the transmission.

Electronic protected health information: Protected health information that meets requirements (i) and (ii) of the definition of protected health information, namely, information that is (i) transmitted by electronic media or (ii) maintained in electronic media.

Emergency access: Documented instructions for obtaining necessary information during a crisis.

Encryption: Use of an algorithmic process to transform data into a form in which there is a low probability of assigning meaning without use of a confidential process or key.

Implementation specification: A required or addressable implementation specification that provides instruction to a covered entity with respect to actions that must be taken to comply with a particular standard.

Information system: Interconnected set of information resources under the same direct management control that shares common functionality. System resources normally include hardware, software, data, information, applications, communications, and people.

Integrity: The property that data or information have not been altered or destroyed in an unauthorized manner.

Password: Confidential authentication information composed of a string of characters.

Protected health information: Individually identifiable health information that is (i) transmitted by electronic media, (ii) maintained in electronic media, or (iii) transmitted or maintained in any other form or media (eg, oral or written health information).

Required or addressable: For a particular safeguard standard, a required implementation specification requires implementation by the covered entity, whereas an addressable implementation specification permits the covered entity to determine the reasonableness and appropriateness of the implementation specification, implement it if it is reasonable and appropriate, and implement an alternative equivalent measure if reasonable and appropriate, with the covered entity documenting its decision making in writing.

Security incident: Attempted or successful unauthorized access, use, disclosure, modification, or destruction of information or interference with system operations in an information system.

User: A person or entity with authorized access.

User identity (ID): A character string that identifies a person or other entity that accesses information systems or applications. User IDs are accompanied by a password or other form of authentication (eg, biometric) known to or possessed by the individual associated with the ID.

Workstation: An electronic computing device, for example, a laptop or desktop computer, tablet, personal data assistant, or any other device that performs similar functions; and electronic media stored in its immediate environment.

The more we adopt technology, the more it seems the stakeholders who developed the framework around administrative simplification, including the technical, physical, and administrative safeguards, may have brought in a fortune-teller to work for them. Previously, the privacy and security policies and procedures your practice was required to adopt may have seemed a little over the top, but they now serve as the platform for the technology you continue to bring into the practice. With a little tweaking, those privacy and security practices are standing the test of time, and they now support the basic infrastructure of health information technology (HIT) exchange.

If you didn't put privacy and security policies and procedures in place before, do it now. Although there have been rapid changes in health care since 2000, the pace of those changes was like that of a turtle crossing the road. Today, health care has moved rapidly into ePrescribing, biometric authentication, personal health records, claims attachments, quality reporting, and clinical decision-support tools.

Case Study

Your patient population has been aging, and you've noticed an increase in patients with orthopaedic, cardiology, and oncology needs. At the same time, the children you once treated for broken bones and sports injuries are now parents, and they are bringing their children in for medical care. As you move from one exam room to another, you find yourself treating a child testing positive for strep; in another room, the 50-something weekend warrior who won't give up soccer; and in exam room 3, a lifelong friend and patient who has been diagnosed with breast cancer.

You are determined to learn all you can about the latest cancer treatment and clinical trials. You access your electronic medical record (EMR) system and click on the link to clinical decision support (CDS). The CDS, with built-in artificial intelligence, detects symptoms coded into the patient record and then connects you with educational material relevant to the assigned diagnosis. You can then print this material and discuss the next step with your friend who is about to join a community of breast cancer fighters and survivors. Also built into the electronic system is your list of oncologist referrals, so you can quickly send a confidential encounter form to the oncology clinic to which you are entrusting her care. Embedded in that report is her medical history, current medication list, and a brief overview of her family and social histories.

Before stepping into the next exam room, you ePrescribe a muscle relaxer for your soccer patient and see that his insurance will cover the prescription you just ordered. Fortunately, you don't have to recall everything that happened at the end of the day, even though that's how you practiced medicine for nearly 20 years.

At the end of the day, as you review the EMR's system audit log, you notice that the scheduler, a neighbor of your breast cancer patient, has logged into the patient record and spent 21 minutes reviewing her health information. Upon further review of the audit logs, you see that the scheduler has been accessing other patient records. When questioned, she says the practice

continued next page

routinely overbooks appointments and it helps if she has enough clinical information to determine whether the patient will show or not show.

You know that the patients' history of shows/no-shows is in the practice management system. And, your policies and procedures are very clear about unauthorized access to patient health information. But now you want to know how the scheduler gained access to the record, because front office personnel are not assigned access to clinical information. What do you do?

With the passage of the HITECH Act provisions of the American Recovery and Reinvestment Act, signed into law by President Obama on February 17, 2009, the pace of change will accelerate over the next several years with new privacy breach notification requirements, incentives for adoption of electronic health record systems, and inclusion of business associates of covered entities that will have to comply with the Security Rule beginning on February 17, 2010. We discuss each of these HITECH Act provisions in the preceding chapter and Appendix B.

Even with nearly 38 percent of physician practices purchasing electronic health records (EHRs), less than 10 percent of practices have experienced the benefits they bring.[1] Utilization requires a much better understanding of EHR capabilities (a process that takes time) as well as an understanding by your workforce of how to make them work (a process of getting comfortable using the system). Your workforce may know the basics of entering a patient's vitals, chief complaint, and reason for visit, but do these values correspond with the findings that are entered during the physical exam? Data accuracy will affect your billing outcomes and your reporting capabilities if you decide to participate in CMS-supported reimbursement incentives. What is the effect

---

[1] The Promises and Pitfalls of Health Information Technology 28, 2:322 doi: 10.1377/hlthaff.28.2.322. 2009.

if your practice plans to contract your clinical staff to an employer-supported health clinic?

Health IT Vendors' Support for Your Policies and Procedures

The American Recovery and Reinvestment Act of 2009 (ARRA), also known as the Stimulus Package, changed the rules for how business associates (BAs) support your policies and procedures. All businesses now must comply with the HIPAA security regulations in the same manner that covered entities comply. This means that BAs must perform security risk analyses and adopt written policies and procedures that address the HIPAA Security Rule's administrative, physical, and technical safeguards standards. Simply signing a BA agreement that states that you will "reasonably and appropriately protect" protected health information will no longer be sufficient. Consult Appendix B for details on how to assist your BAs as they transition to compliance with the Security Rule by February 17, 2010. Between now and the BA compliance date, you must demonstrate the safeguarding of your privacy and security policies and procedures by first securing a BA agreement with all third parties, including system designers, labs, imaging centers, and EMR software vendors. Most EMR vendors have a BA agreement, but the sales team's focus is on closing the sale, and they may overlook getting this agreement signed before handing the practice off to the implementation team.

Language in a BA agreement is the same as what would be used when implementing the Privacy Rule. A sample BA agreement is available for your review at the Office for Civil Rights web site, www.hhs.gov/ocr/hipaa/contractprov.html. If you choose to modify this agreement, consult a health law attorney before presenting it to your EMR vendor so that it does not conflict with your BA's efforts to comply with the Security Rule.

Mapping New Technology to the Security Rule

Since the final Security Rule was published in the *Federal Register* on February 20, 2003,[2] new hardware and software technology has been made available to make your life much easier, including

- single sign-on software that uses a finger image to access password-protected health information;
- ePrescribing and performance measurement with reimbursement incentives;
- convertible notebooks with bar code readers and interchangeable docking stations;
- smartphone capabilities used for e-mail or for downloading content onto a patient's phone;
- wireless bar code scanners and printers for matching patients to medical records; and
- high-speed personal scanners to transfer paper records into electronic files.

In addition, the Health Information Technology Standards Panel released health information exchange standards so that vendors and providers can move information between clinicians across practicing venues (hospitals, physicians, and labs) and between states.

The effective date of the Security Rule for all covered entities, except small health plans, which had an extra year to comply, was April 21, 2003, with the compliance date 2 years later on April 21, 2005.

---

[2] US Department of Health and Human Services, Office of the Secretary. 45 CFR Parts 160, 162, and 164: Health Insurance Reform: Security Standards; Final Rule. *Federal Register*, v. 8, n. 34, Feb. 20, 2003, pp. 8333-8381. Citations to this document hereafter in this chapter are in the standard reference format, eg, 68 *Federal Register* 8333–8381.

This chapter guides you through the analysis of your policies and procedures with a focus on technical and physical safeguards that support ongoing technology development. Critical points are highlighted as reminders as you continue to add technology to your practice. Along with the administrative safeguards discussed in Chapter 1, the technical and physical safeguards discussed in this chapter are the standards and implementation specifications that BAs must comply with starting February 17, 2010.

Technical Standards

By now, 4 years after the covered entity compliance date, your practice has implemented the security safeguards. As security becomes even more important with the growing use of electronic health record (EHR)[3] systems and ePrescribing[4] by health care providers now and in the coming years, you will find the policy and procedures information in this chapter useful as you check on your own policies and procedures. For each implementation specification, the requirement is listed along with an outline on how to comply, a suggested policy,[5] and reminders for reevaluating your policies and procedures.

---

[3] See the following publications on electronic health records (EHRs): Hartley CP, Jones ED III. *EHR Implemention: A Step-by-Step Guide for the Medical Practice*, Foreword by Newt Gingrich, Chicago, IL: AMA Press, 2005; Hartley CP, Jones ED, Ens D, Whitt D. *Technical and Financial Guide to EHR Implementation.* Chicago, IL: AMA, 2007.

[4] Electronic prescribing (ePrescribing) was included in the Medicare Modernization Act (MMA) of 2003. The final rule pertaining to formulary and benefit transactions, medication history transactions, and fill status notifications was published in the *Federal Register* on April 2, 2008. Additional information is available online at www.cms.hhs.gov/eprescribing/.

[5] Suggestions do not constitute legal advice, for which the practice should consult its attorney.

Technical Safeguards

The US Department of Health and Human Services (HHS) defines technical safeguards as "the technology and the policies and procedures for its use that protect electronic protected health information and control access to it."[6] In this section, a distinction is made between *reasonable* and *appropriate* actions, regardless of a practice's size, complexity, or environment of operation, and between *required* and *addressable* implementation specifications. You will need to be familiar with the following key terms, which are defined as follows: technical safeguards are used to protect the *confidentiality, integrity,* and *availability* of your practice's electronic protected health information.

There are five technical safeguard requirements for protecting your practice's information technology assets, including your patients' protected health information that is used, disclosed, transmitted, or stored in an electronic environment (see Table 3-1). It is important to remember that the Security Rule focuses on protection of electronic information, whereas the Privacy Rule covers access to and confidentiality of oral, written, and electronic protected health information. The technical safeguards, then, cover all computer workstations, laptops, handheld devices, database servers, application servers, data management systems, and infrastructure devices.

CRITICAL POINT

As your practice adds new electronic devices, be sure to inventory, reference, and update your written risk analysis and administrative safeguard policies and procedures for using such devices.

---

[6] 68 *Federal Register* 8376.

TABLE 3-1	Technical Safeguard Standards and Implementation Specifications

Security Standard	Implementation Specification	Required or Addressable
Access control	Unique user identification	Required
	Emergency access procedure	Required
	Automatic logoff	Addressable
	Encryption and decryption	Addressable
Audit controls		Required
Integrity	Mechanism to authenticate electronic protected health information	Addressable
Person or entity authentication		Required
Transmission security	Integrity controls	Addressable
	Encryption	Addressable

Many of the technical safeguards discussed in this section may require information from your hardware or software vendor. Be sure to ask your vendor if you have any questions. You may use *reasonable* and *appropriate* measures to demonstrate compliance.

Policies and Procedures

Access Control		
Technical Safeguard Standard	**Federal Register/ 45 CFR[7] Parts**	**Required or Addressable**
Access control	68 *Federal Register* 8378 45 CFR 164.312(a)(1)	Required

Requirement: Implement technical policies and procedures for electronic information systems that maintain electronic protected health information, allowing access only to those persons or software programs that have been granted access rights as specified in the Administrative Safeguard Standard, Information Access Management.

Sample policy: Our practice will implement technical policies and procedures for electronic information systems that maintain electronic protected health information, allowing access only to those persons or software programs that have been granted access rights as specified in the Administrative Safeguard Standard, Information Access Management.

Sample procedures: Our practice will establish policies and procedures to show how our electronic information systems allow persons or software programs to access electronic protected health information in the practice. Operationally, we will do this using control features embedded in our software application, operating system, database, or some combination thereof and by documenting our control procedures in writing as part of our technical safeguard policies.

As appropriate for our workforce and system, we will use one or more of the following approaches to control user access:

- Create a list. Our security official and/or system administrator will assign access to specific applications and add or delete persons, as appropriate.
- Access according to user identity. Access to information is based on user identity and role in the practice. For example, a receptionist may have access to payment information pertaining to a patient in order to collect any co-insurance at check-in but may not have access to the patient's health

---

[7] CFR means *Code of Federal Regulations*.

information. Similarly, a nurse may have access to the patient's health information but not to payment information. A larger practice may have more access restrictions where roles are more specialized in comparison to a small practice where workforce members undertake multiple functions.

■ Access according to role. This procedure is based on a workforce member's specific role in a practice rather than on user identity. If a workforce member performs multiple functions in a practice, then multiple role access permissions may be assigned.

■ Access according to context. This approach elaborates on access control by role by including additional access restrictions. Such restrictions might be time-based for part-time workforce members who work specific shifts or device-based, limiting access to certain workstations.

CRITICAL POINT

Make sure that your practice's responsible party (eg, office manager, chief information officer, or security official) reviews workforce member access on a regular basis according to the practice's method of control.

Unique User Identification

Technical Safeguard Standard	Federal Register/ 45 CFR Parts	Required or Addressable
Access control	68 *Federal Register* 8378 45 CFR 164.312(a)(2)(i)	Required

Requirement: Assign a unique name and/or number for identifying and tracking user identity.

Sample policy: Our security official will assess the practice's needs for access to electronic protected health information and make sure that workforce members only have access to such information required to fulfill their responsibilities. Workforce members shall not share or otherwise disclose user IDs or passwords with other workforce members. Generic or shared user IDs shall not be used to access records containing electronic protected health information.

Sample procedures: Our security official is responsible for assigning a unique user ID to each workforce member.

Our security official will:

■ manage and track user IDs, making any changes or deletions, as appropriate;

■ define the practice's policy regarding sharing and disclosing user IDs and passwords;

■ determine whether single sign-on software will be appropriate for clinicians to log on to both practice management and electronic medical record systems using finger-image access;

■ ensure the initial password assigned by the security official to a user is changed to a user-selected password on initial login; and based on our risk analysis, we will change passwords every <30> <60> <90> days.

CRITICAL POINT

The security official should have each workforce member provide the current password in a sealed envelope for storage in a secure environment in order to provide emergency access.

Emergency Access Procedure

Technical Safeguard Standard	Federal Register/ 45 CFR Parts	Required or Addressable
Access control	68 *Federal Register* 8378 45 CFR 164.312(a)(2)(ii)	Required

Requirement: Establish and implement, as needed, procedures for obtaining necessary electronic protected health information during an emergency.

Sample policy: Our security official will develop methods of accessing information that the practice needs in the event of an emergency or disaster. The security official and a second designated workforce member will be responsible for providing emergency access to electronic protected health information, including restoration or recovery of any loss of such information and the systems required to make the practice's electronic protected health information accessible in a timely manner.

Sample procedures: In our risk analysis, we determined that fire, vandalism, system failure, and natural disaster such as an earthquake, flood, fire, tornado, or hurricane were our primary risks that would result in loss of systems and access to electronic protected health information. An interruption in accessing a patient's medical information could hinder the practice's ability to provide appropriate treatment, thereby posing a risk to the patient's health.

In our risk analysis, our security official developed emergency access procedures and has coordinated them with our physical and administrative policies and procedures.

Our workforce members are fully cognizant of our emergency access control procedures. We will review the procedures periodically and document in writing actions taken in the event of having to execute those procedures.

We also have established a unique password for emergency access with our electronic medical record and practice management system vendors. Our security official, system administrator, and <physician> have access to this emergency password.

CRITICAL POINT

The security official and a designated backup workforce member, such as the office manager, should have the capabilities and resources necessary to provide emergency access to electronic protected health information.

Automatic Logoff		
Technical Safeguard Standard	*Federal Register/* 45 CFR Parts	Required or Addressable
Access control	68 *Federal Register* 8378 45 CFR 164.312(a)(2)(iii)	Addressable

Requirement: Implement electronic procedures that terminate an electronic session after a predetermined time of inactivity.

Sample policy: Our security official shall make sure that automatic logoff procedures are in place on all systems and devices that provide access to electronic protected health information, including desktops, laptops, tablets, and handheld devices.

Based on our risk analysis, we have set the time-out system default to be at the end of <8> <10> minutes of inactivity for nurses and <15> minutes for physicians. (Logoffs in high-traffic areas should be between 2 minutes for large practices and 5 minutes for small practices, and no longer than 10 minutes for any size practice in limited traffic areas.)

Sample procedures: Workforce members in a busy practice frequently leave their workstations without time to completely log off the computer system. The solution is to activate a password-protected screensaver that locks a workstation and prevents unauthorized users from viewing or accessing electronic protected health information but that does not log the user off the system. On the user's return to the workstation, it is only necessary to reenter the password to gain access as before. Your software vendor can help you set up these automatic logoff procedures if they are not already in place.

CRITICAL POINT

Workforce members should log off any computer near a patient when that patient is going to be unattended.

Encryption and Decryption		
Technical Safeguard Standard	**Federal Register/ 45 CFR Parts**	**Required or Addressable**
Access control	68 *Federal Register* 8378 45 CFR 164.312(a)(2)(iv)	Addressable

Requirement: Implement a mechanism to encrypt and decrypt electronic protected health information.[8]

Sample policy: Our notice of privacy practices outlines the practice's policy on communication over *open* networks or computer systems. As a covered entity, our practice is responsible for safeguarding electronic protected health information. As a result, our practice's policy is to inform patients by e-mail that an electronic message can be accessed on the practice's secure server only by the patient providing a unique patient ID and password for access.

NOTE: *A patient is not a covered entity, but may self-authorize release of his or her protected health information in his or her possession to the practice via e-mail, which, upon receipt and thereafter, will be treated as electronic protected health information.*

Sample procedures: Encryption converts information in a file or document from a readable format to an unreadable format, while decryption does the reverse.

---

[8] On August 24, 2009, the Federal Register published the *Guidance Specifying the Technologies and Methodologies That Render Protected Health Information Unusable, Unreadable, or Indecipherable to Unauthorized Individuals* as part of the document, "Office of the Secretary, Department of Health and Human Services, 45 CFR Parts 160 and 164: Breach Notification for Unsecured Protected Health Information; Interim Final Rule," Federal Register, v. 74, n. 162, August 24, 2009, pp. 42742-42743."

The guidance was effective September 23, 2009. Federal enforcement and penalties for failure to follow breach notification requirements are effective for breaches of unsecured protected health information that occur on or after February 22, 2010. Accordingly, in its risk analysis, a practice should evaluate potential risks and costs of breach of unsecured electronic protected health information that becomes accessible to unauthorized users outside of the practice, whether that information is at rest, in use, or in motion, all of which would trigger the new 'breach notification' provisions of the HITECH Act. These breach notification provisions are discussed in Chapter 2 and Appendix B.

Based on our risk analysis, our computing environment functions at least part of the time in an open environment.

Before using email exchanges with patients, we will inform our patient population on how we will handle e-mail communications, and we will only communicate with a patient by e-mail when the patient has acknowledged in writing that the e-mail communication may not be secure, may be intercepted, and may result in a privacy breach.[9]

Most software systems today include encryption routines. Discuss with your software vendor the type of encryption available, and make sure that it is consistent with your risk analysis, especially the potential costs to your practice if electronic protected health information becomes accessible to unauthorized persons.

An example of an open network is the Internet. If you use the Internet for electronic communications such as e-mail, maintain electronic health records using application service provider (ASP) or software as a service (SaaS) network systems, or practice ePrescribing, you must address the protection of electronic protected health information through encryption. If you do not communicate information through an open network, you may not need to implement this specification. You must document your decision in writing.

CRITICAL POINT

The security official should make sure that all communications over *open* networks are encrypted and routinely tested and that the practice's policy with regard to electronic communications is stated in the practice's notice of privacy practices. When a practice is ready to offer virtual office visits, it must revisit this encryption–decryption policy.

---

[9] If your practice uses email to communicate with patients, make sure that it is included in your practice's notice of privacy practices.

Audit Controls		
Technical Safeguard Standard	*Federal Register/* **45 CFR Parts**	**Required or Addressable**
Audit controls	68 *Federal Register* 8378 45 CFR 164.312(b)	Required

Requirement: Implement hardware, software, and/or procedural mechanisms that record and examine activity in information systems that contain or use electronic protected health information.

Sample policy: Our security official must make sure that workforce members are in compliance with the practice's technical safeguards pertaining to use of electronic systems and networks and access to and protection of electronic protected health information. Compliance means that use and access conform to the scope of each workforce member's responsibilities.

As a result of our risk anaysis, our security official shall review audit logs at least once each week for the first six months, thereafter on at least a bi-weekly basis. The practice shall take appropriate actions to correct inappropriate use or accessibility issues or incidents. The security official must make sure that all existing and newly acquired software has auditing capability and that the auditing function is enabled.

Sample procedures: Our audit controls will monitor workforce activity on a practice's electronic systems. Our security official will review audit logs on a routine basis to make sure that activity is appropriate. Such activity includes, but may not be limited to, workforce member logons and logoffs, file accesses, updates, edits, other system activities, and security incidents.

CRITICAL POINT

Failure to exercise this standard on a routine and timely basis may result in proof that the practice had the capability of knowing that inappropriate use or access was occurring but failed to take timely corrective action.

Integrity		
Technical Safeguard Standard	***Federal Register/* 45 CFR Parts**	**Required or Addressable**
Integrity	68 *Federal Register* 8378 45 CFR 164.312(c)(1)	Required

Requirement: Implement policies and procedures to protect electronic protected health information from improper alteration or destruction.

Sample policy: The security official will make sure that the practice has in place user ID and password credentials to authenticate workforce members' system access to appropriate electronic protected health information.

Sample procedure: Our security official will ensure that our electronic health records system maintains mechanisms that authenticate the integrity of confidential health information.

Integrity means that your practice's data are dependable and accurate. It also means that the appropriate person can have access to the appropriate information at the appropriate time and that the data are not altered or destroyed in any manner. Access controls and audit trails can prevent and identify confidentiality breaches, respectively. However, data inaccuracies and data corruptions can arise from several sources, including data entry errors, hacking or tampering, storage device errors, transmission errors, programming bugs, and viruses, among others. Your practice must make sure that its electronic protected health information has not been altered in any way without its knowledge and consent. Integrity of data, along with availability and confidentiality, are key concepts underlying security of your practice's computer systems and electronic protected health information.

Mechanism to Authenticate Electronic Protected Health Information		
Technical Safeguard Standard	***Federal Register/* 45 CFR Parts**	**Required or Addressable**
Integrity	68 *Federal Register* 8379 45 CFR 164.312(c)(2)	Addressable

Requirement: Implement electronic controls to corroborate that electronic protected health information has not been altered or destroyed in an unauthorized manner.

Sample policy: Our security official will make sure that electronic systems and networks have failed login blocks, intrusion detection, protection against mechanical errors, regularly tested backups, synchronized user IDs and passwords across networked electronic systems within the practice, and strictly controlled and limited access to vendor BAs that fulfill business requirements (eg, technical support and maintenance).

Sample procedures: Based on our risk analysis, we identified several areas where information may be damaged or altered, primarily due to human error, data input, or insufficient training. As a result, our practice will ensure that each user has access to training to the extent needed to maintain the highest level of integrity.

Your method of compliance will be determined in part by the stability of the practice's electronic systems and the frequency, if any, of damaged or altered information due to instability of the electronic systems or incorrect information arising from input error. Your software vendor can assist you with software features that will alert the practice if there is an actual or potential threat to data integrity. Such features include programs that check for human input errors, validity of automatically backed-up data to operational database information, intrusion detection systems, and "error-correcting memory and magnetic disk storage . . . as examples of the built-in data authentication mechanisms that are common in hardware and operating systems today."[10]

---

[10] 68 *Federal Register* 8356.

CRITICAL POINT

The security official should regularly conduct integrity checks of your practice's computer systems and networks, operating system, databases, backups, and application software. Your vendor can assist the practice in setting up these checks, some of which may be automatic and continuous. The security official should review the results of these checks to make sure that the results confirm the integrity of the electronic protected health information and that any deficiencies are remediated immediately.

Person or Entity Authentication		
Technical Safeguard Standard	**Federal Register/ 45 CFR Parts**	**Required or Addressable**
Person or entity authentication	68 *Federal Register* 8379 45 CFR 164.312(d)	Required

Requirement: Implement procedures to verify that a person or entity seeking access to electronic protected health information is the person or entity claimed.

Sample policy: Our security official shall make sure that the practice has in place a mechanism to authenticate users that seek access to the practice's computer systems and networks and electronic protected health information. The security official shall make sure that credentials entered into the system match those stored in the system and that discrepancies result in no access until resolved and the person or entity is authenticated.

Sample procedures: Any workforce member, vendor, practice manager, BA, or other person requiring access to confidential health information must provide verification that they are the person accessing the system using an assigned user ID and password or biometric authentication tool, such as a finger image. Audit trails, regularly reviewed by our security official, will authenticate who or what entity is reading, altering, or transmitting electronic protected health information. Our practice's system must require proof of identity that it can authenticate in one of three ways:

- something you know (eg, user ID, mother's maiden name, personal ID number such as a national provider identifier, or password),

- something you have (eg, smart card, token, swipe card, or badge), or

- something you are (eg, biometric such as a finger image, voice scan, iris or retina scan).[11]

CRITICAL POINT

The security official should remind workforce members at least quarterly, and preferably monthly, to change their passwords regularly, using unique but hard-to-identify combinations of personally known alpha and numeric characters; to safeguard knowledge of the password in a secure, locked location; and not to share a password with any other workforce member, other than the security official for emergency situations, as discussed earlier under Access Control (Emergency Access Procedure).

Transmission Security		
Technical Safeguard Standard	Federal Register/ 45 CFR Part	Required or Addressable
Transmission security	68 Federal Register 8379 45 CFR 164.312(e)(1)	Required

---

[11] Hartley CP, et al. *Handbook for HIPAA Security Implementation,* Chicago, IL: AMA Press, 2004, p. 90.

The transmission security standard requires your practice to implement a system to protect your networks. Increasingly, medical practices are tied to outside networks, especially with growing use of application service provider (ASP) and software as a service (SaaS) electronic health record systems, practice management systems, and the use of provider-to-patient e-mail communications and ePrescribing. Use of the Internet, without proper security controls in place, could compromise the availability and integrity of your electronic protected health information. Identifying and evaluating your network applications is a key consideration in your risk analysis. With the rapid changes in technology with respect to hardware, software, and network connections, it is imperative that your practice regularly evaluate the security of your systems vis-à-vis integrity risk. Of particular importance are potential threats that may arise from the growing use of wireless networks that link workstations, notebook and tablet computers, portable hand-held devices, and mobile devices such as cell phones with photographic capabilities.

Integrity Controls		
Technical Safeguard Standard	**Federal Register/ 45 CFR Part**	**Required or Addressable**
Transmission security	68 *Federal Register* 8379 45 CFR 164.312(e)(2)(i)	Addressable

Requirement: Implement security measures to guard against unauthorized access to electronic protected health information over an electronic communications network; ensure that electronically transmitted protected health information is not improperly modified without detection until disposed of.

Sample policy: Our security official shall make sure that the practice has in place controls so that electronic protected health information is not altered without appropriate knowledge and permission.

Sample procedures: Our security official and system administrator will determine when, how, and if electronic protected health information will be shared over an electronic communications network.

Electronic protected health information will not be altered or destroyed in an unauthorized manner, that is, without knowledge or approval of the practice security official.

With assignment of user IDs, passwords, and audit trails, the security official can determine if any unauthorized changes to electronic protected health information have occurred and by whom. If so, the practice can apply appropriate sanctions to the workforce member that made unauthorized changes and remind workforce members of the need to maintain integrity of electronic protected health information.

CRITICAL POINT

The security official should regularly review audit trails and validate user ID/password access to the practice's computer system and networks to make sure that no unauthorized changes have been made to records containing electronic protected health information.

Encryption		
Technical Safeguard Standard	***Federal Register/*** **45 CFR Part**	**Required or Addressable**
Transmission security	68 *Federal Register* 8379 45 CFR 164.312(e)(2)(ii)	Addressable

Requirement: Implement a mechanism to encrypt electronic protected health information whenever deemed appropriate.

Sample policy: The security official shall make sure that all communications across the practice's open networks and that all electronic protected health information on portable devices containing electronic protected health information are encrypted, thereby, creating *secure* data as defined in the August 24, 2009, guidance issued by the U.S. Department of Health and Human Services.[12]

---

[12] See citation in footnote no. 8 and discussion in Appendix B of approved FIPS 140-2 encryption processes.

Sample procedures: Based on our risk analysis, our security official will ensure that transmissions will be encrypted. Portable laptop computers also will be encrypted so that in the event they are misplaced, destroyed, or stolen, electronic protected health information cannot be accessed.

Encryption is appropriate if the practice is using open networks such as the Internet for transmission of electronic protected health information. As practices increasingly use e-mail communications between physician and patient, adopt EHR systems, transmit and receive electronic protected health information, and use ePrescribing to comply with federal regulations, encryption is a must. Your vendor can assist the practice in making sure all communications over open networks are encrypted. Encryption of electronic protected health information also is a must for portable devices that may be mislaid or lost, such as PDAs and portable computers. The practice's notice of privacy practices should address the practice's policy and procedures regarding encryption of electronic protected health information, especially as it relates to physician-to-patient and patient-to-physician e-mail communications.

CRITICAL POINT

The security official should make sure that the practice's notice of privacy practices includes the practice's policy on encrypted communications and that the notice of privacy practices is updated to reflect any changes in the practice's policy regarding encryption.

Physical Safeguards

Physical safeguards are designed to help your practice protect your investments in the facilities and workstations that contain your electronic protected health information. There are four physical safeguard standards, and each standard has implementation specifications, which are either required or addressable.

Safeguarding Your Physical Location

Workforce members in an electronic medical office have a heightened awareness of the physical protections for computers, usually because computers are used in their homes and they have a healthy respect for the financial resources it takes to maintain one.

Networked computers require physical considerations that are more complex than those needed at a home. For example, if you are installing additional servers to accommodate the EMR, e-mail, and data backup, you may need to hire an HVAC service company to ensure you can accommodate the additional heat these servers emit. When considering whether to purchase a locked case around your servers or to keep the door to the server room locked, a locked server room door is generally preferred. If you have 15 minutes of battery power remaining before the system shuts down due to a power failure, it is much easier to unlock the server room door than to unlock the server room door, unlock the case, and then shut down the server.

In the paper world, physicians who regularly take patient files home to review at night may have difficulty changing old habits. If there is concern about theft, tablet PCs and laptops may be a greater risk if they are not encrypted. The security official, who is responsible for the location of these portable computers, should apply bar codes to all computers or otherwise maintain a reliable checkout policy to not only protect the assets but also safeguard the electronic protected health information stored inside them.

The physical safeguard policies and procedures in this chapter will help you determine how to protect your facility, who has access to it, and when access will be allowed or terminated. Table 3-2 summarizes that information.

Facility Access Controls		
Physical Safeguard Standard	***Federal Register/* 45 CFR Part**	**Required or Addressable**
Facility access controls	68 *Federal Register* 8378 45 CFR 164.310(a)(1)	Required

Requirement: Implement policies and procedures to limit physical access to electronic information systems and the facility or facilities in which they are housed, while ensuring that properly authorized access is allowed.

TABLE 3-2 | How To Protect Your Facility

Security Standard	Implementation Specification	Required or Addressable
Facility access controls	Contingency operations	Addressable
	Facility security plan	Addressable
	Access control and validation procedures	Addressable
	Maintenance records	Addressable
Workstation use		Required
Workstation security		Required
Device and media controls	Disposal	Required
	Media re-use	Required
	Accountability	Addressable
	Data backup and storage	Addressable

What Facility Access Controls Mean to Your Practice

This standard requires a physician practice to establish policies and procedures to control access *to* and *within* the physical premises of the practice. Included in this standard are requirements that your practice identify, authorize, and control who has access to electronic information systems.

There are four addressable implementation specifications for this physical safeguard standard:

- contingency operations,

- facility security plan,

- access controls and validation procedures, and

- maintenance records.

These implementation specifications are "applicable to an entity's business location or locations,"[13] and the facility at each location "includes physical premises and the interior and exterior of a building."[14]

The language of the implementation specifications is clear. The way in which your practice implements these specifications is a function of what your practice determines its risks are in the risk analysis. In addressing physical safeguards, be sure to consider each specification separately and how it relates to other administrative and technical safeguards. Of particular importance is the disaster recovery plan.

Many physician practices are small with premises in single business dwellings or in multiple-office structures, such as a medical office building. Physician practices in a single business dwelling must implement the physical safeguard standard so that the physical premises are protected. Physician practices in a multiple-office structure must also implement the physical safeguard standard. However, as a covered entity, the practice must take into consideration the fact that it "retains responsibility for considering facility security even where it shares space within a

---

[13] 68 *Federal Register* 8353.

[14] 68 *Federal Register* 8354.

building with other organizations. Facility security measures taken by a third party must be considered and documented in the covered entity's facility security plan, when appropriate."[15]

CRITICAL POINT

If your physician practice is in a multiple-office structure, acquire a copy of the building security plan, and reference it as an exhibit in your practice's security plan.

Contingency Operations		
Physical Safeguard Standard	**Federal Register/ 45 CFR Parts**	**Required or Addressable**
Facility access controls	68 *Federal Register* 8378 45 CFR 164.310(a)(2)(i)	Addressable

Requirement: Establish (and implement as needed) procedures that allow facility access in support of restoration of lost data under the disaster recovery plan and emergency mode operations plan in the event of an emergency.

Sample policy: Our practice will make sure that the disaster and emergency operations plan is consistent with the Contingency Plan Standard in Administrative Safeguards. Each plan will be based on outcomes from our practice's risk analysis.

NOTE: A practice in Southern California must assess the potential impact of an earthquake; a practice in Kansas must assess the potential impact of damage from a tornado. In either instance, your practice may be without electrical power, impeding access to electronic protected health information. What, then, are your

---

[15] 68 *Federal Register* 8353.

contingency operations? Where would you relocate? How would you make sure your practice was able to access your electronic protected health information and other critical business data? In your planning, make sure that you have identified key personnel from your practice and your software and hardware vendors who will be responsible for executing disaster recovery and that they have access authorizations to make it happen in an emergency.

Sample procedures: Based on our risk analysis, our contingency plan is based on events that have caused us to shut down our practice for a limited amount of time. They include: hurricanes, tornadoes, fire, and lightning.

Our practice has developed a contingency plan that is filed with our security official. At least one person within each department has been trained on our contingency plan and is aware of how to proceed in the event we experience loss of electricity.

All persons have been trained in the event of loss of electricity, for whatever reason, to do the following:

- In the event our servers switch to battery power, our security official will immediately notify each user in the system to shut down his or her computer.
- The security official will then proceed to the server room and manually shut down each server in the appropriate order. Users will not be able to log back into the system until the security official or system administrator notifies them.

CRITICAL POINT

Loss of electricity is the most common reason for having a contingency plan. A procedure for handling this contingency should be in place, with e-mail reminders in place, particularly because servers do not respond well to sudden loss of power.

Facility Security Plan		
Physical Safeguard Standard	***Federal Register/* 45 CFR Parts**	**Required or Addressable**
Facility access controls	68 *Federal Register* 8378 45 CFR 164.310(a)(2)(ii)	Addressable

Requirement: Implement policies and procedures to safeguard the facility and the equipment therein from unauthorized physical access, tampering, and theft.

Sample policy: Our practice will safeguard its facility and systems equipment from unauthorized physical tampering, and theft. Workforce members will comply with our practice policies and procedures to safeguard the practice facility and its equipment from unauthorized physical access, tampering, and theft.

Sample procedures: Our practice owns the building in which we see patients. Based on our risk analysis, our facility security plan covers access to building exteriors, interiors, tampering, and theft. Therefore, we will address intrusion, deliberate impairment of computer systems and electricity supply, and theft of equipment that may contain electronic protected health information.

Our practice's dwelling maintains an electronic security system to safeguard the facility and systems when no workforce members are on site.

OR

Our practice is in a multiple-business structure, with an entrance guard on duty 24/7, and may require strong locks on external and internal doors in order to protect its facility and systems.

During business hours, our practice will achieve reasonable and appropriate levels of protection by strategically placing employees, such as the receptionist, to secure access to the facility and systems internally.

Other reasonable and appropriate policies and procedures can be drawn from the list below.

- Authorizations for individuals to access electronic systems with electronic protected health information
- Control of modes of access of such systems

- Opening and closing procedures for the practice
- Layout, design, and construction of the practice facility
- Lock and key control
- Locking systems for doors, gates, windows, and other access points to the practice's facility
- Access control to and within the facility, as appropriate
- Sign-in and sign-out controls
- Designation of security official responsible for authorizing access to the facility, within the facility, and to systems containing electronic protected health information
- Parking rules to facilitate access control
- Surveillance of facility areas
- Perimeter and barrier protection
- Natural barriers, such as landscape and terrain, to facilitate access control
- Fencing to facilitate access control
- Gate and other type of security checkpoints to control access
- Wall, ceiling, and floor construction to control access
- User IDs and authorized workforce member accompaniment of visitors in high-risk areas
- Security devices on doors and windows to control access to areas with systems containing electronic protected health information
- Firewalls on systems to control access to electronic protected health information
- Alarms, intrusion detection systems, and burglar deterrence devices to control access and to alert practice of unauthorized access
- Environmental controls such as heating, ventilation, and air conditioning to safeguard electronic protected health information

■ Fire protection and detection systems, along with strategically placed fire extinguishers

■ Control of water hazards and protection of systems containing electronic protected health information

■ Awareness and control of contingencies related to potential impairment of the practice's facility and equipment

■ Authorization of persons to manage contingencies related to potential impairment of the practice's facility and equipment

■ Workforce member control of facility entrance and reception areas during business hours

■ Workforce compliance with employee surveillance and vigilance procedures

■ Security official for practice developing a plan to monitor effectiveness of the practice's facility security plan, including periodic testing and evaluation of procedures.

CRITICAL POINT

Most of your practice's facility security plan policies and procedures should already be in the employee handbook that you provide to practice employees. Make sure that any change related to facility and equipment security protections made by your practice's security official are immediately reflected in amendments to your practice's employee handbook, and that workforce members are aware of and understand the change, and acknowledge same, through appropriate training.

Access Control and Validation Procedures

Physical Safeguard Standard	Federal Register/ 45 CFR Parts	Required or Addressable
Facility access controls	68 *Federal Register* 8378 45 CFR 164.310(a)(2)(iii)	Addressable

Requirement: Implement procedures to control and validate a person's access to facilities based on their role or function, including visitor control and control of access to software programs for testing and revision.

Sample policy: Our practice will control and validate a person's access to our practice facility based on that person's role or function. Our practice will control and validate a visitor's access to our practice's software programs for testing, updating, or changing versions. Workforce members of our practice are responsible for complying with our practice's policies and procedures regarding access control and validation.

Sample procedures: Our security official:

- shall be responsible for implementing physical access controls to areas in our practice that contain electronic systems and media.
- shall be responsible for limiting a person's access to electronic systems and media.
- shall make sure that all electronic media containing electronic protected health information in the practice facility—database systems, application servers, device management systems, and infrastructure devices— are configured to control access and are maintained in physically secure locations.
- shall make sure that the practice has an after-hours operable intrusion alarm system to alert authorities and designated workforce members in the event of a break-in to the practice's facility after hours of business operation.
- shall assign facility keys and alarm system codes to designated practice workforce members and maintain written records of such assignments. The security official shall make sure that keys are returned and locks and alarm system codes changed when designated practice workforce members resign or are terminated and as other circumstances warrant.

- shall do the following before any outside party requires access to the practice's electronic media or systems containing electronic protected health information:
  - verify that a business associate (BA) agreement is in place;
  - verify ID and credentials of the BA's representative; and
  - brief the BA representative on the practice's security policies and procedures and acquire written acknowledgment that the representative is aware of and understands them.
- shall regularly monitor and evaluate the effectiveness of the practice's access control and validation procedures.

Our practice will identify and sign in visitors to the practice, and, as appropriate, a workforce member shall escort any visitor in order to safeguard electronic protected health information.

Your practice must have a plan in place that identifies who has control of the practice facility and who has access to software that contains electronic protected health information. Your plan typically is based on job function and need, depending on the scale of your practice and on outcomes from your risk analysis. Function and need must be specified in job descriptions, which are covered in the section on administrative safeguard standards.

With regard to your practice's computer and software systems, vendors may play a critical role in testing, updating, or changing versions of your practice's software programs. It is important that these vendors do so under the provisions outlined in your business associate agreement with the vendors. Further, an important role of the security official is to make sure that such vendors are aware and periodically reminded of the practice's security policies and procedures.

As with other implementation specifications for the facility access controls physical safeguard, this is an addressable specification, indicating what is reasonable and appropriate for your particular practice. There are four procedures that any practice should adopt and they are:

- Verify an individual's authorization to access electronic systems that contain electronic protected health information.
- Control access and movement within the practice.

- Establish a visitor identification, sign-in, and badge system for any visitor in the practice.

- Escort visitors with a need to be in any area containing access to electronic protected health information.

CRITICAL POINT

In a single-physician practice, function and need for each workforce member may be markedly broader than in a multiple-physician practice, where function and need for each workforce member may be more specialized. Do what is reasonable and appropriate and be sure to document your choices in writing.

Maintenance Records

Physical Safeguard Standard	Federal Register/ 45 CFR Parts	Required or Addressable
Facility access controls	68 *Federal Register* 8378 45 CFR 164.310(a)(2)(iv)	Addressable

Requirement: Implement policies and procedures to document repairs and modifications to the physical components of a facility, which are related to security (eg, hardware, walls, doors, and locks).

Sample policy: Our practice documents, in written and electronic formats, all repairs and modifications related to security of our physical facility and equipment, such as locks, doors, walls, and hardware. Workforce members of our practice are responsible for complying with our maintenance records policy and related procedures.

Sample procedures: Our security official:

- documents in a log each repair or modification undertaken to the physical components of the practice's facility that are related to security.

- updates the log in writing within 1 business day of completion of any repair or modification to the physical components of the practice's facility that are related to security.
- maintains the log, in print and electronic format, for a period of 6 years from the date of the last recorded repair or modification to the physical components of the practice's facility that are related to security.

Your security official must make sure that your practice has a log that describes repairs or modifications made to your practice facility's physical security components. The written log must document each repair or modification, including what your practice did and when. The log must be maintained for 6 years following the completion of each maintenance action. Your practice may maintain the log in electronic format, routinely and carefully backed up, and capable of being printed.

Workstation Use		
Physical Safeguard Standard	***Federal Register/* 45 CFR Parts**	**Required or Addressable**
Workstation use	68 *Federal Register* 8378 45 CFR 164.310(b)(2)	Required

Requirement: Implement policies and procedures that specify the proper functions to be performed, the manner in which those functions are to be performed, and the physical attributes of the surroundings of a specific workstation that can access electronic protected health information.

Sample policy: Our practice has specified appropriate functions to be performed on each workstation in the practice, the manner in which they are performed, and the characteristics of the physical surroundings of each workstation or class of workstation that can access electronic protected health information. Workforce members of our practice are responsible for complying with our workstation use policy and related procedures.

Sample procedures:

- Our security official shall be responsible for establishing and implementing workstation use procedures and physical access controls to workstation areas in the practice facility.

- Food and drinks are not allowed near workstations that contain electronic protected health information.
- Our practice shall comply with terms and conditions of software licensing for each workstation and with copyright laws.
- Our practice uses antivirus and other protective software tools; the security official shall verify that each workstation user downloads these tools when they are routed to the user.
- Our practice locates workstations in controlled access areas where practice workstation users and other authorized users (eg, software vendors operating a business associate agreement) only have controlled access, as appropriate for function and need.

The implementation specification for workstation use is specified in the language of the standard and therefore required.

This physical safeguard standard covers workstations that can access electronic protected health information. It requires that your practice ensure that workstations are used appropriately, how such uses are to be performed, and in which physical environment access to electronic protected health information is permitted. Workstations include, but are not limited to, desktop computers, laptop computers, tablet computers, notebook computers, and personal data assistants that transmit, receive, or store electronic protected health information.[16]

One example of an appropriate workstation use would be a policy of workforce members logging off before leaving electronic media unattended. Another example, assuming the workstation is in a controlled access environment in the practice facil-

---

[16] The focus of this standard is on use of workstations in the practice as a controlled environment. Increasingly, workstations are wireless and portable and may be taken out of the practice facility by an authorized member of the workforce, such as a physician with a PDA who may be on call from his home and needs access to his patient's electronic personal health information. If so, it is important that the workstation device be access-controlled by password or biometric and that the electronic protected health information be secured through encryption in such a manner that it is "unusable, unreadable, or indecipherable to unauthorized individuals for purposes of the breach notification requirements under Section 13402 of Title XIII (Health Information Technology for Economic and Clinical Health Act) of the American Recovery and Reinvestment Act of 2009." See citation in footnote 8 and discussion in Appendix B for description of approved FIPS 140-2 ecryption processes.

ity, would be a policy requiring an automatic logoff in the absence of activity on electronic media for a defined period of time, for example, 5 or 10 minutes. Most software systems have this capability built in, and the defined period of time can be easily set in the practice. A final example would be a policy of controlling access to the Internet while working with electronic protected health information in an effort to mitigate the risk of unauthorized access by an outsider to such information.

CRITICAL POINT

A highly vulnerable point of unauthorized access in a practice is the receptionist workstation near the entrance to the practice. The receptionist can be a controlled point of access to the practice, but patient and visitor traffic create potential for risk to electronic protected health information if the workstation is visible. The security official must make sure that the workstations of the receptionist and other workforce members are shielded physically from passersby who are not authorized to have access to electronic protected health information.

Workstation Security		
Physical Safeguard Standard	**Federal Register/ 45 CFR Parts**	**Required or Addressable**
Workstation security	68 *Federal Register* 8378 45 CFR 164.310(c)	Required

Requirement: Implement physical safeguards for all workstations that access electronic protected health information to restrict access to authorized users.

Sample policy: Our practice makes sure that all workstations that access electronic protected health information are secure, restricting access to authorized users. Workforce members of our practice are responsible for complying with our workstation security policy and related procedures.

Sample procedures: Our security official:

- shall establish and implement workstation security procedures and physical access controls to workstation areas in the practice.

- shall periodically inform workforce members that it is their responsibility to safeguard electronic protected health information in the practice facility and on portable media such as laptops, tablets, notebooks, PDAs, tapes, flash drives, and similar devices, regardless of location.

- shall assign passwords to authorized users of electronic media containing electronic protected health information. Our security official also shall implement a time-to-change-passwords procedure, with time to change based on outcomes of the risk analysis, and shall monitor compliance on a regular basis.

- shall require written authorization for any workforce member to take off-site any electronic media device containing electronic protected health information, and any such electronic media device shall have access controls and encryption capabilities if the electronic media device is capable of transmission, such as a PDA.

- shall be responsible for and monitor access of business associates to electronic media containing electronic protected health information.

In addition, our practice:

- enforces a policy that workforce members shall not display written passwords on or near workstations, desktop surfaces, or in drawers, and shall not share passwords with other workforce members in the practice.

- locates workstations containing electronic protected health information in controlled access areas of the practice, to the extent practicable, and limits access only to authorized users—workforce members and software vendor representatives operating under a business associate agreement, as appropriate.

- shall take measures to shield electronic protected health information from unauthorized passersby, including the use of privacy screens, if applicable.

- requires that unattended electronic media have an automatic logoff of 10 minutes or less, with exact time determined by an evaluation of practice business operations and potential risks identified in the risk analysis.

The implementation specification for workstation security is specified in the language of the standard and therefore required.

The workstation security safeguard standard requires practices to secure workstations in such a manner that access is restricted to authorized users. The solution is "dependent on the [covered] entity's risk analysis and risk management process"[17] and may involve controlled access to the workstation or controls on the workstation that restrict access from unauthorized users. The way in which your practice implements this standard will depend on the outcomes of your practice's risk analysis.

One example of an appropriate workstation security requirement would be a policy of workforce members logging off before leaving electronic media unattended. Another example, assuming the workstation is in a controlled access environment in the practice facility, would be a policy requiring an automatic logoff in the absence of activity on electronic media for a defined period of time, for example, 5 or 10 minutes. Most software systems have this capability built in, and the defined period of time can be easily set in the practice. A final example would be a policy of controlling access to the Internet while working with electronic protected health information in an effort to mitigate the risk of unauthorized access by an outsider to such information.

CRITICAL POINT

Device and media controls have been the subject of too many news stories, such as discarded laptops containing electronic Protected Health Information (ePHI) or smart phones returned to stores without destroying a log of patient calls and emails. Electronic media is divided into two categories: (1) electronic storage, such as memory devices, magnetic tapes or disks, optical disks, or digital memory cards; and (2) transmission media such as the Internet, extranet, leased lines, dial-up lines, private networks, or physical transmission or movement such as, paper, fax, voice, or telephone. The security official must

---

[17] 68 *Federal Register* 8354.

make sure that any electronic media device containing ePHI taken off-site from the practice facility has access controls and encryption capabilities if the electronic media device is capable of transmission, such as a PDA.

Device and Media Controls		
Physical Safeguard Standard	Federal Register/ 45 CFR Parts	Required or Addressable
Device and media controls	68 Federal Register 8378 45 CFR 164.310(d)(1)	Required

Requirement: Implement policies and procedures that govern the receipt and removal of hardware and electronic media that contain electronic protected health information into and out of a facility and the movement of these items within the facility.

Your practice's policies and procedures will be based on outcomes from your practice's risk analysis.

At a minimum, your practice should create a written inventory of all practice hardware and electronic media. Maintaining a current inventory enhances your practice's likelihood of risk mitigation in the event of some contingency, such as introduction of a virus or theft of equipment during a break-in. In addition to creating the inventory, the security official needs to track the movement of inventory within the practice, keeping an up-to-date location of each piece of hardware and electronic media. Finally, your practice needs to control introduction of unauthorized electronic media, such as software or flash drives brought into the practice by a workstation member that is extraneous to conducting the practice's business.

Sample policy: Our practice will control the receipt and removal of hardware and electronic media that contain electronic protected health information that enter or leave the practice and will control the movement of hardware and electronic media within the practice facility. Workforce members of our practice are responsible for complying with our device and media reuse security policy and related procedures.

Sample procedures: Our security official:

■ shall establish and implement device and media reuse policies and procedures, including monitoring the movement of electronic protected health information that enters or leaves the practice and tracking the movement of hardware and electronic media within the practice.

■ will make sure that workforce members protect hardware and electronic media to prevent loss or exposure of electronic protected health information, confidential information, or proprietary business information of the practice to unauthorized persons.

■ will make sure that electronic protected health information is routinely backed up and maintained and stored off-site in a physically secure environment and will regularly verify that an exact copy of routinely backed-up information is readily retrievable.

■ will prohibit the introduction or use of unauthorized hardware or electronic media in the practice by any workforce member.

This standard requires your practice to establish policies and procedures that track receipt and removal of hardware and electronic media that contain electronic protected health information that enter the practice and that leave the practice, and control movement of hardware and electronic media within the practice.

This Device and Media Controls Standard has four implementation specifications, of which two are required (R) and two are addressable (A), as noted previously. With respect to the two required implementation specifications, it is important for your practice to remember that *file deletion* and *erasure* functions generally do not delete files and data but rather delete only the file name, not the underlying data content, which may be electronic protected health information. Using these functions prior to disposal or media reuse may not achieve the result your practice intends, namely, elimination of electronic protected health information and proprietary business information of the practice. If you dispose of or reuse electronic media, ask your software vendor or computer store for information on how to delete electronic protected health information and how to *verify* that the information has been deleted.

CRITICAL POINT

Verify that any deletion of electronic protected health information is erased—not just separated from its file name—prior to disposal or reuse of any practice hardware or electronic media.

Disposal		
Physical Safeguard Standard	**Federal Register/ 45 CFR Parts**	**Required or Addressable**
Device and media controls	68 *Federal Register* 8378 45 CFR 164.310(d)(2)(i)	Required

Requirement: Implement policies and procedures to address the final disposal of electronic protected health information and the hardware or electronic media on which it is stored.

Sample policy: Our practice will delete or erase any electronic protected health information prior to final disposal of hardware or electronic media on which it is stored. Workforce members of our practice are responsible for complying with our disposal policy and related procedures.

Sample procedures: Our security official:

■ shall consult with the practice's hardware and software vendors for recommendations concerning final disposition of electronic protected health information and the hardware and electronic media on which it is stored.

■ shall establish and implement procedures for final disposal of electronic protected health information and the hardware and electronic media on which it is stored, based on an examination of appropriate methods of deletion or erasure conducted as part of the risk analysis.

■ shall verify in writing that any electronic protected health information is deleted from hardware or electronic media prior to final disposal.

Your security official must make sure that your practice properly disposes of electronic protected health information and any hardware or electronic media on which it is stored. Failure to delete underlying data content that is electronic protected health information exposes your practice to civil liability should the incident be reported,[18] and your practice may incur significant costs associated in defending and remediating exposure and loss of patient confidence in your practice's ability to secure sensitive medical information.

Your practice should consult its hardware and software vendors for help in deleting electronic protected health information and disposing of the electronic media upon which it resided.

For disposal, consider the following recommendation:

> Render magnetic media such as hard drives, floppy disks, and backup tapes that are unusable or non-repairable completely unusable prior to their disposal. Degaussing is a method whereby a strong magnetic field is applied to magnetic media to fully erase the data. If you don't have access to degaussing equipment, you can physically damage the media beyond repair, eg, drill a hole through it or cut it up with wire cutters or scissors. Optical disks must be physically damaged. Reformatting media is not sufficient to render the data totally inaccessible to people who know how to retrieve it.[19]

In this quote from 2004, there is no mention of flash drives (thumb disks) that connect via USB ports on computers or solid-state storage devices that have no moving parts. Technology moves quickly, and your practice should verify disposal techniques with your hardware and software vendors each time you dispose of hardware or electronic media containing electronic protected health information.

---

[18] An example is disposal of electronic media with files containing electronic protected health information that are accessed by an unauthorized person.

[19] Hartley C, et al. *Handbook for HIPAA Security Implementation.* Chicago, IL: AMA Press, 2004, p. 81.

Media Reuse		
Physical Safeguard Standard	**Federal Register/ 45 CFR Parts**	**Required or Addressable**
Device and media controls	68 *Federal Register* 8378 45 CFR 164.310(d)(2)(ii)	Required

Requirement: Implement procedures for removal of electronic protected health information from electronic media before the media are made available for reuse.

Sample policy: Our practice will delete any electronic protected health information on electronic media prior to reuse of the media. Workforce members of our practice are responsible for complying with our media reuse policy and related procedures.

Sample procedures: Our security official:

- shall consult with our hardware and software vendors to determine the most appropriate way to reuse electronic media within the practice.
- shall determine as part of the risk analysis the trade-off on cost versus risk in determining whether to reuse existing media or purchase new electronic media.[20]
- shall make sure that data are backed up and in secure storage before deleting any electronic protected health information on electronic media.
- shall make sure that electronic media moved from one workstation to another workstation is appropriate for the new user.

Your practice must make sure that it deletes any electronic protected health information on electronic media prior to reuse of the electronic media. Your practice should consult with your practice's hardware and software vendors to determine which methods would work best to delete or erase the electronic protected health information from the practice's hardware or electronic media.

---

[20] Electronic media embedded in workstations and portable electronic media such as external drives and flash drives attached via USB ports are relatively inexpensive and continue to decrease in cost. Accordingly, an appropriate risk mitigation strategy for your practice may be destruction of these devices rather than reuse.

Accountability		
Physical Safeguard Standard	***Federal Register/*** **45 CFR Parts**	**Required or Addressable**
Device and media controls	68 *Federal Register* 8378 45 CFR 164.310(d)(2)(iii)	Addressable

Requirement: Maintain a record of the movements of hardware and electronic media and any person responsible therefore.

Sample policy: Our practice shall keep an inventory of hardware and electronic media, track their movements, and maintain an ongoing record of workforce members responsible for the equipment. Workforce members of our practice are responsible for complying with our accountability policy and related procedures.

Sample procedures: Our security official:

- shall create, or assign a workstation member to create, an inventory of hardware and electronic media for the practice.

- shall maintain written and electronic records of locations and movements of hardware and electronic media in the practice, workforce members responsible for their use, and a backup copy of the inventory information in a secure location.

Your practice should maintain written documentation pertaining to the movement of hardware and electronic media within the practice, including the responsible party for the hardware or electronic media. The outcome of your practice's risk analysis will provide your practice with a framework for compliance with this addressable implementation specification. At a minimum, your practice should include in its inventory of hardware and electronic media a chronology of movements of such equipment within the practice, the responsible party, and whether movement involved disposal or reuse. A sample inventory matrix is provided below for your practice's consideration. Remember, the inventory must be in writing or electronically maintained (such as in a spreadsheet), and retained for

6 years following the most recent change in inventory, with a copy or backup stored in a secure location.[21]

Description of Hardware or Electronic Media _____

Model/Serial Number _____

Manufacturer _____

Purchase Price_____

Date Purchased _____

Date Put in Service _____

Responsible Party _____

Disposal or Reuse _____

This implementation specification recognizes that "small providers would be unlikely to be involved in large-scale moves of equipment that would require systematic tracking, unlike, for example, large healthcare providers or health plans."[22]

CRITICAL POINT

The security official should maintain a current written copy of the inventory list and an electronic version on a flash drive in a secure location outside of the practice, such as in a safety deposit box or with the practice's attorney, accountant, or insurance agent.

---

[21] Such an inventory is a useful part of a disaster recovery plan should the practice experience a disaster or other business contingency.

[22] 68 _Federal Register_ 8354.

Data Backup and Storage		
Physical Safeguard Standard	*Federal Register/* **45 CFR Parts**	**Required or Addressable**
Device and media controls	68 *Federal Register* 8378 45 CFR 164.310(d)(2)(iv)	Addressable

Requirement: Create a retrievable, exact copy of electronic protected health information, when needed, before movement of equipment.

Sample policy: Our practice regularly backs up electronic protected health information and stores it off-site in a secure location. The data are readily available in the event they are needed. Our practice backs up electronic protected health information prior to movement of hardware and electronic media and tests to make sure that it is exact and readily available. Workforce members of our practice are responsible for complying with our data backup policy and related procedures.

Sample procedures: Our security official:

- shall make sure that a retrievable, exact copy of electronic protected health information is available prior to movement of hardware or electronic media on which it is stored.

- shall conduct regular tests of the practice's data backup system and prior to movement of hardware or electronic media on which electronic protected health information is stored.

- shall validate during tests of the practice's data backup system that the backed-up electronic protected health information maintains its integrity as an exact copy of the sourced data.

In addition, our practice conducts daily, weekly, monthly, and quarterly backups of electronic protected health information and practice software and maintains backups in a secure location off-site.

Your practice needs to create an exact copy of electronic protected health information resident on hardware or electronic media just prior to movement of the equipment. If the electronic protected health information is impaired or lost during movement of the equipment, it can be restored. Your practice should maintain a current copy of back-up data in a secure off-site location, where it can be retrieved readily if equipment is damaged in movement or if a disaster or business contingency affects the practice.

CRITICAL POINT

Create and maintain a secure off-site location for backups of the practice's electronic protected health information, critical business software, and proprietary business information.

KEY POINTS

- Defining who has access to health information in an electronic health record (EHR) system is more limiting than in a paper-based practice.

- A review of audit logs should be performed, *at a minimum,* on a weekly basis, but preferably on a random and twice per week basis. The audit trail provides a history of who has accessed health information, what was reviewed or seen, and what and how the accessed information was used.

- Failure to impose and review audit controls may leave the practice culpable, offering proof that the practice had the capability of knowing of inappropriate use and disclosure, but did not act on that information.

- EHR systems today must be able to generate a report identifying how a practice used and disclosed health information, including for treatment, payment, and healthcare operations.

- Do not underestimate the practice's disaster recovery processes; conduct a fire drill to evaluate the strength of its contingency plan.

CHAPTER 4

Performance Measurements and Their Effects on Your Policies and Procedures

IN THIS CHAPTER, YOU WILL LEARN

- How integration of your practice management, laboratory, and pharmacy information systems and electronic medical records can enhance your ability to collect data required for performance measurements
- How transparency through performance measurements may influence where patients choose to seek care
- Policies and procedures that support these initiatives in your practice.

Key Terms

Clinical decision support: Provides clinicians, staff, patients, and other individuals with knowledge and person-specific information, intelligently filtered or presented at appropriate times, to enhance health and health care. It encompasses a variety of tools and interventions such as computerized alerts and reminders, clinical guidelines, order sets, patient data reports and dashboards, documentation templates, diagnostic support, and clinical workflow tools.

Performance measurement: The quantitative assessment of health care processes and outcomes for which an individual physician or other practitioner, health care organization, or health care system may be accountable.

Performance measures: The category of quality improvement tools that seeks to improve the performance and accountability of an organization, process, or program with a quantifiable metrics.

ePrescribing

Case Study

Physician members of Sandhills Physicians IPA reduced health care costs by collectively agreeing to use standard clinical protocols; in the process, they built a performance database that helps them determine how to be better physicians.

The momentum got an early boost when area employers contracting with Doctor's Direct, a care management subsidiary of Sandhills Physicians, reported reduced or stabilized health costs as a result of improved employee health. That's when the physicians began examining what would happen if they exchanged clinical procedures with other physicians to replicate improved health and subsequently increased savings for other employers. The clinical protocols were used by case managers to provide consistent care.

Initial ingredients in the case managers' success formula were divided into the following four basic principles of medical management:

■ precertification,

■ case management,

■ disease management, and

■ wellness management.

In conducting precertification evaluations, 80 employee members of a large employer qualified for gastric bypass surgery as a treatment plan for morbid obesity. Recognizing the need for benefit changes, the physicians in this IPA designed an exercise and nutrition program. Every eligible member signed up for the Lifestyle Management Program and began a 12-week program, which consisted of strength training and educational programs, with a follow-up, 15-month health maintenance program. The lifestyle changes netted the employer a $2 million savings in insurance premiums, which they now share with the physicians as part of their ongoing contractual relationship to provide quality care.

Quality and Reimbursement Go Hand in Hand

For years, physicians have been reimbursed, not according to their skills, years of experience, or patient outcomes, but according to reimbursement contracts negotiated between providers and private and public health plan payers. As a result of a broken health care system marked by reduced reimbursements, increases in patient loads, physician and nurse shortages, and patient misuse of emergency facilities, serious and pervasive deficiencies in quality of care have emerged and taken center stage in quality reports. This compromise in quality care affects all patients, regardless of age, gender, financial resources, or race.[1]

For decades, physicians have pointed to a compromise in quality outcomes and indicated that the reimbursement process is a direct challenge

---

[1] Stead SW. *Physicians' Guide to Implementing Medicare's Physician Quality Reporting Initiative: An Insider's View.* Chicago, IL: American Medical Association. 2008, p. 1.

to the delivery of quality care. But unlike hospitals that have been gathering data for decades, physicians have not had access to data that can be analyzed, reported, and thereby recognized by payer actuaries to build a definitive case that indicates the depth of the problem, or better yet, points to solutions.

Fortunately, this is changing as physicians and health care decision-makers discover what data are available and searchable in electronic medical records and administrative claims, in particular, data that communicate bidirectionally with practice management systems, laboratory information systems, and pharmacy information systems. Physicians are now using real data to tell their story and swing the pendulum in favor of improved quality care. At the same time, payers, including the Centers for Medicare and Medicaid Services (CMS), are saying, "We're tired of paying for care. Now we want to pay for quality of care."[2]

For most physicians, the delivery of quality care is a given. These same physicians have practiced within a frustrating reimbursement system as though it were business as usual. The reimbursement process is changing in small and meaningful steps. A significant goal of performance reimbursement begins by minimizing nonevidence-based differences in practice.[ii] Data, and the protection of that data, then become the physician's allies and tools.

On a larger scale, the CMS Physicians Quality Reporting Initiative (PQRI) offers bonuses to physicians for reporting on a designated set of quality measures (additional information about PQRI is provided later in this chapter). And the ePrescribing Incentive program from CMS offers bonuses to physicians for writing electronic prescriptions. "Run the numbers," says Tom Farmer, market strategist for Sage Software, one of many electronic health record (EHR) companies that

---

[2] For information on Physician Quality Reporting Initiative Guidelines, consult Stead SW, *Physicians' Guide to Implementing Medicare's Physician Quality Reporting Initiative: An Insider's View*. Available at the AMA bookstore: www.ama-assn.org.

offer ePrescribing capabilities. "Keeping your practice afloat is a decision that you make with every penny you save or earn back."

Data Equal Dollars

"Leverage is controlled by who owns the data. Until recently, payers have owned the data," says Julian Bobbitt, JD, who heads the health care practice at Smith, Anderson, Blount, Dorsett, Jernigan, and Mitchell law firm in Raleigh, North Carolina. "Data provide payers with sophisticated resources for negotiation." The lack of detailed and measurable information hinders physicians if they cannot effectively argue their efficiency and disease management successes.

Through data collection engines, such as EHR systems, physicians who are trusted managers and "quarterbacks" in the health care game have the opportunity to achieve the highest rewards because of the benefits they bring to health care. The PQRI represents a small percentage of overall revenue, but Bobbitt says, "PQRI represents big empowerment since doctors control more than 80 percent of where healthcare dollars will be spent."

American industries and businesses understand this reward system. Providing value at high quality with reduced cost attracts and retains customers. In health care, there is a powerful drive to improve patient safety, reduce costs, and motivate consumers to take greater control of their health care. Physicians who participate in that movement should be incentivized with performance bonuses, a process that is common for hospital and insurance executives.

However, as a medical discipline, the provision of measurable information about quality of care and the price for that care is still in the early stage. Some health care providers are tiptoeing into the process of reporting quality of care indicators, while other professions, such as business management, retail, and manufacturing, have embraced the process and developed organization-wide rewards for quality performance.

Quality Reimbursement Programs and How They Affect Your Revenue

American Reinvestment and Recovery Act Funds (ARRA)

In Appendix B, we present an overview of federal initiatives, such as those included in the ARRA Stimulus Act, that are designed to incentivize you (and ultimately de-incentivize you for lack of use) to use certified health information technology systems. Your role in using the system is to demonstrate you are a *meaningful user*. The law requires at a high level, that you participate in the following system-related activities:

- computerized provider order entry (CPOE) that allows you to order and track results from lab tests, pathology or imaging orders, among others.
- ePrescribing,
- submit information to HHS on clinical quality measures, and
- demonstrate to HHS that they are using a certified EHR technology in a meaningful manner.[3]

---

[3] At the time of writing, specific criteria for defining meaningful use was under consideration by the Health IT Policy Committee. See the discussion of meaningful use in Appendix B, and visit the Health IT Policy Committee web site for criteria updates at http://healthit.hhs.gov/portal/server.pt?open=512&objID=1269&parentname= CommunityPag&parentid=26&mode=2&in_hi_userid=11113&cached=true.

ePrescribing

ePrescribing allows physicians to transmit prescriptions electronically to a pharmacy's computer system. It also allows doctors to

- view potential drug interactions and side effects,
- view prescription drug coverage and insurance information,
- receive electronic notification about the need to authorize refills or approve generic substitutions, and
- share simultaneous access to prescription histories and allergies with pharmacies.

What it means: The Medicare Improvement for Patients and Providers Act (H.R. 6331), passed by Congress on July 9, 2008, will provide positive Medicare payment incentives of up to 2 percent for practitioners who use qualified ePrescribing systems in 2009 through 2013 and a reduction in payments of up to 2 percent to providers who fail to ePrescribe by 2012.

A "qualified ePrescribing system" must be able to perform *all* of the following:[4]

- generate a complete active medication list incorporating electronic data received from applicable pharmacy drug plan(s), if available;
- select medications, print prescriptions, electronically transmit prescriptions, and conduct all safety checks
  (A safety check is an automated prompt that offers the provider information on the drug being prescribed, potentially inappropriate dose or route of administration
  of a drug, drug–drug interactions, allergy concerns, and warnings and cautions.);

---

[4] Measure 125, Medicare Improvement for Patients and Providers Act (H.R. 6331). See: www.entnet.org/Practice/upload/125-HIT-Adoption_Use-of-e-Prescribing-specs.pdf

- provide information related to the availability of lower cost, therapeutically appropriate alternatives (if any); and

- provide information on formulary or tiered formulary medications, patient eligibility, and authorization requirements received electronically from the patient's drug plan.

Physicians interested in automating the prescribing process must use a certified ePrescribing or electronic medical record (EMR) system. Several organizations provide certification, including the Pharmacy Health Information Exchange™, operated by SureScripts®, and the Certification Commission for Health Information Technology (CCHIT).

According to the Institute of Medicine Report, *Preventing Medication Errors*, 1.5 million Americans are injured by prescribing errors each year.[5] The Medicare ePrescribing program could save as much as $156 million over the next 5 years from error avoidance and efficiency gains through a newly authorized electronic prescribing incentive program.

Other studies from the SureScripts/RxHub organization suggest that pharmacists make 150 million unnecessary phone calls annually to providers to clarify prescription orders. According to Michael Leavitt, the secretary of the US Department of Health and Human Services (HHS) from 2005 to 2009, there are as many as 530,000 adverse drug events involving Medicare patients every year.

ePrescribing as a stand-alone technology runs about $3,000 per prescriber in one-time acquisition costs, plus ongoing maintenance fees.

---

[5] "Preventing Medication Errors: Quality Chasm Series, Institute of Medicine, 2007. Available to be read for free or purchased as a hard copy at: www.iom.eduhttp://iom.edu/CMS/3809/22526/35939.aspx

Eligible physicians[6] and other authorized prescribers will receive 2 percent bonuses for writing electronic scripts for Medicare beneficiaries in 2009 and 2010 in addition to the 2 percent from participation in with the PQRI. The bonus payments from CMS drop to 1 percent in 2011 and 2012 and to 0.5 percent in 2013.

How to do it:

- Verify that at least 10 percent of your Medicare-allowed charges are associated with prescriptions.

- Ensure that your privacy and security policies and procedures are in place, because these are CMS-required standards that support the infrastructure for electronic exchange of health information.

- Make sure you have a national provider identifier (NPI) number.

- Consult your EMR/EHR vendor or stand-alone ePrescribing vendor about the following capabilities:

  - one or more industry-recognized features designed to prevent unauthorized copying of a completed or blank prescription form;

  - one or more industry-recognized features designed to prevent the erasure or modification of information written on the prescription by the prescriber;

  - one or more industry-recognized features designed to prevent the use of counterfeit prescription forms; and

  - certification to connect to the Pharmacy Health Information Exchange, operated by SureScripts.

---

[6] Physicians are eligible for incentive payments if at least 10 percent of their Medicare-allowed charges are associated with prescriptions. These physicians are the only ones who would face penalties down the road for not using ePrescribing. To obtain the payments, eligible physicians need to report applicable ePrescribing measures established under the Physician Quality Reporting Initiative (PQRI) for their patients with Medicare Part D plans.

To assist its customers in responding to this ePrescribing incentive, most EHR vendors are providing customers with some or all of the following support items:

- a custom external prescription report. This report must contain all of the information that is required for external prescriptions;

- a printer that is specifically designed with tamper-proof security features in place and that interfaces with your practice's EHR system; and

- special prescription paper to be used in the tamper-proof printer.

Physician Quality Reporting Initiative

The PQRI provides bonuses to qualifying physicians. In 2008, if a physician reported on at least three performance measures, incentive payments were based on 80 percent of the eligible patients throughout the full calendar year. For 2009, CMS issued new reporting requirements for measures groups.

In the *Physicians' Guide to Implementing Medicare's Physician Quality Reporting Initiative,* author Stanley W. Stead states, "Performance measures are not clinical guidelines; rather, they are derived from evidence-based clinical guidelines and indicate whether or how often a process of care or outcome of care occurs."[7]

The 2009 bonus is calculated as 2 percent of *all* of a physician's Medicare billings, not just the ones on which he or she reports. This calculation does not include charges for x-ray, MRI, DME, or PT. In 2000, payments will be made to the holder of the taxpayer

---

[7] Stead SW. *Physicians' Guide to Implementing Medicare's Physician Quality Reporting Initiative: An Insider's View.* Chicago, IL: American Medical Association. 2008, p. 2.

identification number (TIN). This means that a multiphysician practice that bills under one TIN will have to decide how to distribute the bonus to individual physicians.

Following are reasons to participate in the PQRI:

- You may earn a bonus of up to 2 percent on *all* of your Medicare billings.

- PQRI, or some version of it, will likely become mandatory in the next several years. This is a way to learn how to report performance measures without penalties.

- Private payers also are implementing pay-for-performance or reporting programs, and this is a way to become familiar with the process. You will get a feedback report outlining how accurately you reported, which will serve as a learning basis as pay-for-performance plans continue to populate the health plan payer arena.

- This particular program takes very little effort on your part.

Following are reasons not to participate in the PQRI:

- If your practice management billing system or your clearinghouse will not accept Current Procedural Terminology® (CPT) Category II codes or Healthcare Common Procedure Coding System (HCPCS) G-codes, it may cost more to modify your system than you recover in the bonus payment.

- If you have to collect data by abstracting information from paper medical charts, the time and cost requirements imposed on your workforce may outweigh the bonus.

- To report the measures by paper, you would append the appropriate CPT Category II codes or G-codes to the CMS 1500 form used to report the service for which the measures are appropriate.

Following are the steps to take in the PQRI application process:

Step 1: Apply for a national provider identifier (NPI), if you have not already done so.

Your data are collected by CMS using the NPI; however, the bonus payment in 2008 and 2009 will be made using the TIN. This means that a multiphysician practice that bills under one TIN will have to decide how to distribute the bonus to individual physicians.

The application for an NPI may seem like a 20-minute exercise. However, there are multiple variables that will affect your reimbursement outcomes, and these need to be considered prior to completing this application. For a quick overview of these variables, consult the NPI Outreach Initiative (NPIOI) white papers, committee advisories, and tip sheets at www.wedi.org/npioi/index.shtml.

You can apply for an NPI using any of the following methods:

Online: https://nppes.cms.hhs.gov/NPPES/Welcome.do

By phone: 1-800-465-3203 (NPI Toll-Free);
1-800-692-2326 (NPI TTY)

By e-mail: customerservice@npienumerator.com

By mail: NPI Enumerator, PO Box 6059, Fargo, ND 58108-6059

Step 2: Ask your practice management software representative if your system can accept CPT Category II codes or G-codes. These alpha-numeric codes are not accepted by all practice management (PM) systems.

Step 3: If you are using a clearinghouse or rebilling company, ask if their service can accept CPT Level II codes or G-codes, as some cannot. Some systems will not accept a zero dollar amount in the field following a CPT code. If that is not the case in your system, insert $.01 into the field.

Step 4: Work with your billing clerk to systematically append the appropriate CPT Level II codes or G-codes to the CMS 1500 forms.

Building the Reporting Engine

New gathering and reporting processes require multiple levels of trust and communication, including trust between patient and physician, accuracy of information, use of data, and new policies and procedures about how to handle confidential patient information, both identified and de-identified. These policies and procedures will have a profound influence on information that can be shared within the federal regulatory environment, including Health Insurance Portability and Accountability Act of 1996 Privacy and Security, Physicians Self Referral (Stark I, II, and III), and Sarbanes–Oxley.

Until recently, patients and their caregivers lacked price and quality information, which impeded their ability to select a physician for quality and efficiency. To the physician, this boosts word of mouth and referrals that may drive more patients to your practice, but to a statistician, anecdotes are poor measures for reimbursement. Even so, the American Medical Association urges organizations conducting outcomes research to ensure the accuracy of data and include relevant physician organizations in all phases so as to provide the opportunity to review and comment on interpretations of results.[8]

Without electronic data, providers struggle through paper records to see how their care measures up to competitors in terms of quality. Without systems to track quality performances of providers and organizations, the inability to view, measure, and report information, providers are rewarded for care rendered, regardless of the level of quality of that care or the efficiency with which care is delivered.[9] In order to match cost and quality, new systems of care now include performance measurement and feedback, transparency and public accountability, and rewards that incentivize provider performance.

---

[8] D-450.988; H-410.965; E-8.056; H-450.941.

[9] Stead, p. 1.

Confidence in reporting is a combination of

- reporting without fear of impunity,
- finding a system that will gather and report quality measures,
- trusting that the practice's users will input information correctly so that it can be gathered and reported, and
- providing policies and procedures that support the first three items.

Performance Measurements

Performance measures are the "category of quality improvement tools that seek to improve the performance and accountability of an organization, process, or program, with a quantifiable metric of results. Performance measurement is the quantitative assessment of health care processes and outcomes for which an individual physician or other practitioner, health care organization, or health care system may be accountable."[10]

Therefore, performance measurement provides the criteria used to define benchmarks for the industry and physicians alike. In the banking industry, a commercial lending officer may receive a bonus based on successful commercial loans opened and successfully managed under his or her leadership. Until recently, performance measures focused largely on health plans, hospitals, and health care organizations.

PQRI Supported by Security Policies and Procedures

If you participate in PQRI, relevant policies and procedures must be in place and support the confidentiality, integrity, and access of

---

[10] Stead, p. 1.

confidential patient information required to support each of the following PQRI reporting activities:

- Select the measures. A threshold of 80 percent must be met on at least three of the measures reported.
- Identify the eligible patient based on the patient's clinical condition.
- Define team roles to ensure data capture.
- Document the encounter.
- Standardize workflows such as patient self-history, vital signs, examinations, and billing.
- Modify billing systems to accept Category II codes.
- Obtain the NPI for report tracking.
- Maintain confidential identity verification, log-in identification, and passwords for secure submission of reports and feedback reports.

Beyond data collection, reporting, and feedback, the physician's team determines what to do with the PQRI results. The results can be used for continuing medical education, practice-wide rewards or incentives, or for marketing or remediation.

Transparency in Value-Driven Health Care

Transparency is a broad-scale initiative that enables consumers and payers to compare the quality and price of health care services in order to make informed choices regarding doctors and hospitals. In cooperation with America's largest employers and the medical profession, this initiative is laying the foundation for pooling and analyzing information about procedures, hospitals, and physician services. When this data foundation is in place, regional health information alliances will turn the raw data into useful information for consumers.[11]

Technical issues inherent in producing valid and reliable information on physician performance are complex not only in the exchange of information from practice to payer but also from physician to physician. Paper medical records, once regarded as the gold standard for health information, included deficiencies relating to access, readability, inaccurate coding, incomplete recording of diagnostic tests, duplicate records, and nonstandard charting practices. These deficiencies limited the accuracy of data extraction and affected use of the data for quality performance.

The EHR is a tool that facilitates more detailed capture of clinical information and assists in making transparent the quality of care and cost that a physician brings to patients. In California's Office of the Patient Advocate, transparency allows patients to stay informed about their rights and responsibilities as health maintenance organization (HMO) enrollees. At its web site, www.opa.ca.gov/report_card, consumers can find quality ratings for health insurance plans, health care providers, and HMOs as well as find guidance about how to choose a health plan or provider.

Ongoing studies that began in 2000 have measured physicians' performance on topics such as quality of delivery of care, communication with patient, getting a treatment and specialty care referral, timeliness of care and service, and coordination of patient care. Under timeliness of care and service, for example, patients responded to questions such as: How long does it take to get an appointment in this practice? and How backed up is the practice upon arrival?

While a practice with numerous patients sitting in the waiting room was once viewed as a thriving practice, practices with delays and long

---

[11] "Transparency: Better Care, Lower Cost." Value Driven Healthcare, posted online at the US Department of Health and Human Services Web site: www.hhs.gov/valuedriven/.

waiting times are now viewed as slow and inefficient. A practice that operates in a timely, efficient manner is indeed one that can use its timeliness of care as a marketing strategy.

The Consumer Assessment of Healthcare Providers and Systems (CAHPS) program, a multiyear initiative of the Agency for Healthcare Research and Quality (AHRQ), supports the assessment of consumers' experiences with health care. The goals of the CAHPS program are twofold:

- develop standardized patient questionnaires that can be used to compare results across sponsors and over time; and

- generate tools and resources that sponsors can use to produce understandable and usable comparative information for both consumers and health care providers.

More information about the CAHPS initiative and how physicians are using quality indicators to improve ambulatory care is available at www.cahps.ahrq.gov.

If you decide to participate in quality measures offered by CMS, health plans, independent physician associations, or other groups, ensure that your workflows, policies and procedures, and documentation protect the privacy and security of confidential patient health information. Sample policies to support these activities are provided at the end of this chapter.

Electronic Health Records Support Transparency and Efficiency

Many EHRs are beginning to conform with certification through organizations such as the CCHIT, a process that measures, verifies, and ensures that EHR clinical and functional information is recognizable and securely exchangeable within the health care industry. CCHIT also is the verification process used by private and public health plan payers to ensure that data created, stored, and exchanged with other health care entities will conform to the same communication standards, much like cell phones and ATMs have conformed with their respective communication and banking industries.

CCHIT does not verify that the information you create in the system is accurate. Accurate data result from a combination of

- tested and verified bidirectional interfaces between your PM and EHR systems;

- ongoing technical support from both PM and EHR software providers;

- excellent and ongoing training;

- excellent and thorough implementation of the EHR system[12]; and

- robust software, good training and implementation, and reliable and consistent data input, with the latter (data input) being the result of your practice's internal customized policies and procedures.

Clinical Decision Support

Clinical decision support (CDS) provides clinicians, staff, patients, and other individuals with knowledge and person-specific information that has been intelligently filtered or presented at appropriate times to enhance health and health care. It encompasses a variety of tools and

---

[12] For details on implementation, consult *Technical and Financial Guide to EHR Implementation:* Hartley CP, Jones, ED, Ens, D. Available in the Practice Management Section of the AMA bookstore: www.ama-assn.org.

interventions such as computerized alerts and reminders, clinical guidelines, order sets, patient data reports and dashboards, documentation templates, diagnostic support, and clinical workflow tools.

CDS has been effective in improving outcomes at some health care institutions and practice sites by making needed medical knowledge readily available to knowledge users. Yet, CDS can be problematic if it is not included in the planning stages of EHR implementation. As a result, relevant medical knowledge that should be brought to bear is not always available or used for many health care decisions in this country.

On the consumer side, efforts to shift the costs of care to consumers will expand patient access to CDS, as the patient–physician team seeks desirable levels of patient safety, care quality, and cost effectiveness. Even so, the content made available to consumers has to be at an understandable level and may not always be in the best interest of that patient's care. Physicians have seen this for years in the direct-to-consumer pharmaceutical ads that bring patients into the office asking for specific medications without fully understanding the side effects or complications that may arise if the patient has multiple health issues.

CDS keeps the physician on the leading edge while minimizing the hours spent searching for the latest health-related knowledge. Its three most beneficial attributes are

- Best knowledge available when needed: The best available clinical knowledge is well organized, accessible to all, and written, stored, and transmitted in a format that makes it easy to build and deploy CDS interventions that deliver the knowledge into the decision-making process
- High adoption and effective use: CDS tools are widely implemented, extensively used, and produce significant clinical value while making financial and operational sense to their end users and purchasers.

- Continuous improvement of knowledge and CDS methods: Both CDS interventions and clinical knowledge undergo continuous improvement based on feedback, experience, and data that are easy to aggregate, assess, and apply.

Policies and Procedures

Quality of Data Input

Sample Policy: It is our practice's goal to ensure that data are input correctly and efficiently so that we can document and verify improved patient population health.

Sample Procedures: Our practice will conduct periodic data validation studies to ensure data are input, stored, and dynamically generated into reports. During the periods immediately before and during our EHR Go-Live, our practice will conduct data validation reports twice each week to ensure our workforce is accurately entering data into the system.

Our practice strongly supports an internal training and support program and will retrain any workforce member needing assistance with capturing documented encounters into the EHR system.

Physician-generated templates will be presented and reviewed by our practice's clinical customization team so that the templates enhance rather than disrupt our reporting capabilities.

Participation in Quality-of-Care Studies

Sample policy: Our practice will participate, as appropriate, in quality-of-care studies to demonstrate the efficiency, quality of care, and patient–physician partnership in the delivery of care. To that end, we will ensure that any information provided to the principal complies with our privacy and security procedures.

Sample procedures: Our practice will inform the privacy and security officials of any intent to participate in quality-of-care studies and ensure that any information provided electronically conforms to our internal privacy and security policies and procedures.

Our privacy and security officials will take an active role in any study to ensure protected health information is safeguarded.

Clinical Decision Support: Use and Documentation

Sample policy: The use of clinical decision support (CDS) technology is compatible with our practice's mission to focus on improved quality of care in ambulatory settings.

Should the quality and safety assurance methods recommended by our vendor's CDS system conflict with what our physicians believe to be in the best interest of the patient, the decision to treat will be made by our physicians.

Sample procedures: In purchasing a system, our practice assigned a higher value to systems that contain CDS capabilities.

Our clinicians will acknowledge safety alerts such as medication advisories and drug–drug, drug–food, and drug–allergy alerts built into the system. In the event the CDS safety alert pop-ups that are built into our EHR system interfere with our ability to provide care, we will not systematically turn these values to an "off" position without first consulting our clinical team and vendor to develop an alternate alerting system.

Our clinicians will provide documentation when the safety alert is not in the best interest of the patient's care.

A clinician in our practice will provide online and/or educational material to our patients, as appropriate, so that they have online access to additional health information relevant to their care.

ePrescribing

Sample policy: Our practice will participate in ePrescribing under the following conditions:

- The ePrescribing application is an integrated component within our electronic medical record (EMR) software and it is certified to connect to the Pharmacy Health Information Exchange™ or has achieved Certification Commission for Health Information Technology (CCHIT) ePrescribing certification.

- The ePrescribing application is a separate application but is certified to connect to the Pharmacy Health Information Exchange™ or has achieved ePrescribing CCHIT certification, and it can import the HL7 Medication Order message we send into the patient's file in our EMR.

- The ePrescribing message will be signed using the prescriber's digital signature, according to our policies and procedures.

Sample procedures: Our security and privacy officials will

- ensure that our privacy and security policies and procedures are in place;
- ensure the national provider identifiers (NPIs) are in place for the prescribing physicians;
- ensure the practice follows policies and procedures for digital signatures;
- notify our patients that we are participating in ePrescribing to improve the quality of care, notify them of insurance coverage as provided to us from the ePrescribing software, and check medications against food or drug allergies;
- ensure our practice management system captures billing orders supporting the medication order; and
- ensure our practice uses, as backup, tamper-proof prescription pads and a tamper-proof printer that interfaces with our practice's EMR system in the event of a transmission error.

Digital Signatures		
Safeguard: Administrative	*Federal Register*	**Required or Addressable**
Security awareness and training	21 CFR Part 11: Electronic Records: Electronic Signatures Final Rule; Paperwork Reduction Act of 1980 (P.L. 96-511) Computer Matching and Privacy Act of 1987, 5-USC-522a (as amended) Computer Security Act of 1987 FIPSPUB46-1, Data Encryption Standard; Jan. 22, 1988 FIPSPUB140A, General Security Requirements for Equipment Using the Data Encryption Standard; April 14, 1982	Addressable

Sample policy: Our practice is committed to support the implementation of integrated electronic processing applications as a way to expedite the workload and reduce duplicate activities, consistent with applicable policies regarding electronic record-keeping and security.

An electronic signature will be deemed as legally binding as a paper signature, provided each application is developed, implemented, and monitored in accordance with our privacy and security policies and procedures.

The provider is responsible for reviewing each document for accuracy prior to affixing his/her electronic signature. The provider should identify any discrepancies in the report and dictate an addendum when necessary. Both the original report and the addendum will be authenticated and maintained as part of the permanent electronic record.

Sample procedures: Digital signatures will be adopted and used at our discretion and when the decision has been made to fully automate a paper-based system that employs digital signatures.

The security official must approve the use of an electronic signature.

Our system administrator and security official will control password usage so that only authorized individuals can apply their specific electronic signature. All physicians will conform to the use of electronic signatures.

All electronic-signature users will certify, in writing, that they will not disclose their user identification and password to anyone, which would permit someone to use their electronic signature.

Manually signed reports will not be accepted if electronic signatures are available. The system incorporating digital signatures must meet the following requirements:

- Signature authentication:
  - The electronic signature must establish sender/user authenticity.
  - It must be possible to ensure, with a reasonable degree of certainty, that the sender's signature has not been forged.
  - Sufficient audit trails must be provided to resolve disputes, with a reasonable degree of certainty, especially involving cases where an individual disavows sending a message.
  - The integrity of the electronic signature will be protected from alteration.

- Message authentication:
  - Through testing prior to full usage, and at regular intervals, it must be possible to ensure, with a reasonable degree of certainty, that a document and its signature have not been changed after it has been signed.

Data Quality Management and Reporting

Sample policy: Our practice will participate in data quality reporting. We understand our practice management system is capable of processing CPT Category II codes, and the interfaces between our practice management system and electronic health record system are secure and meet our security safeguard policies and procedures.

Sample procedures: Our practice will determine which quality improvement programs are appropriate for our participation, and our security official will evaluate the privacy, security, and confidentiality risks of our participation.

Our quality improvement team will build and support the clinical, coding, and administrative workflow infrastructure as appropriate for our participation.

According to the clinical requirements and documentation required to participate, our practice will de-identify confidential patient records for reporting purposes.

Our security official, along with our quality control officer (may be the same person), will provide training to clinicians participating in data quality management and include the following topics:

- use and disclosure of confidential health information,
- risks and our practice's efforts to manage those risks,
- privacy and security safeguards and responsibilities, and
- how our practice will use the outcomes.

Disease Management Information Exchange

Sample policy: From time to time, our practice participates in studies that enhance public health and Healthy People 2010 outcomes. We may participate in public health service reporting systems such as providing epidemiologic information to improve diagnostic accuracy (alerts of outbreaks), surveillance of regional data, access to immunization records, provider alerts for best-practice health management and out-of-norm test results for chronic disease management, notification, and public health information distribution.

Sample procedures: Our practice will consult our security and privacy officials prior to exchanging health information to ensure that we conform to our policies and procedures and our notice of privacy practices. Failure to coordinate with our privacy and security officials on disease management information exchange will result in sanctions imposed on the person or persons who authorized such an exchange.

Our security official, at a minimum, will review the following before authorizing participation:

- our consent and authorization policies and procedures;
- use and disclosure of confidential health information for treatment, payment, and health care operations;
- safe harbors for exchange of disease management information with payers, public health agencies, clinical research organizations, or other agencies related to this request;
- our notice of privacy practices;
- our business associate agreements; and
- authentication of electronic data.

Performance Measurements

Sample policy: Our practice views performance measurements in two separate and distinct arrangements:

- A valuable tool that measures the security of information systems for our decision-makers. Our technical safeguards require our security official to oversee the security of our information systems.
- Practice guidelines that provide practitioners with tools to measure the quality of care they provide by defining specific, measurable elements. It is the second performance measurement addressed here.

Our policy is to participate in performance measurement activities as appropriate, which may include the Physicians Quality Reporting Initiative, ePrescribing, health system performance measurement, or other programs that assist us in quality improvement. It is our expectation that our efforts will be open and forthright and that we will learn from performance feedback, and that our reports will not mislead or confuse any party as we strive to improve our delivery of care.

Sample procedures: Our security official, in collaboration with our practice attorney, will review performance measurement contracts prior to our participation. Our security official will ensure that the data provided to the evaluation team is safeguarded in accordance with our privacy and security policies and procedures.

Results from performance measurement evaluations shall not be used solely for the discipline of a workforce member. Rather, performance measurement results are to be used to constructively assist in improving the patient–physician relationship and delivery of care.

KEY POINTS

- Several performance measurement initiatives reward physicians financially for demonstrating they can securely exchange health information with other providers involved in the patient's care, and demonstrating improved patient outcomes.

- Performance measurement provides the criteria to define benchmarks. In health care, physicians like to know how they are doing compared to other physicians in the same specialty and subspecialty.

- Give patients a reason to select you or your practice over another practice or physician by showing them how well your practice performs in quality improvement measures.

- Clinical decision support keeps a physician on the leading edge while minimizing the hours spent researching the latest health-related knowledge.

CHAPTER 5

Managing the Personal Health Record

IN THIS CHAPTER, YOU WILL LEARN

- How federal incentive programs designed to help you adopt health information technology (such as ARRA), will impact the way you communicate with your patients
- How to prepare your practice for patients who want to be involved in managing their health information
- Key components of a personal health record
- Recent guidance that clarifies health information you can provide to family, friends, and caregivers
- Standards that are waived in a presidential-declared emergency.

Key Terms

Designated record set: Records maintained by or for the health care provider including medical records, billing records, and other records used in whole or in part to make decisions regarding the patient. A personal health record created and maintained by the patient is not part of your designated record set.

Patient portals: Health care–related online applications that allow patients to interact and communicate with their health care providers, such as physicians and hospitals.

Personal health record: All health care information from all sources, compiled, maintained, and held by the patient.

Smart card, chip card, or integrated circuit card (ICC): Any pocket-sized card with embedded integrated circuits that can process data. This implies that it can receive input that is processed by way of the ICC applications and delivered as an output. There are two broad categories of ICCs: memory cards contain only non-volatile memory storage components and perhaps some specific security logic, and microprocessor cards contain volatile memory and microprocessor components. The card is generally made of plastic. The card may embed a hologram to prevent counterfeiting. Use of smart cards is a form of strong security authentication for single sign-on within large companies and organizations.

Virtual office visit: A visit that, by logging onto a secure web portal, a physician and a preexisting patient can address a medical problem without having to physically travel to the office. A virtual office visit is not designed to treat emergencies or to take the place of face-to-face office visits for such needs as refills of controlled medications, routine prescription refills, or other situations that usually require further testing.

Long Time Coming, Short Time to Get There

In earlier books, practices were asked to envision their practice, customers, and business market 3 years into the future. These practices saw health information technology coming and made many financial

Case Study

It's 2011. For more than a decade, credit and debit card companies, in partnership with banks, have offered card-swiping capabilities to their members. But now, embedded in the card's computer chip is the capability to include the patient's current demographic and clinical patient information.

A local bank's market research indicates their commercial customers are very concerned about increasing health care costs. The bank has teamed up with private health plan payers to offer health savings accounts (HSAs) as a way to provide benefits and also attract and keep a competent workforce. To that end, the bank, in partnership with its commercial customers and pharmacies, has been offering mini-workshops to demonstrate how employees can build a combined patient and financial personal health record (PHR) using the bank's smart card and seamlessly manage their flexible spending accounts (FSA).

Step now into your practice. Several of your patients have brought their cards, USB drives, and smart phones into the practice in hopes of building a PHR. Taking advantage of their privacy rights to access medical information under the Health Insurance Portability and Accountability Act (HIPAA), they have asked you to provide them with health information that they can download into their files. Regardless of the bank's training, your patients are tired of providing the same demographic, payer, and medical history information over and over again to specialists, hospitals, and other practitioners. They have discovered the PHR to be a real time-saver and patient safety measure, especially in emergencies.

Your policies and procedures, in harmony with HIPAA's Privacy Rule, say you have 30 days to respond to these requests. To comply with previous requests, the physicians in your practice asked the nurses to review the paper medical records and create a summary report (continuity of care record), and you've been able to keep up with the small number of requests. However, the bank's enthusiasm has bogged your nurses down to a point that they are begging for relief. How will you handle this problem?

and organizational decisions to prepare. It wasn't easy, and you aren't done yet. But you're getting there.

Baby boomers have begun to flood Medicare, and health care expenditures are still a higher percentage of gross domestic product. The Obama Administration has been successful in changing the health care landscape in terms of fostering faster adoption of electronic business tools for practices. And health care stakeholders are going to expect quicker response and easier access to important, but protected, health care information.

The vision of patients building their personal medical records has been a long time in coming, but the time is almost here due to several factors that are influencing the timeline, including

- ePrescribing capabilities and transparency through reimbursement incentives;
- proactive legislation and more government funding that supports the testing of health information exchange;
- certification processes for interoperability and in-patient and emergency care;
- a reduction in employer benefits and an increase in flexible spending accounts and health savings accounts;
- the banking industry's increasing revenue stream for supporting electronic remittance to health care providers; and
- consumers' slow but steady interest in making decisions about their own health care.

This chapter will help you analyze new electronic medical record (EMR)-related content of your notice of privacy practices that you developed during implementation of HIPAA's Privacy and Security Rules. You can prepare now by making sure you understand that patients' rights are safeguarded as health care continues to incorporate technology in all areas, including

- ePrescribing to ensure security and confidentiality during the transaction,
- marketing, including reuse of protected health information,
- sharing health information in an emergency and when it becomes appropriate,
- biometric proof (digital photo, finger image) that a patient is who he or she says, and
- virtual office visits.

What Is a Personal Health Record (PHR)?

In 2002, the Markle Foundation established "Connecting for Health," a public–private collaborative whose mission was to bring greater visibility and coordination to the government, provider, and industry efforts that were being made to speed up the adoption of electronically connected health information systems. In phase I of the project, the Markle Foundation recommended that the American public engage in the creation of developing PHRs.

In phase 2, the foundation built working groups on policies for electronic information sharing between doctors and patients. A recent Markle Foundation report, which reflected concerns over the use of PHRs, influenced stepped up privacy and security measures attached to the American Recovery and Reconstruction Act's health information technology (IT) incentives.

Today, many disease-specific associations, such as the American Association of Kidney Patients, American Heart Association, and the National Cancer Institute, are helping patients build PHRs in paper and electronic format to help them become active decision-makers in their care, as well as to provide information to caregivers. To assist in standardizing health information between primary health care providers, specialists, and other caregivers, the Certification Commission for Health Information Technology (CCHIT), in October 2008, added personal health records (PHRs) to its list of certification activities that may launch in late 2009. In certifying EHRs, the certification process has ensured physicians selecting EHR software that it has criteria for technical competency, such as functionality, interoperability, and security. If an EHR system is certified, the potential buyer can focus on the specific needs of their office. For patients who want to manage their care, communicate with physicians, or have critical information available in emergencies, CCHIT plans to apply similar standards to PHRs.

There are several types of PHRs, many of which have been in place for years. They include

- Paper-based records. These are the files that people have in their homes stored in spiral notebooks or paper files. The files contain information from doctors, insurance companies, pharmacies, and hospitals. Some also contain information regarding allergies, vitamins, insurance, and emergency contacts. This is the most common style of PHR.

- Personal computer (PC)–based records. Health information is typed or scanned into software or generic applications and stored on personal computers. This information is usually the least accessible by health care providers, because they do not have immediate access to a desktop PHR or laptop.

- Web-based records. This type of PHR allows consumers to maintain their information in private, online accounts, which they access by logging in with a unique user name and password. Web-based platforms do not require software other than a Web browser. They may include secure email, document sharing, and video-conferencing for home consultations. The American Health Information Management Association maintains a fairly detailed list of PHR products at

http://library.ahima.org/xpedio/groups/public/documents/ahima/
bok1_027459.hcsp?dDocName=bok1_027459.

- Hybrid desktop/Web-based records. The typical hybrid solution allows individuals to maintain their PHRs on their PCs and provides an upload facility to a secure Web server. The Web server provides around-the-clock access to the information. The access is primarily read-only, with the update capability restricted to the individual's PC. In most cases, individuals are allowed to upload all or part of their medical information as they desire.

- Smart phones and other portable devices. This category represents the most rapidly expanding method for storing and transporting health information between patient and physician. Devices include smart cards, personal digital assistants, smart phones, and memory devices such as USB drives.

Minimum Common Data Elements

A standardized PHR includes common data elements in order to ensure its use among different care settings and different providers. Suggested categories of common data elements include,

- personal demographic information,
- general medical information,
- allergies and drug sensitivities,
- conditions,
- hospitalizations,
- surgeries,
- medications,
- immunizations,
- clinical tests, and
- pregnancy history.

Patient Rights and Access to Medical Information

The following are patient rights defined by HIPAA's Privacy Rule.

1. Patients can ask and get a copy of their health records. Patients may not be able to get all of their information in special cases, eg, if something in the record would endanger the patient or someone else. A practice has 30 days to provide this information to the patient and can extend this for another 30 days if the patient is given a reason for the delay. A practice may charge for the cost of copying and mailing.

2. Patients can ask to have corrections added to their health information. A patient can ask to change any wrong information in or add information if it is incomplete. For example, if the hospital sends the wrong result for a test, even if the hospital believes the test result is correct, a patient has a right to note the disagreement in his or her file. In most cases, the file should be changed within 60 days.

3. Patients can receive a notice on how a practice's health information is shared. The new provision in the HITECH Act discussed in Appendix B also gives patients the right to ask where their health records and information have been electronically used and disclosed, including for treatment, payment, and health care operations. This may be the most misinterpreted patient right, as demonstrated by the number of complaints filed with US Department of Health and Human Services (HHS's) Office for Civil Rights (OCR). To help patients better understand their rights and also help patients understand that a physician's practice must share confidential information for reimbursement and caregiver purposes, OCR issued a patient guide, "When Health Care Providers May Communicate About You with Your Family, Friends, or Others Involved in Your Care."[1] A copy of this guidance is included in Appendix A.

---

[1] When Health Care Providers May Communicate About You with Your Family, Friends, or Others Involved in Your Care. Available online at: www.hhs.gov/ocr/hipaa/consumer_ffg.pdf.

In general, health information cannot be given to a patient's employer, used or shared for things such as sales calls or advertising, or used or shared for any other purposes unless permission is given by signing an authorization form. This authorization form must identify who will get the information and what the information will be used for.

4. Patients can ask to be reached somewhere other than home. A patient can make reasonable requests to be contacted at different places or in a different way. For example, a patient can have the nurse call at the office instead of home or send mail in an envelope instead of on a postcard. If sending information to the patient at home may endanger the patient, the patient should provide a place where he or she can be reached. If the request is reasonable and does not interfere with the practice's ability to conduct health care operations, including reimbursement, the practice should try to comply.

5. Patients can ask that health information not be shared. Patients can ask the provider or health insurer not to share their health information with certain people, groups, or companies. If patients pay in full for their visits, and request the practice not to share their health records or information with anyone or organization, including the payer, the practice is required to honor their requests. If patients do not pay in full, and ask the practice not to share their health records or information, the practice, in this case, does not have to agree or honor their requests. Document the decision in the notes section of the patient's EMR.

6. Patients can file a complaint if they believe their confidentialities have been breached. If patients believe their health information were used or shared in a way that is not allowed under the privacy law or patients were not able to exercise their rights, patients can file a complaint with the practice's privacy official or with the secretary of HHS via its web site at www.hhs.gov/ocr/hipaa.

CRITICAL POINT

Included in the American Reinvestment and Recovery Act (ARRA) are beefed up security provisions designed to help safeguard confidential protected health information. These include:

- accounting of all electronic disclosures outside treatment, payment, and health care operations, upon patient request

- requirement that the practitioner notify HHS if an unencrypted portable computer, laptop, or PDA is compromised by theft, lost or stolen.

- requirement that if more than 500 patient records can be accessed by the compromised and unencrypted portable device, that the incident is reported to the media in all media markets where your patients reside.

- state attorney generals can initiate an investigation on a health information privacy breach with the intention of protecting consumers from potential identity theft. HHS may also step in and take precedence on a state-initiated investigation.

Enterprise-wide Health Care Portals

Although the PHR is created, owned, and maintained by the patient, local health communities are increasingly finding ways to share secure patient information that benefits the patient's treatment. These processes also allow patients to communicate and interact securely with their health care providers, such as hospitals and physicians. Information sharing via portals is typically governed by the practice's notice of privacy practices.

Portals can be stand-alone Web sites that draw information from multiple EMR vendors or they can be implemented into one vendor's existing application. You may already be familiar with the following types of portals.

- *Clinical portals* typically provide the physician and clinical team with access to the patient's medical information created at other locations, such as radiology and picture archiving and communication systems (PACS), cardiology, laboratory, or similar system.

- *Patient portals* are health care–related online applications that allow patients to interact and communicate with their health care providers, such as physicians and hospitals. Typically, portal services are available on the Internet at all hours of the day. Patient portals can also be used to complete administrative tasks, such as appointment scheduling, completing preregistration information, generating privacy and security acknowledgments, and similar notices.

- Some patient portal applications are stand-alone Web sites, and services are sold to health care providers. Other patient portal applications are a component of the hospital vendor's health IT system.

- *Consumer portals* allow consumers to search for reliable health information, receive reminders and alerts, securely communicate with patients managing similar diseases, and participate in online classes.

- *Employee portals* provide a central filing and communication system that typically includes the employer's benefits packages, internal policies and procedures, and employee notices. Where the employer offers in-house medical care, this portal also provides benefits and care-management guidance.

User authentication, firewalls, and additional layers of proprietary security protect access to all of these portals.

Privacy and Security Tested and Clarified in New Guidances

Since the privacy and security rules have become enforceable, the United States has experienced natural disasters and emergencies where HIPAA's rules were used as an excuse to not disclose information. In other instances, the rules regarding confidential exchange of critical information were misunderstood. Because we now live in an environment that includes possible attacks from foreign nations, disaster preparedness agencies and health care communities have become partners in the mission to deliver quality care. To help early responders and physicians at the point of care, the Department of Health and Human Services Office for Civil Rights (OCR) released additional guidance and preparedness tools to ensure that the delivery of health care continues without interruption or fear of disclosure breaches in the event of an emergency.

Privacy and Security in Disasters or Emergencies

As it relates to sharing personal health information in an emergency or disaster, reference the privacy and security in disasters or emergencies policies and procedures located in Chapter 1.

If the president declares an emergency or disaster *and* the secretary of HHS declares a public health emergency, the secretary may waive sanctions and penalties against a covered hospital that does not comply with certain provisions of the HIPAA Privacy Rule, as noted here:

- the requirements to obtain a patient's agreement to speak with family members or friends involved in the patient's care (45 CFR 164.510(b));
- the requirement to honor a request to opt out of the facility directory (45 CFR 164.510(a));
- the requirement to distribute a notice of privacy practices (45 CFR 164.520);

- the patient's right to request privacy restrictions (45 CFR 164.522(a)); and
- the patient's right to request confidential communications (45 CFR 164.522(b)).

When and to what entities does the waiver apply? If the secretary issues such a waiver, it only applies:

- in the emergency area and for the emergency period identified in the public health emergency declaration
- to hospitals that have instituted a disaster protocol. The waiver would apply to all patients at such hospitals.
- for up to 72 hours from the time the hospital implements its disaster protocol.

When the presidential or secretarial declaration terminates, a hospital must then comply with all requirements of the Privacy Rule for any patient still under its care, even if 72 hours has not elapsed since implementation of its disaster protocol.

Regardless of the activation of an emergency waiver, the HIPAA Privacy Rule permits disclosures for treatment purposes and certain disclosures to disaster relief organizations. For instance, the Privacy Rule allows covered entities to share patient information with the American Red Cross so it can notify family members of the patient's location. See 45 CFR 164.510(b)(4).[2]

Resources. Following are resources you can use when building your emergency disaster and recovery plan.

1. OCR, the agency named to oversee privacy of confidential health information and, as of July 27, 2009, enforcement of the HIPAA Security Rule. This is HHS's primary site for assisting you in emergency preparedness and disaster recovery planning

---

[2] Available online at: www.hhs.gov/ocr/hipaa/emergencyPPR.html.

and response. At its Web site, www.hhs.gov/ocr/hipaa/
emergencyPPR.html, OCR provides links to its own planning
documents and links to other agencies inside and outside of
HHS that have developed disaster recovery guidance tools (see
number 2 in this list); other links will take you to the National
Aging Network.

2. Agency for Healthcare Research and Quality (AHRQ). At the
   AHRQ's web site, www.ahrq.gov/path/katrina.htm, you will
   find links to multiple tools and resources to assist in response
   and recovery efforts. Those that are most likely to affect a physician practice include:

   a. personal protective equipment, decontamination, isolation/
      quarantine, and laboratory capacity

   b. computer staffing model for disaster preparedness response

   c. alternate site locator

   d. health Emergency Assistance Line and Triage Hub model.

3. Decision tool to help you determine who, when, and how health
   information can be disclosed in emergencies is available at
   www.hhs.gov/ocr/hipaa/decisiontool/tool/source1.html.

Family Members Involved as Caregivers

Communicating patient needs and treatment also has been a con-
tentious area that OCR has addressed. Even though HIPAA requires
health care providers to protect patient privacy, providers are permitted, in most circumstances, to communicate with the patient's family,
friends, or others involved in their care or payment for care. As a way
to help clarify the communication, OCR released a guide to clarify
HIPAA requirements so that health care providers do not unnecessarily withhold a patient's health information from these persons.[3] A copy
of the guidance is included in Appendix A.

---

[3] Guidance on Communications with Family, Friends, or Others Involved in a
Patient's Care. Sept. 16, 2008, Office for Civil Rights. Available online at:
www.hhs.gov/ocr/hipaa/privacy.html.

Using Patient Information in Marketing

Under HIPAA's current rules, *marketing* is defined as "making a communication about a product or service that encourages the recipients of the communication to purchase or use the product or service." Report 19, "Patient Information in the Electronic Medical Record," by the American Medical Association's board of trustees, provides the following guidance: "Those organizations using patient health information for purposes other than the direct patient care should be responsible for plainly disclosing the purpose(s) for which that information will be used and should have transparent policies and procedures indicating how the privacy of this information will be secured."[4]

If you use protected health information that is personally identifiable to the patient to market your products or services, you generally must obtain the patient's prior written authorization with the following exception. In HHS-issued guidance about marketing, the agency reiterated that authorization is always required prior to such use except in three instances:

- the marketing takes place during an in-person meeting, such as a medical appointment.
- the marketing concerns products or services are of "nominal value."
- The covered entity is marketing health-related products and services, is identified as such, and gives the individual the opportunity to opt out of any additional marketing.

The key to understanding marketing is to first determine whether the activity is marketing or "communications that enhance the individual's access to quality health care." Communications includes providing information about or recommendations of treatment, case management, coordination of care, and new or alternative therapies or services.

---

[4] American Medical Association, Board of Trustees, Report 19 of the Board of Trustees (A-07), 2006.

There are three general categories that will help you make
this determination.

1. Is the activity for "case management" or "care coordination"?
   This covers information provided to individual patients for the
   purpose of furthering or managing the treatment of an individual, such as directing or recommending alternative treatments,
   therapies, health care providers, or care facilities.

   a. Are you using the patient's health information to encourage
      the purchase of a product or service? If yes, the activity is
      considered marketing, and you will need an authorization.

   b. If you are describing a service that is part of the patient's ben-
      efit plan, it is not considered marketing.

2. The "health-related" or "value added" exception.

   a. Are you providing information about entities participating in
      services provided and benefits covered by a provider network
      or health plan (which also includes replacements to and
      enhancements of coverage under the plan but does not include
      communications of discounts or other items that are available
      to the general public)? This is not considered marketing.

   b. If you wish to provide protected health information to a
      pharmaceutical company or alternative medicine organiza-
      tion, you will need an authorization. For example, a drug
      company wants to convert all patients taking a weekly med-
      ication to a monthly dosage. You will need an authorization
      to provide health information.

3. The communications that "promote health in a general manner"
   exception, which covers newsletters and other general circulation
   information promoting health, as long as they do not endorse a
   specific product or service. For example, you want to use or disclose protected individually identifiable health information to
   target a group of patients with a particular diagnosis to distribute
   a discount coupon or rebate offer for a product or service.

a. The covered entity could distribute calendars, pens, and other merchandise without authorization.

If the communications qualify as a communication activity defined in one of these three situations, these activities may be conducted either by the covered entity or via a "business associate" with whom you have a business associate agreement. If the activity does not meet the requirements in these three situations, it is considered marketing, and the patient must sign an authorization for you to release identifying information. In that authorization, the covered entity must make certain disclosures, such as letting the patient know whether the individual has been targeted based on health status and whether the covered entity is being compensated for such marketing.

Pharmaceutical industry's interest in marketing. Pharmaceutical companies are increasingly seeking ways to learn more about how well their direct-to-consumer or direct-to-physician advertising campaigns are working, even if it means using de-identified patient information. Often, the answer to their questions is embedded in the physician comments and medication orders stored in the physician's database. Recently, pharmaceutical companies have begun looking into business relationships with electronically connected physician practices to mine de-identified data, with the goal of learning about drug efficiencies, drug prescribing habits, competitor inefficiencies, and improved disease management outcomes.

This new approach to market research is changing the historic process of selling to physicians, ie, where a sales representative stops by to visit the physician, learns about the drug's use efficacy, and also provides free drug samples to the physician. Today, drug representatives must provide information that is more advanced than what the patient has already learned on the Internet. Added economic pressures on the industry and the vast amounts of health information provided online are causing pharmaceutical companies to rethink the traditional sales process to physicians.

Marketing also has affected the health payer industry through Medicare Advantage's open health and drug plan enrollment period. This has caused the OCR to release new guidance on how confidential health information can be used and disclosed for marketing purposes. The marketing policies and procedures included in this book reflect this new guidance.

Policies and Procedures

Patient Rights		
Safeguard: Administrative	**Federal Register/ CFR Parts**	**Required or Addressable**
Notice of privacy practices, electronic communication	67 *Federal Register* 45 CFR 164.520	Required

Sample policy: Our practice has designated <name> as our privacy official. <Name> continues to be responsible for implementing the privacy policies and procedures explained in our notice of privacy practices (NPP) and is the practice's primary contact for patient privacy questions or complaints. Our privacy official will review our NPP as our practice develops new electronic communication strategies, such as those outlined in the policy, with our patients.

As it relates to electronic communications with our patients, we have adopted and will train our workforce on the following policies.

Virtual Office Visit Patient Communication

Sample policy: Our clinical staffs are the only ones who can determine how to manage a patient's care on a virtual office visit. For example, we may decide to issue a prescription, ask the patient to come into the practice, or recommend a specialist.

Sample procedures: We will not disclose confidential health information with patients using unsecure e-mail servers. If we receive an e-mail with confidential health information from a patient, we will respond using a generic response asking them to communicate with us using our secure e-mail portal or call the practice at our primary telephone number.

ePrescribing Patient Communication

Sample policy: Our patients will be informed of any medication that is sent via electronic processes to their local pharmacy. We will disclose confidential medication prescriptions only via certified ePrescribing software (certified as an ePrescriber by CCHIT or certified to connect to the Pharmacy Health Information Exchange), and in accordance with our ePrescribing policy, to the pharmacy designated in writing by the patient, as part of our treatment, payment, and health care operations identified in our NPP.

Patient Acknowledgment of NPP by E-mail

Sample policy: Our patients can download our NPP from our Web site and acknowledge receipt of that NPP.

Sample procedures: Instruct either in person, by phone, or via the Internet how the patient can download and complete the NPP using the following instructions:

- completing specific fields, such as the initial and date of birth fields on our Web site, as an indication that they received the NPP,
- sending us a secure e-mail through a link provided that they read and reviewed our NPP, or
- printing a copy of our NPP acknowledgments page and bringing a signed copy with them to the office visit.

Use of Patient Portals in Patient Communication

Sample policy: Communication with patients via our patient portal is made available only to our existing patients. All new patients must make an appointment to see a practitioner before they can access our patient portal.

Sample procedures: We will provide brochures or pamphlets inviting patients to sign up to join our patient portal.

Online Payments

Sample policy: Patients will know their credit or debit card transactions will be conducted in a secure and firewalled environment.

Sample procedures:

- Our NPP is presented to patients in accordance with HIPAA's Privacy Rule, a process that we have implemented.

- Our practice will determine how we will be reimbursed for virtual office visits and will coordinate that health care component with our billing, front office, and clinical staffs.

- Virtual office visits are for existing patients only and cannot be utilized by new patients. Virtual office visits will be conducted using the same policies we have established for office visits in person at our facility.

- Our privacy and security officials will oversee the implementation of technical, physical, and administrative safeguards to protect the patient's confidential health information.

Patient Portal

Sample policy: Our practice will participate in the secure, interoperable exchange of protected health information and will notify our patients when that portal is available for them to use.

Sample procedures:

- New patients will be directed to the patient portal to review administrative documentation, including our NPP, authorization forms, consent forms, patient's rights, and other routine information that expedites the patient's visit.

- New patients cannot schedule a virtual office visit unless they have first seen the physician in the office for a physical exam.

- Patients wishing to participate in our patient portal will be assigned a user ID and password. Our physicians will establish protocols that determine how much information will be made available to patients on our portal. For example, we may decide to share normal lab results but not abnormal results.

- When communicating with patients via our patient portal, an e-mail will be sent to the patient's unsecure e-mail notifying them that the physician has posted a note on the portal, along with instructions to sign in to retrieve the message.
- Patients participating in online care management programs will be asked to create a patient profile that secures and protects their identity. Care management programs will be audited. One person from the practice will act as reviewer to ensure the privacy and security of our patient population is secure.

Online Reimbursement

Sample policy: Our workforce will comply with Red Flag Rules, described in Chapter 2, to protect the identity of patients making payments to our practice by check, cash, credit or debit card, or online transaction.

Marketing

Safeguard: Administrative	*Federal Register/* *CFR Parts*	Required or Addressable
Notice of privacy practices, electronic communication	67 *Federal Register* 45 CFR 164.520	Required

Sample policy: With limited exceptions, our practice will secure an authorization from the patient permitting us to use protected health information for marketing purposes. Our privacy and security officials will assist in determining whether an activity is deemed to be marketing or patient communication.

Sample procedures: Prior to releasing protected health information for marketing purposes, our privacy and security officials will review the intent of the message and determine whether the message is of a marketing or communication nature in terms of how protected health information will be used. The officials will establish a method for overseeing the administration of authorizations, as appropriate, and will ensure that signed authorizations will be scanned and stored electronically.

Patients Rights: Accounting of Disclosures

Sample policy: Our policy is to document all disclosures of personal health information made by our practice or our business associates on our behalf, except for the following types:

- disclosures to carry out treatment, payment, or health care operations, and
- incidental disclosures in compliance with our policies and procedures for incidental disclosures.

Sample procedures: Our security official will ensure that the electronic medical record system we select can and will automatically capture electronic disclosures that are sent outside of our practice. This is in addition to the disclosure log that we maintain as protected health information on paper is sent outside the practice.

KEY POINTS

- To participate in ARRA Stimulus funds, the selected EHR system must be able to report if patients have electronic access to a personal health record (PHR). This question needs to be added to the intake processes.
- ARRA allows patients to ask the practice for a list of all persons/facilities that have been provided or disclosed their protected health information, *including* for treatment, payment, and health care operations.
- HHS has guidelines that clarify the HIPAA privacy and security conversations a physician may have with friends and family, as well as guidance on exchange of health information in an emergency or disaster.
- Consult the practice's privacy and security officials and policies and procedures before agreeing to participate in pharmaceutical marketing programs.

GLOSSARY

Application: Shortened form of *application program* designed to perform a specific function directly for the user or for another application program. Examples of applications include word processing programs; database programs; Web browsers; development tools; drawing, painting, and image-editing programs; and communication programs.

Authentication: Corroboration that a person seeking access to information is the one claimed.

Audit controls: Mechanisms employed to record and examine system activity.

Audit trail: Information regarding activity on the network, which provides the basis for a security audit.

Auto expand: System feature that allows you to string words together and then repeat that string each time you type the first few letters of the string. Auto expands are particularly helpful when building repetitive encounter summaries.

Bandwidth: The maximum amount of information (bits per second) that can be transmitted along a channel.

Benchmarking: Continuous process whereby an enterprise measures and compares all of its functions, systems, and practices against strong competitors, identifying quality gaps in the organization and striving to achieve competitive advantage locally and globally.[1]

Client-server network: A self-contained network within a building that is made up of a central server that shares information with remote client computers.

Client: A remote computer attached to the central server. See also *Fat Client* and *Thin Client*.

Clinical flow sheets: Collection of clinical observations made over time, arranged in a row/column matrix, tailored to clinical guidelines.

---

[1] SixSigma, www.isixsigma.com/dictionary/Benchmarking-1.htm. Accessed 02/04/09.

Clinical practice guidelines: Systematically developed statements to assist the practitioner and patient make decisions about appropriate health care for specific circumstances.

Clinical decision support: Active knowledge systems that use two or more items of patient data to generate case-specific guidance.

Consolidated Health Informatics (CHI): A federal initiative that requires federal agencies that engage in health care activities to adopt a common set of clinical, administrative, and messaging standards.

Data authentication: The corroboration that data have not been altered or destroyed in an unauthorized manner.

Data storage: Computer storage is the holding of data in an electromagnetic form for access by a computer processor. Primary storage are data in random access memory (RAM) and other "built-in" devices. Secondary storage are data on hard disk, tapes, and other external devices.

Digital signature: An electronic signature, which serves as a unique identifier for an individual, much like a written signature, in which an algorithm authenticates the integrity of the signed data and the identity of the signatory.[2]

ePrescribe: Describes a prescriber's ability to electronically send an accurate, error-free, and understandable prescription directly to a pharmacy from the point-of-care. ePrescribing was included as a provision in the Medicare Modernization Act (MMA) of 2003.

ePrescribing: The process of moving a prescription through a digital environment, such as from a handheld device or tablet PC to the pharmacy and also accepted by a payer for reimbursement according to the patient's benefit plan. The e-prescribing process is intended to also inform the physician whether the patient picked up the prescription.

Encryption: Encryption is a method of converting an original message of regular text into encoded text. The text is encrypted by means of an algorithm (type of formula). If information is encrypted, there would be a low probability that

---

[2] US Department of Commerce/National Institute of Standards and Technology (NIST), "Digital Signature Standards (DSS)," FIPS Pub 186-2, Jan. 27, 2000, http://csrc.nist.gov/publications/fips/fips186-2/fips186-2-change1.pdf.

anyone other than the receiving party who has the key to the code or access to another confidential process would be able to decrypt (translate) the text and convert it into plain, comprehensible text. Two specific examples of encryption that have been deemed to meet HIPAA's Security Rule standard: (1) for data at rest, encryption consistent with National Institute of Standards and Technology Special (NIST) Publication 800-111 and; (2) for data in transit, encryption that complies with Federal Information Processing Standard 140-2.

Electronic media: (1) Electronic storage media, including memory devices in computers (hard drives) and any removable/transportable digital memory medium, such as magnetic tape or disk, optical disk, or digital memory card; or (2) transmission media used to exchange information already in electronic storage media. Transmission media include the Internet (wide open), extranet (using Internet technology to link a business with information accessible only to collaborating parties), leased lines, dial-up lines, private networks, and the physical movement of removable/transportable electronic storage media. Written communications sent via facsimile (not from one computer to another) and oral information exchanges are not considered electronic media.

Electronic medical record (EMR): An application environment composed of the clinical data repository, clinical decision support, controlled medical vocabulary, order entry, computerized provider order entry, pharmacy, and clinical documentation applications.

Electronic health record (EHR): A secure, real-time, interoperable point-of-care, patient-centric information resource for clinicians. The EHR aids clinicians in decision making by providing access to patient health record information where and when they need it and by incorporating evidence-based decision support. The EHR automates and streamlines the clinicians' workflow, closing loops in communication and response that result in delays or gaps in care. The EHR also supports the collection of data for uses other than direct clinical care, such as billing, quality management, outcomes reporting, resource planning, and public health disease surveillance and reporting.

Electronic protected health information (ePHI): Confidential health information that is transmitted by electronic media or maintained in electronic media.

Electronic signature: Comparable to a seal. An electronic signature must identify the signing individual, assure the integrity of a document's content, and provide for no repudiation. The signature must provide strong and substantial evidence that will make it difficult for the signer to claim that the electronic representation is not valid. Currently, the only technically mature electronic signature meeting the above criteria is the digital signature.

Enterprise-wide EMR: A system that allows large groups of employees to share and disseminate information using multiple medical record systems (e.g., access to databases) and analyze or compute procedures based on their access to information, often for quality control, predictive care, inventory, purchasing, supply chain, and accounts receivable. In a practice, the practice management system (PMS) and EMR working together become a small scale enterprise-wide EMR.

Evidence-based medicine: The conscientious, explicit, and judicious use of current best evidence in making decisions about the care of individual patients. The practice of evidence-based medicine means integrating individual clinical expertise with the best available external clinical evidence from systematic research.

Evidence-based practice centers: Institutions contracted under Agency for Healthcare Research and Quality (AHRQ) to develop evidence reports and technology assessments on topics relevant to clinical, social science/behavioral, economic, and other health care organization and delivery issues.

Fat Client: or *Rich Client* is a computer (client) in client-server architecture networks that typically provides rich functionality independently of the central server. A fat client will include memory, a hard drive, and adequate computing power to process data locally, independently of a central server.

Go-live: A point of time when you and the vendor determine to officially begin entering data into the system. To a vendor, go-live means the date you accept the system, make your final licensing payment, or the vendor's implementation team hands you off to their technical support team.

Health information technology (HIT): Approach that allows comprehensive management of medical information and its secure exchange between health care consumers and providers. The US Department of Health and Human Services (HHS) promotes countrywide adoption of electronic health record (EHR) systems by 2014 in the hopes that hundreds of thousands of health care IT systems throughout the United States will be able to exchange information. Broad use of HIT will

- improve health care quality
- prevent medical errors
- reduce health care costs
- increase administrative efficiencies
- decrease paperwork
- expand access to affordable care

Health Insurance Portability and Accountability Act (HIPAA): Enacted by the US Congress in 1996 to protect health insurance coverage for workers and their families when they change or lose their jobs; it also requires the establishment of national standards for electronic health care transactions and national identifiers for providers, health insurance plans, and employers.

Health Level 7 (HL7): One of several American National Standards Institute (ANSI)–accredited standards developing organizations (SDOs) operating in the health care arena. Most SDOs produce standards (sometimes called *specifications* or *protocols*) for a particular health care domain such as pharmacy, medical devices, imaging, or insurance (claims processing) transactions. HL7's domain is clinical and administrative data.

Health savings account: Tax-deferred employee contributions paid into a self-managed fund used to pay for health care services purchased by an employee and/or his or her beneficiaries.

Implementation: All activity involved in moving a practice from paper to electronic, including planning, research, system installation, software training, change management, privacy and security assessment, analysis of health information exchange partners, computer literacy training, and staff comfort with the new system.

Implementation specification: In the HIPAA Security Rule, this is a detailed statement that provides instruction to a covered entity on actions that must be taken to comply with a particular standard.

Information system: An interconnected set of information resources under the same direct management control that shares common functionality. A system normally includes hardware, software, information, data, applications, communications, and people.

Installation: The process of bringing software and hardware into a practice and connecting (interfacing) electronic systems among the practice management, laboratory, pathology, and/or hospital systems so that information can be exchanged.

Interface: To export data from one database to a file, usually a comma-delimited file that looks like a string of values, each separated by a comma (name, address, phone number, etc.). The interface software program then sends that file to another computer where the other database resides. It then imports the data from the file into the other database. Interface software programs are made up of three components: the part that exports, the part that sends, and the part that imports. Both the EHR program and PM program have to be configured and tweaked in order for the information to flow back and forth properly.

Sometimes that involves a third software program that does nothing but manage the flow of data between the EHR and practice management system. When a company offers an interfaced product, there are almost always costs associated with maintaining the interface and for upgrading it; in some cases, the physician will have to purchase a third program that manages the data flow.

Interfaced systems: In an EMR, vendors connect characteristics such as data fields, application, presentation, and operational issues using HL7 standards. Systems built in this way are often referred to as a *Best of Breed solution.*

Integrity: The property that data or information have not been altered or destroyed in an unauthorized manner.

Integrated: An integrated product means that the EHR and the practice management system are both in one program. There is no Health Level 7 (HL7) interface necessary because the two programs are made together. Typically, integrated products offer a more natural, less cumbersome transition between patient charting and billing.

Integrated systems: In an EMR, the vendor builds the system using the same characteristics arranged in the broad categories of data issues, application issues, presentation issues, and operational issues. Systems built in this way are often referred to as a *Single Source solutions*.

Interoperability: The ability of different information technology systems, software applications, hardware, and networks to communicate, exchange, and use information that has been exchanged (usually in a large heterogeneous network made up of several local area networks). Interoperability includes uniform:

- movement of data
- presentation of data
- user controls
- safeguarding of data security and integrity
- protection of patient confidentiality

Local Area Network (LAN): covers a small physical area, like a home, office, or small group of buildings, such as a school or an airport. The defining characteristics of LANs, in contrast to a Wide Area Network (WAN) include their usually higher data-transfer rates, smaller geographic place, and lack of a need for leased telecommunication lines.

Login monitoring: The system is capable of identifying who is logging in to the system, filing a report on repeated unsuccessful attempts, and the security official can read and respond to monitoring reports.

Network: A constellation of computers that share information.

Office of the National Coordinator for Health Information Technology (ONC): Formerly known by the acronym ONCHIT, was established by Executive Order in April 2004 with a mission to provide "leadership for the development and nationwide implementation of an interoperable health information technology infrastructure to improve the quality and efficiency of health care and the ability of consumers to manage their care and safety."

Password: Confidential authentication information composed of a string of characters.

Pay-for-performance: The use of incentives to encourage and reinforce the delivery of evidence-based practices in the health care system transformation that promotes better outcomes as efficiently as possible.

Performance improvement: Process for achieving desired institutional and individual results.

Personal health record: The health care consumer's health information record, which they own and manage. Sharing or allowing access is based on the patient's consent/permission.

Process management: The execution and monitoring of repeatable business processes that have been defined by a set of formal procedures.

Request for information (RFI): A simple form used to gather information to help make a decision on what steps to take next. An RFI is an invitation to vendors to let you know whether they believe they would be a good fit for your practice. An RFI can be sent to many vendors. Once you narrow the selection, you may either send an RFP or ask for a quote from the vendor.

Request for proposal (RFP): A compilation of factors the buyer will consider before making a purchase. An RFP is typically sent to two or more potential responders and always contains a due date

and contact person in the event those bidding on the proposal have additional questions.

Return on investment (ROI): The profit or loss resulting from an investment transaction, usually expressed as an annual percentage return.

Quality measure: Mechanism to assign a quantity to quality of care by comparison to a criterion.[3]

Risk analysis: Identification of vulnerabilities in resources and the threats to those resources to determine appropriate safeguards or controls.

Security incident: The attempted or successful unauthorized access, use, disclosure, modification, or destruction of information or interference with system operations in an information system.

Security or security measures: All administrative, physical, and technical safeguards in an information system.

Site visit: A scheduled three- to five-hour visit at a location determined by the vendor and host site that allows the practice purchasing the same software to see that software

---

[3] National Quality Measures Clearinghouse, www.qualitymeasures.ahrq.gov/submit/glossary.aspx. Accessed 02/04/09.

and interfaces in action. Most purchasers want to observe the new workflows and how well the interfaces work, as well as learn implementation tips.

Server: A central computer that houses the database.

Short list: A list of the ICD-9 and CPT codes that are typically used by your specialty and/or subspecialty so that you do not have to search through the entire ICD and CPT indices during each assessment and plan. Short lists are built during the implementation from your super bills or patient invoices.

Team building: Philosophy of in which employees are viewed as members of interdependent teams instead of individual workers.

Template: Archetypes (or models) that define what, in a specific local context, needs to be documented. Physicians often create templates for their own specialty and subspecialty that mirror the information they need to gather to determine diagnosis, procedures, and treatment.

Timeline development: In EMR implementation, the process of coordinating activities within the practice to minimize downtime.

Workflow: The tasks, procedural steps, and organizations or people required to input and output information or other outcomes.

Thin client: A computer that does not have a hard drive, sometimes called a *dumb terminal.*

Training: In the implementation of electronic health records (EHRs), training refers to educational services designed to help you understand how the software works. It is usually provided by the software vendor to your practice staff.

Treatment protocols: A precise and detailed plan for the study of a medical or biomedical problem and plans for a regimen of therapy.

Wide Area Network (WAN): network that covers a broad area (ie, any network whose communications links cross metropolitan, regional, or national boundaries. The largest and most well-known example of a WAN is the Internet.

Resources and Guidance For The HIPAA Privacy Rule

Communicating with a Patient's Family, Friends, or Others Involved in the Patient's Care

U.S. Department of Health and Human Services • Office for Civil Rights

This guide explains when a health care provider is allowed to share a patient's health information with the patient's family members, friends, or others identified by the patient as involved in the patient's care under the Health Insurance Portability and Accountability Act of 1996 (HIPAA) Privacy Rule. HIPAA is a federal law that sets national standards for how health plans, health care clearinghouses, and most health care providers are to protect the privacy of a patient's health information.[1]

[1.] The HIPAA Privacy Rule applies to those health care providers that transmit any health information in electronic form in connection with certain standard transactions, such as health care claims. See the definitions of "covered entity," "health care provider," and "transaction" at 45 C.F.R. § 160.103.

Even though HIPAA requires health care providers to protect patient privacy, providers are permitted, in most circumstances, to communicate with the patient's family, friends, or others involved in their care or payment for care. This guide is intended to clarify these HIPAA requirements so that health care providers do not unnecessarily withhold a patient's health information from these persons. This guide includes common questions and a table that summarizes the relevant requirements.[2]

Common Questions About HIPAA

1. If the patient is present and has the capacity to make health care decisions, when does HIPAA allow a health care provider to discuss the patient's health information with the patient's family, friends, or others involved in the patient's care or payment for care?

If the patient is present and has the capacity to make health care decisions, a health care provider may discuss the patient's health information with a family member, friend, or other person if the patient agrees or, when given the opportunity, does not object. A health care provider also may share information with these persons if, using professional judgment, he or she decides that the patient does not object. In either case, the health care provider may share or discuss only the information that the person involved needs to know about the patient's care or payment for care.

Here are some examples:

- An emergency room doctor may discuss a patient's treatment in front of the patient's friend if the patient asks that her friend come into the treatment room.

[2.] The full text of these requirements can be found at 45 C.F.R. § 164.510(b). Note that this guide does not apply to a health care provider's disclosure of psychotherapy notes, which generally requires a patient's written authorization. See 45 C.F.R. § 164.508(a)(2).

- A doctor's office may discuss a patient's bill with the patient's adult daughter who is with the patient at the patient's medical appointment and has questions about the charges.

- A doctor may discuss the drugs a patient needs to take with the patient's health aide who has accompanied the patient to a medical appointment.

- A doctor may give information about a patient's mobility limitations to the patient's sister who is driving the patient home from the hospital.

- A nurse may discuss a patient's health status with the patient's brother if she informs the patient she is going to do so and the patient does not object.

BUT:

- A nurse may <u>not</u> discuss a patient's condition with the patient's brother after the patient has stated she does not want her family to know about her condition.

2. If the patient is not present or is incapacitated, may a health care provider still share the patient's health information with family, friends, or others involved in the patient's care or payment for care?

Yes. If the patient is not present or is incapacitated, a health care provider may share the patient's information with family, friends, or others as long as the health care provider determines, based on professional judgment, that it is in the best interest of the patient. When someone other than a friend or family member is involved, the health care provider must be reasonably sure that the patient asked the person to be involved in his or her care or payment for care. The health care provider may discuss only the information that the person involved needs to know about the patient's care or payment.

Here are some examples:

- A surgeon who did emergency surgery on a patient may tell the patient's spouse about the patient's condition while the patient is unconscious.
- A pharmacist may give a prescription to a patient's friend who the patient has sent to pick up the prescription.
- A hospital may discuss a patient's bill with her adult son who calls the hospital with questions about charges to his mother's account.
- A health care provider may give information regarding a patient's drug dosage to the patient's health aide who calls the provider with questions about the particular prescription.

BUT:

- A nurse may <u>not</u> tell a patient's friend about a past medical problem that is unrelated to the patient's current condition.
- A health care provider is <u>not</u> required by HIPAA to share a patient's information when the patient is not present or is incapacitated, and can choose to wait until the patient has an opportunity to agree to the disclosure.

3. Does HIPAA require that a health care provider document a patient's decision to allow the provider to share his or her health information with a family member, friend, or other person involved in the patient's care or payment for care?

No. HIPAA does not require that a health care provider document the patient's agreement or lack of objection. However, a health care provider is free to obtain or document the patient's agreement, or lack of objection, in writing, if he or she prefers. For example, a provider may choose to document a patient's agreement to share information with a family member with a note in the patient's medical file.

4. May a health care provider discuss a patient's health information over the phone with the patient's family, friends, or others involved in the patient's care or payment for care?

Yes. Where a health care provider is allowed to share a patient's health information with a person, information may be shared face-to-face, over the phone, or in writing.

5. If a patient's family member, friend, or other person involved in the patient's care or payment for care calls a health care provider to ask about the patient's condition, does HIPAA require the health care provider to obtain proof of who the person is before speaking with them?

No. If the caller states that he or she is a family member or friend of the patient, or is involved in the patient's care or payment for care, then HIPAA doesn't require proof of identity in this case. However, a health care provider may establish his or her own rules for verifying who is on the phone. In addition, when someone other than a friend or family member is involved, the health care provider must be reasonably sure that the patient asked the person to be involved in his or her care or payment for care.

6. Can a patient have a family member, friend, or other person pick up a filled prescription, medical supplies, X-rays, or other similar forms of patient information, for the patient?

Yes. HIPAA allows health care providers to use professional judgment and experience to decide if it is in the patient's best interest to allow another person to pick up a prescription, medical supplies, X-rays, or other similar forms of information for the patient.

For example, the fact that a relative or friend arrives at a pharmacy and asks to pick up a specific prescription for a patient effectively verifies that he or she is involved in the patient's care. HIPAA allows the pharmacist to give the filled prescription to the relative or friend. The patient does not need to provide the pharmacist with their names in advance.

7. May a health care provider share a patient's health information with an interpreter to communicate with the patient or with the patient's family, friends, or others involved in the patient's care or payment for care?

Yes. HIPAA allows covered health care providers to share a patient's health information with an interpreter without the patient's written authorization under the following circumstances:

- A health care provider may share information with an interpreter who works for the provider (e.g., a bilingual employee, a contract interpreter on staff, or a volunteer).

For example, an emergency room doctor may share information about an incapacitated patient's condition with an interpreter on staff who relays the information to the patient's family.

- A health care provider may share information with an interpreter who is acting on its behalf (but is not a member of the provider's workforce) if the health care provider has a written contract or other agreement with the interpreter that meets HIPAA's business associate contract requirements.

For example, many providers are required under Title VI of the Civil Rights Act of 1964 to take reasonable steps to provide meaningful access to persons with limited English proficiency. These providers often have contracts with private companies, community-based organizations, or telephone interpreter service lines to provide language interpreter services. These arrangements must comply with the HIPAA business associate agreement requirements at 45 C.F.R. 164.504(e).

- A health care provider may share information with an interpreter who is the patient's family member, friend, or other person identified by the patient as his or her interpreter, if the patient agrees, or does not object, or the health care provider determines, using his or her professional judgment, that the patient does not object. For example, health care providers sometimes see patients who speak a certain language and the provider has no employee, volunteer, or contractor who can competently interpret that language. If the provider is aware of a telephone interpreter service that can help, the provider may have that interpreter tell the patient that the service is available. If the provider decides, based on professional judgment, that the patient has chosen to continue using the interpreter, the provider may talk to the patient using the interpreter.

8. Where can I find additional information about HIPAA?

The Office for Civil Rights, part of the Department of Health and Human Services, has more information about HIPAA on its Web site. Visit www.hhs.gov/ocr/hipaa for a wide range of helpful information, including the full text of the Privacy Rule, a HIPAA Privacy Rule Summary, fact sheets, over 200 Frequently Asked Questions, as well as many other resources to help health care providers and others understand the law.

A PATIENT'S GUIDE TO THE HIPAA PRIVACY RULE

When Health Care Providers May Communicate About You with Your Family, Friends, or Others Involved In Your Care

U.S. Department of Health and Human Services • Office for Civil Rights

The U.S. Department of Health and Human Services (HHS) enforces the Federal privacy regulations commonly known as the **HIPAA Privacy Rule (HIPAA)**. HIPAA requires most doctors, nurses, pharmacies, hospitals, nursing homes, and other health care providers to protect the privacy of your health information. Here is a list of common questions about HIPAA and when health care providers may discuss or share your health information with your family members, friends, or others involved in your care or payment for care.

Common Questions About HIPAA

1. If I do not object, can my health care provider share or discuss my health information with my family, friends, or others involved in my care or payment for my care?

Yes. As long as you do not object, your health care provider is allowed to share or discuss your health information with your family, friends, or others involved in your care or payment for your care. Your provider may ask your permission, may tell you he or she plans to discuss the information and give you an opportunity to object, or may decide, using his or her professional judgment, that you do not object. In any of these cases, your health care provider may discuss only the information that the person involved needs to know about your care or payment for your care.

Here are some examples:

- An emergency room doctor may discuss your treatment in front of your friend when you ask that your friend come into the treatment room.

- Your hospital may discuss your bill with your daughter who is with you at the hospital and has questions about the charges.

- Your doctor may talk to your sister who is driving you home from the hospital about your keeping your foot raised during the ride home.

- Your doctor may discuss the drugs you need to take with your health aide who has come with you to your appointment.

- Your nurse may tell you that she is going to tell your brother how you are doing, and then she may discuss your health status with your brother if you did not say that she should not.

BUT:

- Your nurse may not discuss your condition with your brother if you tell her not to.

2. If I am unconscious or not around, can my health care provider still share or discuss my health information with my family, friends, or others involved in my care or payment for my care?

Yes. If you are not around or cannot give permission, your health care provider may share or discuss your health information with family, friends, or others involved in your care or payment for your care if he or she believes, in his or her professional judgment, that it is in your best interest. When someone other than a friend or family member is asking about you, your health care provider must be reasonably sure that you asked the person to be involved in your care or payment for your care. Your health care provider may share your information face to face, over the phone, or in writing, but may only share the information that the family member, friend, or other person needs to know about your care or payment for your care.

Here are some examples:

- A surgeon who did emergency surgery on you may tell your spouse about your condition, either in person or by phone, while you are unconscious.
- A pharmacist may give your prescription to a friend you send to pick it up.
- A doctor may discuss your drugs with your caregiver who calls your doctor with a question about the right dosage.

BUT:

- A nurse may not tell your friend about a past medical problem that is unrelated to your current condition.

3. Do I have to give my health care provider written permission to share or discuss my health information with my family members, friends, or others involved in my care or payment for my care?

HIPAA does not require that you give your health care provider written permission. However, your provider may prefer or require that you give written permission. You may want to ask about your provider's requirements.

4. If my family or friends call my health care provider to ask about my condition, will they have to give my provider proof of who they are?

HIPAA does not require proof of identity in these cases. However, your health care provider may have his or her own rules for verifying who is on the phone. You may want to ask about your provider's rules.

5. Can I have another person pick up my prescription drugs, medical supplies, or X-rays?

Yes. HIPAA allows health care providers (such as pharmacists) to give prescription drugs, medical supplies, X-rays, and other health care items to a family member, friend, or other person you send to pick them up.

6. Can my health care provider discuss my health information with an interpreter?

Yes. HIPAA allows your health care provider to share your health information with an interpreter who works for the provider to help communicate with you or your family, friends, or others involved in your care. If the interpreter is someone who does not work for your health care provider, HIPAA also allows your provider to discuss your health information with the interpreter so long as you do not object.

7. How can I help make sure my health care providers share my health information with my family, friends, or others involved in my care or payment for my care when I want them to?

Print a copy of this document and discuss it with your health care provider at your next appointment. You may also want to share this information with your family members, friends, or others involved in your care or payment for your care.

8. Where can I get more information about HIPAA?

The HHS Office for Civil Rights web site at www.hhs.gov/ocr/hipaa/ has a variety of resources to help you understand HIPAA.

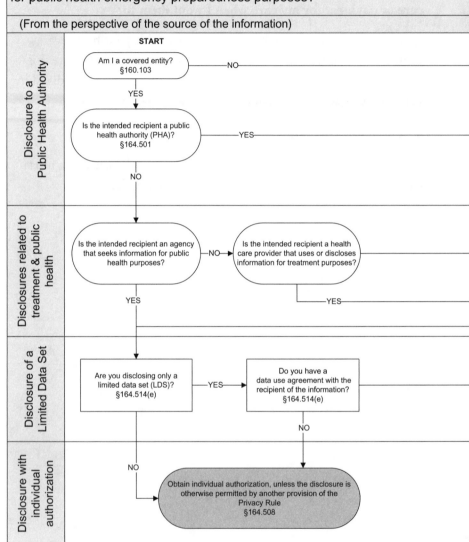

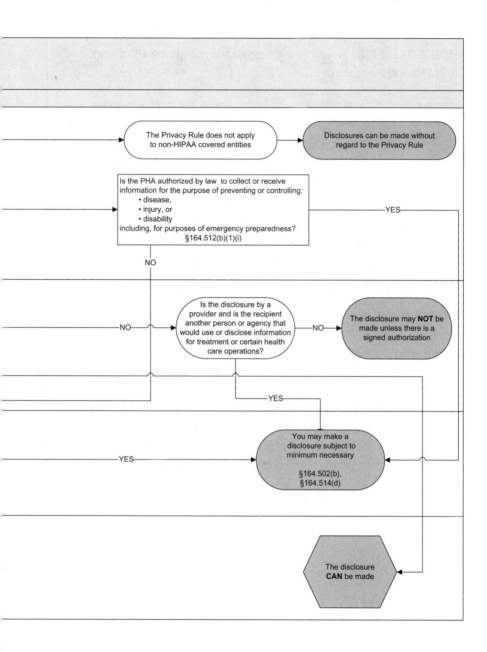

The Privacy Rule does not apply to non-HIPAA covered entities

Disclosures can be made without regard to the Privacy Rule

Is the PHA authorized by law to collect or receive information for the purpose of preventing or controlling:
- disease,
- injury, or
- disability
including, for purposes of emergency preparedness?
§164.512(b)(1)(i)

YES

NO

Is the disclosure by a provider and is the recipient another person or agency that would use or disclose information for treatment or certain health care operations?

NO

NO

The disclosure may **NOT** be made unless there is a signed authorization

YES

You may make a disclosure subject to minimum necessary

§164.502(b),
§164.514(d)

YES

The disclosure **CAN** be made

HHS GUIDANCE: President-Declared Emergency Planning and Disaster Recovery

Sample policy: If the president of the United States declares an emergency or disaster and the secretary of the US Department of Health and Human Services declares a public health emergency, our practice, in collaboration with the hospital, will support the urgent delivery of care and waive the immediate need to:

- obtain a patient's agreement to speak with family members or friends involved in the patient's care (45 CFR 164.510(b))
- honor a request to opt out of the facility directory (45 CFR 164.510(a))
- distribute a notice of privacy practices (45 CFR 164.520)
- request privacy restrictions (45 CFR 164.522(a))
- request confidential communications (45 CFR 164.522(b))

Sample procedures: We understand that waiving these privacy obligations extends to hospitals first and may not apply to our practice, unless we are brought into the declared emergency, and that waiving these patient rights is in force for no more than 72 hours from the time we implement our disaster protocol.

When the presidential or secretarial declaration terminates, we then will comply with all the requirements of the Privacy Rule for any patient still under our care, even if 72 hours has not elapsed since implementation of our disaster protocol.

HIPAA Privacy Rule Disclosures to a Patient's Family, Friends, or Others Involved in the Patient's Care or Payment for Care Family Member or Friend Other Persons

	Family Member or Friend	Other Persons
Patient is present and has the capacity to make health care decisions	Provider may disclose relevant information if the provider does one of the following: (1) obtains the patient's agreement (2) gives the patient an opportunity to object and the patient does not object (3) decides from the circumstances, based on professional judgment, that the patient does not object Disclosure may be made in person, over the phone, or in writing.	Provider may disclose relevant information if the provider does one of the following: (1) obtains the patient's agreement (2) gives the patient the opportunity to object and the patient does not object (3) decides from the circumstances, based on professional judgment, that the patient does not object Disclosure may be made in person, over the phone, or in writing.

	Family Member or Friend	Other Persons
Patient is not present or is incapacitated	Provider may disclose relevant information if, based on professional judgment, the disclosure is in the patient's best interest. Disclosure may be made in person, over the phone, or in writing. Provider may use professional judgment and experience to decide if it is in the patient's best interest to allow someone to pick up filled prescriptions, medical supplies, X-rays, or other similar forms of health information for the patient.	Provider may disclose relevant information if the provider is reasonably sure that the patient has involved the person in the patient's care and in his or her professional judgment, the provider believes the disclosure to be in the patient's best interest. Disclosure may be made in person, over the phone, or in writing. Provider may use professional judgment and experience to decide if it is in the patient's best interest to allow someone to pick up filled prescriptions, medical supplies, X-rays, or other similar forms of health information for the patient.

COMPLIANCE AND ENFORCEMENT

How OCR Enforces the HIPAA Privacy Rule

The Office for Civil Rights (OCR) is responsible for enforcing the HIPAA Privacy Rule (45 C.F.R. Parts 160 and 164, Subparts A and E). One of the ways that OCR carries out this responsibility is to investigate complaints filed with it. OCR may also conduct compliance reviews to determine if covered entities are in compliance, and OCR performs education and outreach to foster compliance with the Privacy Rule's requirements.

OCR may only take action on certain complaints. See What OCR Considers During Intake and Review of a Complaint for a description of the types of cases in which OCR cannot take an enforcement action.

If OCR accepts a complaint for investigation, OCR will notify the person who filed the complaint and the covered entity named in it. Then the complainant and the covered entity are asked to present information about the incident or problem described in the complaint.

OCR may request specific information from each to get an understanding of the facts. Covered entities are required by law to cooperate with complaint investigations.

If a complaint contains information about an incident or problem that could also be a violation of the HIPAA Security Rule (45 C.F.R. Parts 160 and 164, Subparts A and C), OCR coordinates its investigation with the Centers for Medicare & Medicaid Services (CMS), which is the agency within HHS that is responsible for enforcing the Security Rule. (Effective July 27, 2009, the OCR is responsible for enforcement of the HIPAA Security Rule. See *Secretary Delegates HIPAA Security Rule to OCR*, which is available online at www.hhs.gov/ocr/privacy/hipaa/administrative/srdelegationofauthoritytoocr.html.) If a complaint describes an action that could be a violation of the criminal provision of HIPAA (42 U.S.C. 1320d-6), OCR may refer the complaint to the Department of Justice for investigation.

OCR reviews the information, or evidence, that it gathers in each case. In some cases, it may determine that the covered entity did not violate the requirements of the Privacy Rule. If the evidence indicates that the covered entity was not in compliance, OCR will attempt to resolve the case with the covered entity by obtaining:

Voluntary compliance;

Corrective action; and/or

Resolution agreement.

Most Privacy Rule investigations are concluded to the satisfaction of OCR through these types of resolutions. OCR notifies the person who filed the complaint and the covered entity in writing of the resolution result.

If the covered entity does not take action to resolve the matter in a way that is satisfactory, OCR may decide to impose civil money penalties (CMPs) on the covered entity. If CMPs are imposed, the covered entity may request a hearing in which an HHS administrative law judge decides if the penalties are supported by the evidence in the case. Complainants do not receive a portion of CMPs collected from covered entities; the penalties are deposited in the U.S. Treasury.

What OCR Considers During Intake & Review of a Complaint

The Office for Civil Rights (OCR) is the agency within the U. S. Department of Health and Human Services that investigates complaints about failures to protect the privacy of health information. It does so under its authority to enforce the Privacy Rule.

OCR carefully reviews all complaints that it receives. Under the law, OCR only may take action on complaints that meet the following conditions.

- **The alleged action must have taken place after the dates the Rules took effect.** Compliance with the Privacy Rule was not required until April 14, 2003. Compliance with the Security Rule was not required until April 20, 2005. Therefore, OCR can not investigate complaints about actions that took place before these dates.

- The **complaint must be filed against an entity that is required by law to comply with the Privacy and Security Rules.** Not all organizations are covered by the Privacy and Security Rules. Entities subject to the Privacy and Security Rules are considered "covered entities." Briefly, a covered entity is:

  - a health plan:

    including but not limited to

    - health insurance companies,

    - company health plans; or

- a health care provider that electronically transmits any health information in connection with certain financial and administrative transactions (such as electronically billing insurance carriers for services): including but not limited to
  - doctors,
  - clinics,
  - hospitals,
  - psychologists,
  - chiropractors,
  - nursing homes,
  - pharmacies, and
  - dentists; or
- a health care clearinghouse.
- **Examples of organizations that are not required to comply** with the Privacy and Security Rules include
  - life insurers,
  - employers,
  - workers compensation carriers,
  - many schools and school districts,
  - many state agencies like child protective service agencies,
  - many law enforcement agencies,
  - many municipal offices
- A complaint must **allege an activity that, if proven true, would violate the Privacy or Security Rule.** For example, OCR generally could not investigate a complaint that alleged that a physician sent a person's demographic information to an insurance company to obtain payment, because the Privacy Rule generally permits doctors to use and disclose such information to bill for their services.

- Complaints **must be filed within 180 days** of when the person submitting the complaint knew or should have known about the alleged violation of the Privacy or Security Rule. OCR may waive this time limit if it determines that the person submitting the complaint shows good cause for not submitting the complaint within the 180 day time frame (e.g., such as circumstances that made submitting the complaint within 180 days impossible).

OCR must know the identity of the person who filed the complaint, and have a way to contact that person, to investigate the complaint. If it cannot reach the person to discuss the case, OCR will close the case.

During an investigation, OCR often must reveal the name of the person who filed the complaint. For example, a person complains about being denied access to her medical record by her doctor. For OCR to find out what happened in this case, the OCR investigator would need to tell the doctor the name of the person who made the complaint. In these cases, OCR needs to first **obtain that person's written consent.** If the person refuses to grant consent, OCR will close the complaint. OCR will not disclose the name of the person if it can investigate the complaint without doing so.

In some cases in which OCR cannot take enforcement action, it may be able to refer the matter to another agency that can respond to it, or provide suggestions to the complainant about other avenues to follow for resolution. In addition, many organizations may be subject to other federal or state laws requiring privacy protections that OCR does not enforce.

YOUR HEALTH INFORMATION PRIVACY RIGHTS

PRIVACY IS IMPORTANT TO ALL OF US

You have privacy rights under a federal law that protects your health information. These rights are important for you to know. You can exercise these rights, ask questions about them, and file a complaint if you think your rights are being denied or your health information isn't being protected.

Who must follow this law?

- Most doctors, nurses, pharmacies, hospitals, clinics, nursing homes, and many other health care providers
- Health insurance companies, HMOs, most employer group health plans
- Certain government programs that pay for health care, such as Medicare and Medicaid

Providers and health insurers who are required to follow this law must comply with your right to...

Ask to see and get a copy of your health records

You can ask to see and get a copy of your medical record and other health information. You may not be able to get all of your information in a few special cases. For example, if your doctor decides something in your file might endanger you or someone else, the doctor may not have to give this information to you.

- In most cases, your copies must be given to you within 30 days, but this can be extended for another 30 days if you are given a reason.

- You may have to pay for the cost of copying and mailing if you request copies and mailing.

Have corrections added to your health information

You can ask to change any wrong information in your file or add information to your file if it is incomplete. For example, if you and your hospital agree that your file has the wrong result for a test, the hospital must change it. Even if the hospital believes the test result is correct, you still have the right to have your disagreement noted in your file.

- In most cases the file should be changed within 60 days, but the hospital can take an extra 30 days if you are given a reason.

Receive a notice that tells you how your health information is used and shared

You can learn how your health information is used and shared by your provider or health insurer. They must give you a notice that tells you how they may use and share your health information and how you can exercise your rights. In most cases, you should get this notice on your first visit to a provider or in the mail from your health insurer, and you can ask for a copy at any time.

Decide whether to give your permission before your information can be used or shared for certain purposes

In general, your health information cannot be given to your employer, used or shared for things like sales calls or advertising, or used or shared for many other purposes unless you give your permission by signing an authorization form. This authorization form must tell you who will get your information and what your information will be used for.

PRIVACY IS IMPORTANT TO ALL OF US

Other privacy rights

You may have other health information rights under your state's laws. When these laws affect how your health information can be used or shared, that should be made clear in the notice you receive.

For more information

This is a brief summary of your rights and protections under the federal health information privacy law. You can ask your provider or health insurer questions about how your health information is used or shared and about your rights. You also can learn more, including how to file a complaint with the U.S. Government, at the website at www.hhs.gov/ocr/hipaa/.

Get a report on when and why your health information was shared

Under the law, your health information may be used and shared for particular reasons, like making sure doctors give good care, making sure nursing homes are clean and safe, reporting when the flu is in your area, or making required reports to the police, such as reporting gunshot wounds. In many cases, you can ask for and get a list of who your health information has been shared with for these reasons.

- You can get this report for free once a year.
- In most cases you should get the report within 60 days, but it can take an extra 30 days if you are given a reason.

Ask to be reached somewhere other than home

You can make reasonable requests to be contacted at different places or in a different way. For example, you can have the nurse call you at your office instead of your home, or send mail to you in an envelope instead of on a postcard. If sending information to you at home might put you in danger, your health insurer must talk, call, or write to you where you ask and in the way you ask, if the request is reasonable.

Ask that your information not be shared

You can ask your provider or health insurer not to share your health information with certain people, groups, or companies. For example, if you go to a clinic, you could ask the doctor not to share your medical record with other doctors or nurses in the clinic. However, they do not have to agree to do what you ask.

File complaints

If you believe your information was used or shared in a way that is not allowed under the privacy law, or if you were not able to exercise your rights, you can file a complaint with your provider or health insurer. The privacy notice you receive from them will tell you who to talk to and how to file a complaint. You can also file a complaint with U.S. Government.

Published by:

U.S. Department of Health & Human Services

Office for Civil Rights

HIPAA Security Rule At-a-Glance: Administrative, Physical, and Technical Safeguards

TABLE A-1 | Administrative Safeguards

Standards	Implementation Specifications	Required (R)/ Addressable (A)
Security Management Process	Risk Analysis	(R)
	Risk Management	(R)
	Sanction Policy	(R)
	Information System Activity Review	(R)
Assigned Security Responsibility		(R)

Standards	Implementation Specifications	Required (R)/ Addressable (A)
Workforce Security	Authorization and/or Supervision	(A)
	Workforce Clearance Procedure	(A)
	Termination Procedures	(A)
Information Access Management	Isolating Health Care Clearinghouse Function	(R)
	Access Authorization	(A)
	Access Establishment and Modification	(A)
Security Awareness and Training	Security Reminders	(A)
	Protection from Malicious Software	(A)
	Log-in Monitoring	(A)
	Password Management	(A)
Security Incident Procedures	Response and Reporting	(R)
Contingency Plan	Data Backup Plan	(R)
	Disaster Recovery Plan	(R)
	Emergency Mode Operation Plan	(R)
	Testing and Revision Procedure	(A)
	Applications and Data Criticality Analysis	(A)
Evaluation		(R)
Business Associate Contracts	Written Contract or Other Arrangement	(R)

TABLE A-2 | Physical Safeguards

Standards	Implementation Specifications	Required (R)/ Addressable (A)
Facility Access Controls	Contingency Operations	(A)
	Facility Security Plan	(A)
	Access Control and Validation Procedures	(A)
	Maintenance Records	(A)
Workstation Use		(R)
Workstation Security		(R)
Device and Media Controls	Disposal	(R)
	Media Re-use	(R)
	Accountability	(A)
	Data Backup and Storage	(A)

TABLE A-3 | Technical Safeguards

Standards	Implementation Specifications	Required (R)/ Addressable (A)
Access Control	Unique User Identification	(R)
	Emergency Access Procedure	(R)
	Automatic Logoff	(A)
	Encryption and Decryption	(A)

Standards	Implementation Specifications	Required (R)/ Addressable (A)
Audit Controls		(R)
Integrity	Mechanism to Authenticate Electronic Protected Health Information	(A)
Person or Entity Authentication		(R)
Transmission Security	Integrity Controls	(A)
	Encryption	(A)

Additional Resources

For a companion guide on how to implement HIPAA's Security Rule in your practice, consult the following additional resources:

- Root J, et al. *Field Guide to HIPAA Implementation, Revised Edition.* Chicago, Ill: American Medical Association; 2004.
- Hartley C, Jones E. *HIPAA Plain & Simple.* Chicago: American Medical Association; 2004.
- Amatayakul M, et al. *Handbook for HIPAA Security Implementation.* Chicago: American Medical Association; 2004.

Sample HIPAA Security Risk Assessment For A Small Practice

Review the following implementation specifications to determine your potential risks; then develop and implement policies according to the risks you identified.

TABLE A-4 | **Administrative Safeguards**

Standard	Required (R)/ Addressable (A)	Activity	Risk (Check All That Applies)			Policy (Check All That Applies)		Assigned To
			Risk For Us	Could Be A Risk	Not A Risk	Policy In Place	Need Policy	
		Security Risk Management						
		Team: Security Official, Physician, Workforce Members						
General Questions	Required	Can you identify where ePHI is located (computers, laptops, handhelds, tablet PCs etc)?						
	Required	Have you implemented the safeguards component of HIPAA's Privacy Rule?						
Inventory	Required	Have you developed an inventory of hardware and software owned by the practice?						

Standard	Required (R)/ Addressable (A)	Activity	Risk (Check All That Applies)			Policy (Check All That Applies)		Assigned To
			Risk For Us	Could Be A Risk	Not A Risk	Policy In Place	Need Policy	
		Security Risk Management						
		Team: Security Official, Physician, Workforce Members						
	Required	Do you know where the inventory is kept?						
Assets	Required	Do you know the current approximate value of your hardware and software?						
	Required	Does the inventory contain contact information of service providers?						
	Required	Do you control the information contained on your information system?						

continued next page

TABLE A-4 | Administrative Safeguards—continued

Standard	Required (R)/ Addressable (A)	Activity	Risk (Check All That Applies)			Policy (Check All That Applies)		Assigned To
			Risk For Us	Could Be A Risk	Not A Risk	Policy In Place	Need Policy	
		Security Risk Management Team: Security Official, Physician, Workforce Members						
	Required	Do you take portable computers containing electronic patient information (ePHI) home?						
	Required	Has there been a significant investment in your information systems in the last 2 years?						
Privacy	Required	Does a vendor have access to confidential patient data?						

Security Risk Management

Team: Security Official, Physician, Workforce Members

Standard	Required (R)/ Addressable (A)	Activity	Risk (Check All That Applies)			Policy (Check All That Applies)		Assigned To
			Risk For Us	Could Be A Risk	Not A Risk	Policy In Place	Need Policy	
	Required	Can a vendor change confidential patient data?						
Risk Management	Required	Has there been a prior risk analysis completed for your practice?						
	Required	Do you control who has access to your ePHI?						
	Required	Do you have control over persons and systems that cannot have access to ePHI?						

continued next page

TABLE A-4 | Administrative Safeguards—continued

Standard	Required (R)/ Addressable (A)	Activity	Risk (Check All That Applies)			Policy (Check All That Applies)		Assigned To
			Risk For Us	Could Be A Risk	Not A Risk	Policy In Place	Need Policy	
		Security Risk Management						
		Team: Security Official, Physician, Workforce Members						
	Required	Do you have control over who can change content on your medical records?						
Sanctions Policy	Required	Have you developed written sanctions against workforce members who do not abide by your policies?						
	Required	Have you explained those sanctions to your workforce members?						

Standard	Required (R)/ Addressable (A)	Activity	Risk (Check All That Applies)			Policy (Check All That Applies)		Assigned To
			Risk For Us	Could Be A Risk	Not A Risk	Policy In Place	Need Policy	
		Security Risk Management						
		Team: Security Official, Physician, Workforce Members						
	Required	Have you been challenged on your sanctions?						
Information System Activity Review	Required	Do you regularly review system audit logs?						
	Required	Do you regularly review reports on who has access to ePHI?						
	Required	Would you know if someone was trying to hack into your system? (Do you regularly review security incident reports?)						

continued next page

TABLE A-4 | Administrative Safeguards—continued

Standard	Required (R)/ Addressable (A)	Activity	Risk (Check All That Applies)			Policy (Check All That Applies)		Assigned To
			Risk For Us	Could Be A Risk	Not A Risk	Policy In Place	Need Policy	
		Assigned Security Responsibility Team: Physician, Security Official, Privacy Official						
Assigned Security Responsibility	Required	Have you appointed a security official?						
	Required	Does the security official work closely with the privacy official?						
		Workforce Security Team: Security Official, Privacy Official						
Authorization and Supervision	Addressable	Do you have written job descriptions that define specific levels of access to ePHI?						

Standard	Required (R)/ Addressable (A)	Activity	Risk (Check All That Applies)			Policy (Check All That Applies)		Assigned To
			Risk For Us	Could Be A Risk	Not A Risk	Policy In Place	Need Policy	
		Workforce Security Team: Security Official, Privacy Official						
		Are persons with access to ePHI supervised?						
Workforce Security	Addressable	Do you check references and educational background before hiring employees?						
		Do you conduct additional background checks on key workforce members?						
Termination Procedure	Addressable	Do you immediately deactivate a workforce member's access upon termination?						

continued next page

TABLE A-4 | Administrative Safeguards—continued

Standard	Required (R)/ Addressable (A)	Activity	Risk (Check All That Applies)			Policy (Check All That Applies)		Assigned To
			Risk For Us	Could Be A Risk	Not A Risk	Policy In Place	Need Policy	
		Workforce Security Team: Security Official, Privacy Official						
		Do you notify your IS vendor of an employee's termination within a specific time?						
		Is there a standard checklist of action items (return keys, close and payment of credit cards, return software and hardware) when an employee leaves?						

Standard	Required (R)/ Addressable (A)	Activity	Risk (Check All That Applies)			Policy (Check All That Applies)		Assigned To
			Risk For Us	Could Be A Risk	Not A Risk	Policy In Place	Need Policy	
Workforce Security Team: Security Official, Privacy Official								
		Are there different policies for employees who leave voluntarily and those terminated for cause?						
Information Access Management Team: Security Official, Physician								
Isolating healthcare clearinghouse functions	Addressable	Does your business associate agreement address clearinghouse functions?						
Access authorization	Addressable	Does your IT system have the capacity to set access controls?						

continued next page

TABLE A-4 | **Administrative Safeguards—continued**

Standard	Required (R)/ Addressable (A)	Activity	Risk (Check All That Applies)			Policy (Check All That Applies)		Assigned To
			Risk For Us	Could Be A Risk	Not A Risk	Policy In Place	Need Policy	
		Information Access Management Team: Security Official, Physician						
		Is access to ePHI based on the employee's role?						
		Does everyone on your workforce have access to all ePHI?						
Access establishment and modification	Addressable	Do you periodically review whether workforce members have the appropriate access to ePHI?						

Security Awareness and Training
Team: Security Official, with input from Privacy Official

Standard	Required (R)/ Addressable (A)	Activity	Risk (Check All That Applies)			Policy (Check All That Applies)		Assigned To
			Risk For Us	Could Be A Risk	Not A Risk	Policy In Place	Need Policy	
Security Reminders	Addressable	Have there been lapses in privacy safeguards policies that need refreshers?						
		Have you identified your security training priorities?						
		Are security reminders posted in a visible location?						
		Are vendors aware of your security reminders?						
		Do workforce members know where to find a copy of your security policies and procedures?						

continued next page

TABLE A-4	Administrative Safeguards—continued						
Standard	Activity	Risk (Check All That Applies)			Policy (Check All That Applies)		Assigned To
Required (R)/ Addressable (A)		Risk For Us	Could Be A Risk	Not A Risk	Policy In Place	Need Policy	
	Security Awareness and Training Team: Security Official, with input from Privacy Official						
	Do workforce members understand the consequences of noncompliance with those policies?						
	Are workforce members with laptops, PDAs, or cell phones aware of security issues and how to handle them?						
	Do you discuss security awareness with new hires?						

Standard	Required (R)/ Addressable (A)	Activity	Risk (Check All That Applies)			Policy (Check All That Applies)		Assigned To
			Risk For Us	Could Be A Risk	Not A Risk	Policy In Place	Need Policy	
		Security Awareness and Training Team: Security Official, with input from Privacy Official						
		Would workforce members say they received adequate security training?						
		Do you have a security training budget?						
Protection from malicious software	Addressable	Have you installed virus protection software on your computers?						
		Do workforce members update the virus protection software when it's routed to them?						

continued next page

TABLE A-4 | Administrative Safeguards—continued

Standard	Required (R)/ Addressable (A)	Activity	Risk (Check All That Applies)			Policy (Check All That Applies)		Assigned To
			Risk For Us	Could Be A Risk	Not A Risk	Policy In Place	Need Policy	
		Security Awareness and Training						
		Team: Security Official, with input from Privacy Official						
		Do you allow workforce members to download software (family pictures, games, books, music etc) from home?						
Login monitoring	Addressable	Does the security official regularly monitor audit logs?						
		Is the security official notified of unsuccessful logins?						

Standard	Required (R)/ Addressable (A)	Activity	Risk (Check All That Applies)			Policy (Check All That Applies)		Assigned To
			Risk For Us	Could Be A Risk	Not A Risk	Policy In Place	Need Policy	
		Security Awareness and Training Team: Security Official, with input from Privacy Official						
		Do workforce members know what to do if they cannot access the system?						
Password management	Addressable	Are sanctions in place if workforce members share passwords?						
		Do workforce members know what to do if they forget a password?						
		Are you providing password management reminders?						

continued next page

TABLE A-4 | Administrative Safeguards—continued

Standard	Required (R)/ Addressable (A)	Activity	Risk (Check All That Applies)			Policy (Check All That Applies)		Assigned To
			Risk For Us	Could Be A Risk	Not A Risk	Policy In Place	Need Policy	
		Security Incident Procedures						
		Team: Security Official, Practice Management Vendor						
Response and reporting	Required	Do you know if your security system has ever been breached?						
	Required	Have you prioritized what must first be restored in the event of a disruption?						
	Required	Have you identified contacts in the event of a security incident?						

Standard	Required (R)/ Addressable (A)	Activity	Risk (Check All That Applies)			Policy (Check All That Applies)		Assigned To
			Risk For Us	Could Be A Risk	Not A Risk	Policy In Place	Need Policy	
		Security Incident Procedures						
		Team: Security Official, Practice Management Vendor						
		Do you require workforce members to tell you if they suspect a compromise to your system?						
	Required	Have you made a list of possible security incidents?						
		Contingency Plan						
		Team: Security Official, Privacy Official, Physician						
Data Backup Plan	Required	Does your practice backup your electronic data?						
	Required	Do you store the backup data at the medical practice's location?						

continued next page

TABLE A-4 | Administrative Safeguards—continued

Standard	Required (R)/ Addressable (A)	Activity	Risk (Check All That Applies)			Policy (Check All That Applies)		Assigned To
			Risk For Us	Could Be A Risk	Not A Risk	Policy In Place	Need Policy	
		Contingency Plan						
		Team: Security Official, Privacy Official, Physician						
	Required	Do you know whom to call to restore data?						
Disaster Recovery	Required	Do you have a list of critical hardware, software, and workforce members stored offsite?						
Emergency Mode Operations	Required	Do you have a plan to temporarily relocate if you lost access (because of fire, system failure, vandalism, natural disaster, etc) to your physical location?						

Contingency Plan

Team: Security Official, Privacy Official, Physician

Standard	Required (R)/ Addressable (A)	Activity	Risk (Check All That Applies)			Policy (Check All That Applies)		Assigned To
			Risk For Us	Could Be A Risk	Not A Risk	Policy In Place	Need Policy	
	Required	Would ePHI be safeguarded in this temporary location?						
	Required	Are formal agreements in place for that relocation?						
	Required	Have you trained staff on your contingency plan?						
	Required	Is there a contingency plan coordinator?						
	Required	Do you have an emergency call list?						

continued next page

TABLE A-4 | **Administrative Safeguards—continued**

Standard	Required (R)/ Addressable (A)	Activity	Risk (Check All That Applies)			Policy (Check All That Applies)		Assigned To
			Risk For Us	Could Be A Risk	Not A Risk	Policy In Place	Need Policy	
		Contingency Plan						
		Team: Security Official, Privacy Official, Physician						
	Required	Have you identified situations where your contingency plan must be activated?						
	Required	Is there a plan to restore systems to your normal operations?						
Testing and Revision	Addressable	Have you tested your contingency plan?						

Standard	Required (R)/ Addressable (A)	Activity	Risk (Check All That Applies)			Policy (Check All That Applies)		Assigned To
			Risk For Us	Could Be A Risk	Not A Risk	Policy In Place	Need Policy	
Contingency Plan								
Team: Security Official, Privacy Official, Physician								
Applications and Data Criticality	Analysis Addressable	Do you have a plan to restore your practice activities, beginning with what is most critical to your practice?						
Evaluation								
Team: Security Official, Privacy Official, Physician								
Evaluation	Addressable	Has your security official determined acceptable levels of risk in its business operations and mitigation strategies?						

continued next page

TABLE A-4 | Administrative Safeguards—continued

Standard	Required (R)/ Addressable (A)	Activity	Risk (Check All That Applies)			Policy (Check All That Applies)		Assigned To
			Risk For Us	Could Be A Risk	Not A Risk	Policy In Place	Need Policy	
		Do you have a plan to evaluate your systems at least annually or at any time a risk warrants a review?						
		Business Associate Contracts and Other Arrangements Team: Security Official, Privacy Official, Physician						
Business Associate Contract	Required	Do business associate agreements ensure that ePHI will be protected?						
	Required	Are there new organizations or IT vendors that require a business associate agreement?						

TABLE A-5 | **Physical Safeguards**

Standard	Required (R)/ Addressable (A)	Activity	Risk (Check All That Applies)			Policy (Check All That Applies)		Assigned To
			Risk For Us	Could Be A Risk	Not A Risk	Policy In Place	Need Policy	
		Facility Access Controls Team: Security Official, Privacy Official, Physician						
Contingency Operations	Addressable	Do you know who needs access to the facility in the event of a disaster?						
		Do you have a backup plan for access, including who has the authority to access the facility in a disaster?						
Facility security plan	Addressable	Do you have an inventory of facilities?						

continued next page

TABLE A-5 | Physical Safeguards—continued

Standard	Required (R)/ Addressable (A)	Activity	Risk (Check All That Applies)			Policy (Check All That Applies)		Assigned To
			Risk For Us	Could Be A Risk	Not A Risk	Policy In Place	Need Policy	
		Facility Access Controls						
		Team: Security Official, Privacy Official, Physician						
		Is there a contingency plan in place?						
Access control and validation procedures	Addressable	Do you have policies and procedures in place that control who has access to the facility?						
		Is there a history of break-ins that require monitoring equipment?						

Standard	Required (R)/ Addressable (A)	Activity	Risk (Check All That Applies)			Policy (Check All That Applies)		Assigned To
			Risk For Us	Could Be A Risk	Not A Risk	Policy In Place	Need Policy	
		Facility Access Controls						
		Team: Security Official, Privacy Official, Physician						
Maintenance records	Addressable	Do you document repairs and modifications that ensure security to the facility?						
		Workstation Use						
		Team: Security Official, Privacy Official, Physician						
Workstation Use	Required	Have you documented how workstations are to be used in the physician practice?						
	Required	Are there wireless tools used as workstations?						
	Required	Can unauthorized persons view content of workstations?						

continued next page

TABLE A-5 | Physical Safeguards—continued

Standard	Required (R)/ Addressable (A)	Activity	Risk (Check All That Applies)			Policy (Check All That Applies)		Assigned To
			Risk For Us	Could Be A Risk	Not A Risk	Policy In Place	Need Policy	
		Workstation Use						
		Team: Security Official, Privacy Official, Physician						
	Required	Do you have an inventory of workstations?						
		Workstation Security						
		Team: Security Official, Privacy Official, Physician, IT Vendor						
Workstation security	Required	Is access to ePHI restricted to authorized users?						
	Required	Is there a logoff policy before leaving computers unattended?						
	Required	Is there a policy that controls Internet access while working with ePHI?						

Standard	Required (R)/ Addressable (A)	Activity	Risk (Check All That Applies)			Policy (Check All That Applies)		Assigned To
			Risk For Us	Could Be A Risk	Not A Risk	Policy In Place	Need Policy	
		Device and Media Controls						
		Team: Security Official, Privacy Official, Physician, IT Vendor						
Disposal	Required	Do you destroy data on hard drives and file servers before disposing the hardware?						
Media Reuse	Required	Are workforce members trained on security risks to ePHI when reusing hardware and software?						
Accountability	Addressable	Do you periodically check the inventory to be sure workstations are where they are supposed to be?						

continued next page

TABLE A-5	Physical Safeguards—continued						
Standard	Required (R)/ Addressable (A)	Activity	Risk (Check All That Applies)			Policy (Check All That Applies)		Assigned To
			Risk For Us	Could Be A Risk	Not A Risk	Policy In Place	Need Policy	
		Device and Media Controls						
		Team: Security Official, Privacy Official, Physician, IT Vendor						
		Do you document where they've been moved?						
		Is the inventory list part of your disaster recovery files?						
Data backup and storage	Addressable	Do you regularly backup data on hardware and software and maintain backup files off-site?						
		Has staff been trained on backup policies?						

TABLE A-6 | Technical Safeguards

Standard	Required (R)/ Addressable (A)	Activity	Risk (Check All That Applies)			Policy (Check All That Applies)		Assigned To
			Risk For Us	Could Be A Risk	Not A Risk	Policy In Place	Need Policy	
		Access Controls						
		Team: Security Official, Privacy Official, Physician, IT Vendor						
Unique User Identification	Required	Has the security official assigned a unique user identity to each member of the workforce?						
	Required	Are passwords unique to each individual and not shared?						
	Required	Is there a sanction policy on sharing passwords?						

continued next page

TABLE A-6 | Technical Safeguards—continued

Standard	Required (R)/ Addressable (A)	Activity	Risk (Check All That Applies)			Policy (Check All That Applies)		Assigned To
			Risk For Us	Could Be A Risk	Not A Risk	Policy In Place	Need Policy	
		Access Controls						
		Team: Security Official, Privacy Official, Physician, IT Vendor						
	Required	Do workforce members have access to the minimum ePHI necessary to do the job?						
Emergency Access Procedure	Required	Does the security official have a unique user ID that is only used in emergencies?						
	Required	Is there a process to notify another leader in the practice when the emergency ID is used?						

Standard	Required (R)/ Addressable (A)	Activity	Risk (Check All That Applies)			Policy (Check All That Applies)		Assigned To
			Risk For Us	Could Be A Risk	Not A Risk	Policy In Place	Need Policy	
		Access Controls						
		Team: Security Official, Privacy Official, Physician, IT Vendor						
Automatic Logoff	Addressable	Do your computers automatically logoff after a specific period of inactivity?						
		Is there a shorter logoff period for computers in high traffic areas?						
Encryption and Decryption	Addressable	Have you installed encryption software to your servers and/or portable computers?						

continued next page

TABLE A-6 | Technical Safeguards—continued

Standard	Required (R)/ Addressable (A)	Activity	Risk (Check All That Applies)			Policy (Check All That Applies)		Assigned To
			Risk For Us	Could Be A Risk	Not A Risk	Policy In Place	Need Policy	
		Access Controls						
		Team: Security Official, Privacy Official, Physician, IT Vendor						
		Is the email sent over an open network or web-based email?						
		Audit Controls						
		Team: Security Official, IT Vendor						
Audit Controls	Required	Is there a policy in place to monitor and audit who has had access to ePHI?						
	Required	Is one person responsible for conducting audit processes and reporting results?						

Standard	Required (R)/ Addressable (A)	Activity	Risk (Check All That Applies)			Policy (Check All That Applies)		Assigned To
			Risk For Us	Could Be A Risk	Not A Risk	Policy In Place	Need Policy	
		Audit Controls						
		Team: Security Official, IT Vendor						
	Required	Has your IT vendor explained how to conduct audits?						
		Integrity						
		Team: Security Official, Privacy Official, Physician, IT Vendor						
Mechanism to authenticate ePHI	Addressable	Are users required to authenticate themselves when logging into the system?						
		Is there a feature that locks out users after a specific number of failed login attempts?						

continued next page

TABLE A-6	Technical Safeguards—continued

Standard	Required (R)/ Addressable (A)	Activity	Risk (Check All That Applies)			Policy (Check All That Applies)		Assigned To
			Risk For Us	Could Be A Risk	Not A Risk	Policy In Place	Need Policy	
Integrity								
		Team: Security Official, Privacy Official, Physician, IT Vendor						
		Are data transmitted through standard network protocols?						
		Have you identified sources that would jeopardize the integrity of ePHI (vandalism, hackers, system failures, viruses etc)?						

Standard	Required (R)/ Addressable (A)	Activity	Risk (Check All That Applies)			Policy (Check All That Applies)		Assigned To
			Risk For Us	Could Be A Risk	Not A Risk	Policy In Place	Need Policy	
		Person or Entity Authentication Team: Security Official, Privacy Official, Physician, IT Vendor						
Person or Entity Authentication	Required	Does your system require users to identify themselves using a password and user name?						
	Required	Does the system allow you to conduct audit trails on users?						
		Transmission Security Team: Security Official, IT Vendor						
Integrity Controls	Addressable	Does the software allow you to track and audit users who transmit and alter ePHI?						

continued next page

TABLE A-6	Technical Safeguards—continued						
Standard	**Required (R)/ Addressable (A)**	**Activity**	**Risk** (Check All That Applies)			**Policy** (Check All That Applies)		**Assigned To**
			Risk For Us	**Could Be A Risk**	**Not A Risk**	**Policy In Place**	**Need Policy**	
		Transmission Security Team: Security Official, IT Vendor						
		Is there an auditing process in place?						
		Does the IT vendor ensure that information is not altered in transmission?						
Encryption	Addressable	Do you need a mechanism (secure network) to encrypt email?						

Standard	Required (R)/ Addressable (A)	Activity	Risk (Check All That Applies)			Policy (Check All That Applies)		Assigned To
			Risk For Us	Could Be A Risk	Not A Risk	Policy In Place	Need Policy	
Transmission Security								
Team: Security Official, IT Vendor								
		Are you sending ePHI via handhelds or wireless laptops?						
		Do workforce members know how to respond to emails containing ePHI?						

NPI TIP SHEET

April 2006 – Tips for Health Care Professionals –
Preparing Your Office Staff for NPI

EVERY provider completing electronic transactions **MUST** use only the NPI to identify covered healthcare providers in standard transactions by May 23, 2007. This means you MUST **apply for and receive** an NPI to use on HIPAA claims transactions before May 23, 2007. (See important web links below).

Health care professionals who are health care providers need to prepare themselves and their staff for the upcoming NPI compliance date. Careful preparation for, and use of, the NPI will help minimize claim errors and delays in payment.

Getting Started

As health care professionals, you need to:

- Get your NPI.
- Familiarize yourself with information available from CMS, private industry groups (eg, WEDI) and your business partners.

- Determine if there are any State laws or requirements that impact obtaining an NPI.

- Communicate with the health plans with which you do business to determine their NPI implementation timelines.

- Identify your vendors, trading partners and business associates – contact them and determine their readiness to deal with NPI.

- Ensure that any health plan, clearninghouse or other vendor that you use is accepting the NPI before you use it in your transactions.

- Get your NPI soon and share it with trading partners and other colleagues who need it to bill for services or your cashflow may be disrupted after the compliance date.

Implementing the NPI in Your Business – Training Staff

Once you've done your research and obtained your NPI, then you must begin implementation. Staff training is important; all staff should have an understanding of the NPI and anticipate the changes in business practices due to the implementation of NPI. Certain staff members will need to know the requirements of its use and where it appears in transactions.

Training should include:

- Any new responsibilities or business processes that come about as a result of the NPI, such as: how and when to disseminate a provider's NPI, how to protect it, and when to collect it from other providers for use in HIPAA standard transactions.

- Staff will need to know what to do if another provider's NPI is needed in a HIPAA standard transaction and is unknown (eg, ordered or referred services).

- Developing a plan for who will be responsible for ensuring that the NPIs are kept up to date.

- Plan and educate your staff on how NPIs from other organizations or peers will be collected and validated for use in HIPAA standard referral transactions.

- Create a process for sharing your NPI with your business partners for billing purposes.

Impact on Business Processes

In addition to impacting the HIPAA standard transactions, the implementation of the NPI could impact several additional business processes and systems that health care professionals rely on every day. Stay ahead of the curve and begin proactively reviewing these processes to see if NPIs should be used in them and, if so, plan for NPI implementation.

Business processes that should be reviewed include:

- Business computer systems and software, such as the Practice Management System, to identify all places that a provider identifier is used.

  - Do you have Electronic Medical Records?

  - Do you participate in ePrescribing? Do you use a CPOE (computerized physician order entry) system?

Internal staff who work with these systems must understand the impact of using the NPI in place of all other provider identifiers.

- Any document imaging or archival system that you may use to determine if it needs updating to accommodate the NPI.

- Workflow processes – to see if a provider identifier is used for routing or indexing. Both internal and external reports could be affected.

■ ALL HIPAA standard transactions are impacted by the NPI – not just electronic claims. For example, make sure that you review the needs of the payment and remittance advice, claims status inquiry and response, and eligibility inquiry and response.

Finally, stay on top of the timelines for NPI implementation that are established by your trading partners. As the compliance date of May 23, 2007 nears, some health plans may request that all transactions submitted as of a certain date contain both the old legacy identifier and the NPI.

Stay connected with up-to-the-minute-information available from:

CMS
www.cms.hhs.gov/NationalProvIdentStand and

WEDI
www.wedi.org/npioi/

This tip sheet was prepared as a service to the public and is not intended to grant rights or impose obligations. This tip sheet may contain references or links to statutes, regulations, or other policy materials. The information provided is only intended to be a general summary. It is not intended to take the place of either the written law or regulations. We encourage readers to review the specific statutes, regulations and other interpretive materials for a full and accurate statement of their contents.

RISK MITIGATION TOOLS

The following are examples of risk mitigation tools you can use to manage and mitigate risks. This book provides security safeguard standards, policies and procedures along with strategies on how to build and implement your policies. Your health IT coordinator, whether an employee or outsourced personnel, should be able to demonstrate knowledge of each of these tools.

Risk Mitigation Tools

- Security safeguard standards, policies, and procedures

- Security training

- Physical security access controls (eg, doors, locks, guards)

- Proximity badges and smart cards

- Intrusion detection systems

- Shredders (disposal of paper and diskettes)

- Disaster recovery services (hardware, software, and data backup)

- Application criticality analysis

- Emergency downtime procedures

- Copied data storage at different locations

- Risk management software

- Malicious software protection (virus control)

- Audit trails

- Monitoring

- Firewalls

- Secure modems

- Dialers to identify modems

- Virtual private networks

- Laptop tracking software

- Wireless network access and control tools

- Authentication controls (password standards)

- Encryption

- Automatic log-off of inactive workstations

HITECH Act

President Obama signed into law the American Recovery and Reinvestment Act of 2009 (ARRA) on February 17, 2009. Included in the so-called stimulus bill was the Health Information Technology for Economic and Clinical Health Act (HITECH Act). The HITECH Act comprises Title XIII (Health Information Technology of Division A of ARRA (pp. 112-165) and Title IV (Medicare and Medicaid Health Information Technology; Miscellaneous Medicare Provisions) of Division B of ARRA (pp. 353–382).[1]

The HITECH Act provisions of ARRA in Title XIII included important changes in Privacy (Subtitle D), two of which are discussed here: Application of Security Provisions and Penalties to Business Associates of Covered Entities (Section 13401 on page 146 of ARRA), and Notification in the Case of Breach (Section 13402 on pages 146–149).

---

[1] ARRA, as signed by President Obama, is available online in portable document format (pdf) at http://frwebgate.access.gpo.gov/cgi-bin/getdoc.cgi?dbname=111_cong_bills&docid=f:h1enr.pdf.

We close our discussion of the HITECH Act with an outline of the Medicare financial incentive program for physicians to adopt certified electronic health record systems and to *meaningfully use* them.

Security Rule and Business Associates

Because of the importance of this new HITECH Act requirement that business associates of covered entities comply with the HIPAA Security Rule by February 17, 2010, we reproduce below the definition of business associate.[2] You will note that the definition focuses on the handling of individually identifiable health information and covers a number of functions that a practice may contract outside of its workforce.

Definition of a Business Associate

(1) Except as provided in paragraph (2) of this definition, business associate means, with respect to a covered entity, a person who:

(i) On behalf of such covered entity or of an organized health care arrangement (as defined in Sec. 164.501 of this subchapter) in which the covered entity participates, but other than in the capacity of a member of the workforce of such covered entity or arrangement, performs, or assists in the performance of:

(A) A function or activity involving the use or disclosure of individually identifiable health information, including claims processing or administration, data analysis, processing or administration, utilization review, quality assurance, billing, benefit management, practice management, and repricing; or

(B) Any other function or activity regulated by this subchapter; or

---

[2] 45 CFR 160.103, which is available online at http://edocket.access.gpo.gov/cfr_2004/octqtr/pdf/45cfr160.103.pdf. CFR is Code of Federal Regulations.

(ii) Provides, other than in the capacity of a member of the workforce of such covered entity, legal, actuarial, accounting, consulting, data aggregation (as defined in Sec. 164.501 of this subchapter), management, administrative, accreditation, or financial services to or for such covered entity, or to or for an organized health care arrangement in which the covered entity participates, where the provision of the service involves the disclosure of individually identifiable health information from such covered entity or arrangement, or from another business associate of such covered entity or arrangement, to the person.

(2) A covered entity participating in an organized health care arrangement that performs a function or activity as described by paragraph (1)(i) of this definition for or on behalf of such organized health care arrangement, or that provides a service as described in paragraph (1)(ii) of this definition to or for such organized health care arrangement, does not, simply through the performance of such function or activity or the provision of such service, become a business associate of other covered entities participating in such organized health care arrangement.

(3) A covered entity may be a business associate of another covered entity.

By no later than February 17, 2010, business associates must implement HIPAA Administrative Simplification Security Rule administrative, physical, and technical safeguards, based on having conducted a risk analysis; related policies and procedures; and written documentation and workforce training requirements. Compliance "shall apply to a business associate of a covered entity in the same manner that such sections apply to the covered entity. The additional requirements of this title that relate to security and that are made applicable with respect to covered entities shall also be applicable to such a business associate and shall be incorporated into the business associate agreement between the business associate and the covered entity."[3] The additional requirements include civil and criminal penalties, notification provisions for a breach, and application of "guidance on the most effective and appropriate technical safeguards" as determined by the Secretary of Health and Human Services (HHS), amongst other requirements.

Application of the Security Rule to business associates of covered entities is a significant compliance change. Previous to the change, if there were a breach involving a business associate of which the covered entity were aware, then the covered entity could just terminate the contract if the breach was not remedied. Responsibility and liability rested with the covered entity. With the change in the HITECH Act privacy provisions, the business associate now has responsibility and liability directly for a breach as well as the covered entity.

We recommend that physician practices and their business associates read an April 2009 <u>Baseline Magazine</u> article by Corinne Bernstein entitled: "The Cost of Data Breaches."[4] This article reports on a Ponemon Institute study of incidents and costs incurred at 43 organizations in 17 industry sectors. Here are several highlights from the article:

- "Lost business accounted for nearly 70 percent of a data breach in 2008.

- "[S]ectors suffering the highest customer losses were health care. . . and financial services.

- "The biggest cause of breaches. . . is insider negligence. . . 88% of all cases in 2008.

- "The number of breaches involving third-party organizations continues to climb."

---

[3] 13401 *HITECH Act* 146.

[4] This article is available online at www.baselinemag.com/c/a/Security/The-Cost-of-Data-Breaches-380742/?kc=rss.

The article concludes with the following quotation:

> "'Organizations are getting better at detecting breaches,' says the institute's Larry Ponemon. 'But to reduce the incidence of data breaches, they need to use better security technologies, such as encryption and identity access management, and they must provide more training to their employees.'"

In addition to responsibility and liability, physician practices—and all other covered entities—and their business associates must safeguard individually identifiable health information and train their workforce members to protect their businesses and avoid the costs of losing customers because of a breach. In short, as the Bernstein article indicates, a data breach will cost an affected organization big dollars, customer losses, and maybe the business as well.

Breach Notification

The HITECH Act provides a new, statutory definition of a breach[5], as follows:

"(1) Breach

  (A) In General. The term 'breach' means the unauthorized acquisition, access, use, or disclosure of protected health information which compromises the security or privacy of such information, except where an unauthorized person to whom such information is disclosed would not reasonably have been able to retain such information.

  (B) Exceptions. The term 'breach' does not include-

    (i) Any unintentional acquisition, access, or use of protected health information by an employee or individual acting under the authority of a covered entity or business associate if-

---

[5] 13400 *HITECH Act* 144.

(I) Such acquisition, access, or use was made in good faith and within the course and scope of the employment or other professional relationship of such employee or individual, respectively, with the covered entity or business associate; and

(II) Such information is not further acquired, accessed, used, or disclosed by any person; or

(ii) Any inadvertent disclosure from an individual who is otherwise authorized to access protected health information at a facility operated by a covered entity or business associate to another similarly situated individual at same facility; and

(iii) Any such information received as a result of such disclosure is not further acquired, accessed, used, or disclosed without authorization by any person."

A breach requires notification, which is triggered when there is an incident of "unauthorized acquisition, access, use, or disclosure of 'unsecured protected health information.'"[6] Notification to affected persons must be accomplished "without unreasonable delay and in no case later than 60 calendar days after the discovery of a breach by the covered entity involved (or business associate involved in the case of a notification [to the covered entity following discovery of a breach])." The notification provision requires covered entities to notify affected parties directly and individually in a timely manner, and to use appropriate public media for cases involving over 500 individuals. The Department of Health and Human Services (HHS) Office of Civil Rights (OCR) has additional information on breach notification procedures, which is available at www.hhs.gov/ocr/privacy/hipaa/administrative/breachnotificationrule/index.html.

---

[6] The information in this paragraph is from 13402 *HITECH Act* 146-149.

On April 17, 2009, as required by the HITECH Act, the Secretary of Health and Human Services issued *Guidance Specifying the Technologies and Methodologies That Render Protected Health Information Unusable, Unreadable, or Indecipherable to Unauthorized Individuals for Purposes of the Breach Notification Requirements under Sections 13402 of Title XIII (Health Information Technology for Economic and Clinical Health Act) of the American Recovery and Reinvestment Act of 2009.*[7] The Guidance was effective on the date of issuance, and the Secretary requested public comment prior to including the Guidance in an Interim Final Rule pertaining to breach notification.

On August 24, 2009, the *Federal Register* published the HHS Secretary's Interim Final Rule, *Breach Notification for Unsecured Protected Health Information.*[8] The Interim Final Rule effective date was September 23, 2009. The Interim Final Rule stated that federal criminal and civil sanctions for violations would not be enforced until February 22, 2010, and only for breaches and failures to notify affected persons that occur on or after that date. That enforcement limitation does not apply to possible state enforcement actions and penalties in the event of a breach prior to that date, nor relieve the covered entity of notification requirements in the event of a breach.

We reproduce here the definition of breach from the Interim Final Rule[9]:

> "Breach means the acquisition, access, use, or disclosure of protected health information in a manner not permitted under subpart E [Privacy of Individually Identifiable Health Information] of this part [164, Security and Privacy] which compromises the security or privacy of the protected health information.

---

[7] This 20-page document is available in PDF at www.hipaa.com or www.hhs.gov/ocr/privacy/hipaa/understanding/coveredentities/hitechrfi.pdf.

[8] Department of Health and Human Services, Office of the Secretary, "45 CFR Parts 160 and 164: Breach Notification for Unsecured Protected Health Information; Interim Final Rule," *Federal Register*, v. 74, n. 162, August 24, 2009, pp.42739-42770.

[9] 74 *Federal Register* 42767-42768.

(1)

(i) For purposes of this definition, *compromises the security or privacy of the protected health information* means poses a significant risk of financial, reputational, or other harm to the individual.

(ii) A use or disclosure of protected health information that does not include the identifiers listed at § 164.514(e)(2), date of birth, and zip code does not compromise the security or privacy of the protected health information.[10]

(2) Breach excludes:

(i) Any unintentional acquisition, access, or use of protected health information by a workforce member or person acting under the authority of a covered entity or a business associate, if such acquisition, access, or use was made in good faith and within the scope of authority and does not result in further use or disclosure in a manner not permitted under subpart E of this part.

(ii) Any inadvertent disclosure by a person who is authorized to access protected health information at a covered entity or business associate to another person authorized to access protected health information at the same covered entity or business associate, or organized health care arrangement in which the covered entity participates, and the information received as a result of such disclosure is not further used or disclosed in a manner not permitted under subpart E of this part.

(iii) A disclosure of protected health information where a covered entity or business associate has a good faith belief that an unauthorized person to whom the disclosure is made would not reasonably have been able to retain such information."

---

[10] This refers to a de-identified data set.

Note in the regulatory definition of breach that analysis and measurement of harm is a consideration in breach notification [Section (1)(i)], requiring risk analysis, and that breach of de-identified protected health information is specifically excluded from breach notification [Section (1)(ii)].

The August 24, 2009, Interim Final Rule contained *Guidance Specifying the Technologies and Methodologies that Render Protected Health Information Unusable, Unreadable, or Indecipherable to Unauthorized Individuals.*[11]

The Guidance from the Interim Final Rule is reproduced below:

> B. *Guidance Specifying the Technologies and Methodologies that Render Protected Health Information Unusable, Unreadable, or Indecipherable to Unauthorized Individuals* Protected health information (PHI) is rendered unusable, unreadable, or indecipherable to unauthorized individuals if one or more of the following applies:
>
> (a) Electronic PHI has been encrypted as specified in the HIPAA Security Rule by 'the use of an algorithmic process to transform data into a form in which there is a low probability of assigning meaning without use of a confidential process or key' [45 CFR 164.304, definition of 'encryption'] and such confidential process or key that might enable decryption has not been breached. To avoid a breach of the confidential process or key, these decryption tools should be stored on a device or at a location separate from the data they are used to encrypt or decrypt. The encryption processes identified below have been tested by the National Institute of Standards and Technology (NIST) and judged to meet this standard.[12]

---

[11] 74 *Federal Register* 42742-42743. The Guidance will be updated annually, as necessary, beginning in April 2010.

[12] NIST documents cited in the Guidance are available at www.csrc.nist.gov.

(i) Valid encryption processes for data at rest are consistent with NIST Special Publication 800-111, *Guide to Storage Encryption Technologies for End User Devices.*[13]

(ii) Valid encryption processes for data in motion are those which comply, as appropriate, with NIST Special Publications 800-52, *Guidelines for the Selection and Use of Transport Layer Security (TLS) Implementations;* 800-77, *Guide to IPsec VPNs;* or 800-113, *Guide to SSL VPNs,* or others which are Federal Information Processing Standards (FIPS) 140-2 validated.

(b) The media on which the PHI is stored or recorded has been destroyed in one of the following ways:

(i) Paper, film, or other hard copy media have been shredded or destroyed such that the PHI cannot be read or otherwise cannot be reconstructed. Redaction is specifically excluded as a means of data destruction.

(ii) Electronic media have been cleared, purged, or destroyed consistent with NIST Special Publication 800-88, *Guidelines for Media Sanitization* [available at http://www.csrc.nist.gov], such that the PHI cannot be retrieved."

It is important to note that "[c]overed entities and business associates that implement the specified technologies and methodologies with respect to protected health information are not required to provide notifications in the event of a breach of such information—that is, the information is not considered 'unsecured' in such cases."[14]

---

[13] NIST Roadmap plans include the development of security guidelines for enterprise-level storage devices, and such guidelines will be considered in updates to this guidance, when available.

[14] 74 *Federal Register* 42741. The definition of "unsecured protected health information" in the Interim Final Rule is "protected health information that is not rendered unusable, unreadable, or indecipherable to unauthorized individuals through the use of a technology or methodology specified by the Secretary in the guidance...." 74 *Federal Register* 42768.

In the Interim Final Rule, HHS clarified the type of data comprising protected health information that was covered by the guidance[15]:

- *Data in motion* includes data that is moving through a network, including wireless transmission, whether by e-mail or structured electronic interchange.
- *Data at rest* includes data resides in databases, file systems, flash drives, memory, and any other structured storage method.
- *Data in use* includes data in the process of being created, retrieved, updated, or deleted.
- *Data disposed* includes discarded paper records or recycled electronic media.

Data in those states are secured or unsecured—the choice is left up to the covered entity and business associate, as encryption is an addressable implementation specification under the HIPAA Security Rule.

A covered entity physician practice must rely on outcomes of its risk analysis to determine whether encryption is necessary. In that risk analysis, the covered entity should evaluate potential risks and costs of breach of unsecured electronic protected health information that becomes accessible to unauthorized users outside of the covered entity, whether data are at rest, in use, or in motion, which would trigger the new 'breach notification' provisions of the HITECH Act. If a covered entity does not encrypt electronic protected health information, then it must document its decision and explain why this implementation specification does not apply. Even in the absence of exposure to an open network, a covered entity should consider in its risk analysis costs and benefits of encrypting electronic protected health information at rest on its closed electronic information system.

With expected increased use of electronic transactions in healthcare, such as ePrescribing, and electronic communications via email, say,

---

[15] 74 *Federal Register* 42742.

between a physician practice and a patient, most covered entities will be using open systems and will have need for encryption tools. We recommend that you contact your electronic information system hardware and software vendors for advice on encryption, and that you also consult the National Institute for Standards and Technology (NIST) Special Publication 800-53, Revision 3: *Recommended Security Controls for Federal Information Systems and Organizations* (Initial Public Draft), February 2009,[16] and NIST Special Publication 800-66, Revision 1, *An Introductory Resource Guide for Implementing the Health Insurance Portability and Accountability Act (HIPAA) Security Rule,* October 2008.[17]

HHS's Health IT Policy Committee Releases Draft Recommendations on *Meaningful Use* for Public Comment

The HITECH Act provides an electronic health record (EHR) adoption incentive program for healthcare providers who adopt certified[18] electronic health records **and** *use* them in a *meaningful* way to improve

---

[16] This document is available online at http://csrc.nist.gov/publications/drafts/800-53/800-53-rev3-markup-02-05-2009.pdf.

[17] This document is available online at http://csrc.nist.gov/publications/nistpubs/800-66-Rev1/SP-800-66-Revision1.pdf, or can be downloaded at www.hipaa.com.

[18] Since 2006, the Certification Commission for Health Information Technology (CCHIT) has been certifying electronic health record systems. Visit www.cchit.org for more information on CCHIT and certification criteria under that program. CCHIT was not named in the HITECH Act as the certifying authority for the Medicare EHR incentive program. According to the HITECH Act, "[t]he National Coordinator, in consultation with the Director of the National Institute of Standards and Technology , shall keep or recognize a program or programs for the voluntary certification of health information technology as being in compliance with applicable certification criteria adopted under this subtitle." See 3001(c)(5) *HITECH Act* 118.

patient care.[19] The Medicare incentive program begins in January 2011 and terminates at the end of 2014 for new *meaningful user* physician adopters of certified electronic health record technology, as illustrated in Table B-1.

TABLE B-1	HITECH Act Medicare EHR Incentive Program

Incentive Year   Year Adopted

Incentive Year	2011	2012	2013	2014	2015+
2011	$18,000[20]	—	—	—	—
2012	$12,000	$18,000	—	—	—
2013	$8,000	$12,000	$15,000	—	—
2014	$4,000	$8,000	$12,000	$12,000	—
2015	$2,000	$4,000	$8,000	$8,000	0
2016	0	$2,000	$4,000	$4,000	0
2017	0	0	0	0	0
Total	$44,000	$44,000	$39,000	$24,000	0
Health Shortage Area[21]	+10% $48,400	+10% $48,400	+10% $42,900	+10% $26,400	

---

[19] The HITECH Act provisions pertaining to healthcare professionals are located at 4101 *HITECH Act* 353–363.

[20] Amounts shown in this table are per physician.

[21] There is an additional 10 percent incentive payment for physicians who adopt and deploy certified electronic medical record systems in health shortage areas. See 4101 *HITECH Act* 354

As defined in the HITECH Act, meaningful use of certified electronic health record technology includes:

- "use of electronic prescribing as determined to be appropriate by the [HHS] Secretary;

- "electronic exchange of health information to improve the quality of health care, such as promoting care coordination.

- "in a form and manner specified by the Secretary on such clinical quality measures and such other measures as selected by the Secretary."[22]

HHS' Health Information Technology (Health IT) Policy Committee released on June 16, 2009, two documents pertaining to the definition of "meaningful use" for public comment by 5 PM ET, Friday, June 26, 2009.[23] These documents are the *Meaningful Use Preamble*[24] and *Meaningful Use Matrix*[25]. These documents likely will be updated during the second half of 2009, and we recommend that readers periodically visit the Health IT Policy Committee web site for updates.[26]

We also recommend that physician practices read the draft recommendations on *meaningful use* and become familiar with the activities that

---

[22] 4101 *HITECH Act* 356.

[23] See the HHS Press Release, which is available at www.hhs.gov/news/press/2009pres/06/20090616a.html.

[24] This document is available in PDF at http://healthit.hhs.gov/portal/server.pt/gateway/PTARGS_0_11113_872720_0_0_18/Meaningful%20Use%20Preamble.pdf and www.hipaa.com.

[25] This document is available in PDF at http://healthit.hhs.gov/portal/server.pt/gateway/PTARGS_0_11113_872719_0_0_18/Meaningful%20Use%20Matrix.pdf and www.hipaa.com. For your convenience, it is reproduced at the end of Appendix B.

[26] The Health IT Policy Committee web site is: http://healthit.hhs.gov/portal/server.pt?open=512&objID=1269&parentname=CommunityPage&parentid=26&mode=2&in_hi_userid=11113&cached=true, where you can also find other information on the Health IT Policy Committee and its activities.

will comprise meaningful use. We recommend that you read the 3-page *Meaningful Use Preamble:* "Meaningful Use: A Definition–Recommendations from the Meaningful Use Workgroup to the Health IT Policy Committee, June 16, 2009," prior to examining the *Meaningful Use Matrix.*

Here, we take a high level view of the content of the matrix, reproducing *Health Outcomes Policy Priorities,* embedded *Care Goals,* and summary *Objectives* for each of the years 2011, 2013, and 2015, and *Measures* for tracking objective performance in each of those years. Then, we reproduces *Objectives* and *Measures* for 2011, the first year for which healthcare providers will be eligible for incentives under Medicare. You will note in a review of the matrix that *meaningful use* objectives evolve in two- year intervals from the initial objectives.

Meaningful Use Matrix Priorities and Goals

The meaningful use matrix outlines in Column 1 of eight columns five *Health Outcomes Policy Priorities* (P), and for each priority, in Column 2, *Care Goals* (G):

- (P) Improve quality, safety, efficiency, and reduce health disparities
  - (G) Provide access to comprehensive patient health data for patient's health care team
  - (G) Use evidence-based order sets and CPOE [computerized physician order entering]
  - (G) Apply clinical decision support at the point of care
  - (G) Generate lists of patients who need care and use them to reach out to patients (e.g., reminders, care instructions, etc.)
  - (G) Report to patient registries for quality improvement, public reporting, etc.
- (P) Engage patients and families

- (G) Provide patients and families with access to data, knowledge, and tools to make informed decisions and to manage their health
- (P) Improve care coordination
  - (G) Exchange meaningful clinical information among professional health care team
- (P) Improve population and public health
  - (G) Communicate with public health agencies
- (P) Ensure adequate privacy and security protections for personal health information
  - (G) Ensure privacy and security protections for confidential information through operating policies, procedures, and technologies and compliance with applicable law
  - (G) Provide transparency of data sharing to patient.

For each set of priorities and embedded goals, there are three combinations of objectives and measures for three years:

- 2011
  - To electronically capture in coded format and to report health information and to use that information to track key clinical conditions
- 2013
  - To guide and support care processes and care coordination
- 2015
  - To achieve and improve performance and support care processes and on key health system outcomes.

The *Meaningful Use Preamble* from the Health IT Policy Committee recognizes that meaningful use will evolve over time as "considerable gaps in EHR-generated measures available to monitor key desired policy outcomes (e.g., efficiency, patient safety, care coordination)" are closed.

Hence, the objectives and measures for 2013 build on those of 2011, and those of 2015 build on those of the preceding years.

The Centers for Medicare & Medicaid (CMS) expects to issue a notice of proposed rulemaking (NPRM) relating to the EHR adoption incentive program and definition of meaningful use late in 2009.

Above, we outlined Health Outcomes Policy Priorities and Care Goals, and described the Meaningful Use Preamble and Meaningful Use Matrix. Here, we reproduce the draft recommendation 2011 Objectives and Measures for each of the five Health Outcomes Policy Priorities. Public comment on these draft recommendations ended on June 26, 2009.[27] Be sure to visit the Health IT Policy Committee web site cited earlier for updates on the 2011 Objectives and Measures.

Meaningful Use Matrix Draft Objectives and Measures for 2011

The meaningful use matrix outlines in Column 1 of eight columns five Health Outcomes Policy Priorities (P), and in Columns 3 and 4 2011 Objectives (O) and 2001 Measures (M), respectively.

- ■ **(P) Improve quality, safety, efficiency, and reduce health disparities**
  - ■ (O) Use CPOE for all order types including medications (OP, IP)
  - ■ (O) Implement drug-drug, drug-allergy, drug-formulary checks (OP, IP)

---

[27] The Health IT Policy Committee sought "feedback on how to best frame these measures including measurement of key public health conditions, measuring health care efficiency, and measuring the avoidance of certain adverse events. These comments will be used to help revise the recommended measurement strategy to include more extensive and refined outcome measures for 'meaningful use' in 2013 and beyond." See *Preamble*, p.3.

- (O) Maintain and up-to-date problem list (OP, IP)_Generate and transmit permissible prescriptions electronically (eRX)(OP)

- (O) Maintain active medication list (OP, IP)

- (O) Record primary language, insurance type, gender, race, ethnicity (OP, IP)

- (O) Record vital signs including height, weight, blood pressure (OP, IP)

- (O) Incorporate lab-test results in EHR (OP, IP)

- (O) Generate lists of patients by specific condition to use for quality improvement, reduction of disparities, and outreach (OP)

- (O) Send reminders to patients per patient preference for preventive/follow-up care (OP, IP)

- (O) Document a progress note for each encounter (OP)

- (M) Report quality measures, including

- % diabetics with A1c under control (OP)

- % hypertensive patients with BP under control (OP)

- % of patients with LDL under control (OP)

- % of smokers offered smoking cessation counseling (OP, IP)

- (M) % of patients with recorded BMI (OP)

- (M) % eligible surgical patients who received VTE prophylaxis (IP)

- (M) % of orders entered directly by physicians through CPOE

- (M) Use of high-risk medications in the elderly (OP, IP)

- % of patients over 50 with annual colorectal cancer screenings (OP)

- (M) % of females over 50 receiving annual mammograms (OP)

- (M) % patients at high-risk for cardiac events on aspirin prophylaxis (OP)

- (M) % of patients with current pneumovax (OP)
- (M) % eligible patients who received flu vaccine (OP)
- (M) % lab results incorporated into EHR in coded format (OP, IP)
- (M) Stratify reports by gender, insurance type, primary language, race, ethnicity (OP, IP)

- **(P) Engage patients and families**
  - (O) Provide patients with electronic copy of–or electronic access to–clinical information (including lab results, problem list, medication lists, allergies) per patient preference (e.g., through PHR)(OP, IP)
  - (O) Provide access to patient-specific educational resources (OP, IP)
  - (O) Provide clinical summaries for patients for each encounter (OP, IP)
  - (M) % of all patients with access to personal health information electronically (OP, IP)
  - (M) % of all patients with access to patient-specific educational resources (OP, IP)
  - (M) % of encounters for which clinical summaries were provided (OP, IP)

- **(P) Improve care coordination**
  - (O) Exchange key clinical information among providers of care (e.g., problems, medications, allergies, test results) (OP, IP)
  - (O) Perform medication reconciliation at relevant encounters (OP, IP)
  - (M) Report 30-day readmission rate (IP)
  - (M) % of encounters where med reconciliation was performed (OP, IP)

- (M) Implemented ability to exchange health information with external clinical entity (specifically labs, care summary and medication lists)(OP, IP)

- (M) % of transitions in care for which summary care record is shared (e.g., electronic, paper, eFax)(OP, IP)

- **(P) Improve population and public health**

  - (O) Submit electronic data to immunization registries where required and accepted (OP, IP)

  - (O) Provide electronic submissions of reportable lab results to public health agencies (IP)

  - (O) Provide electronic syndrome surveillance data to public health agencies according to applicable law and practice (IP)

  - (M) Report up-to-date status for childhood immunizations (OP)

  - (M) % reportable lab results submitted electronically (IP)

- **(P) Ensure adequate privacy and security protections for personal health information**

  - (O) Compliance with HIPAA Privacy and Security Rules and state laws

  - (O) Compliance with fair data sharing practices set forth in the Nationwide Privacy and Security Framework [released by HHS' Office of the National Coordinator for Health Information Technology on December 15, 2008, and available on the HIPAA.com site]

  - (M) Full compliance with HIPAA Privacy and Security Rules

  - (M) An entity under investigation for a HIPAA privacy or security violation cannot achieve meaningful use until the entity is cleared by the investigating authority

  - (M) Conduct or update a security risk assessment and implement security updates as necessary.

The 2011 Objectives are described in the Meaningful Use Matrix header to Column 3 as follows:

"Goal is to electronically capture in coded format and to report health information and to use that information to track by clinical conditions."

The Meaningful Use Preamble elaborates further:

"Although some recommended measure used to assess meaningful use in 2011 may apply to specific chronic diseases, the recommended 2011 objective are meant to establish a foundation for affecting a more comprehensive set of health outcomes in the future. . . . In identifying potential criteria for 'meaningful use' of an electronic health record, it became apparent that that there are considerable gaps in EHR-generated measures available to monitor key desired policy outcomes (e.g., efficiency, patient safety, care coordination). . . . [T]hese measures will not be required for Medicare and Medicaid incentive payments until 2013. . . ."

Health Outcomes Policy Priority	Care Goals	2011[1] Objectives — Goal is to electronically capture in coded format and to report health information and to use that information to track key clinical conditions		2011[1] Measures	2013 Objectives — Goal is to electronically capture in coded format and to report health information and to use that information to track key clinical conditions		2013 Measures	2015 Objectives — Goal is to achieve and improve performance and support care processes and on key health system outcomes	2015 Measures
		Eligible Providers	**Hospitals**		**Eligible Providers**	**Hospitals**			

Improve quality, safety, efficiency, and reduce health disparities	• Provide access to comprehensive patient health data for patient's health care team
	
	• Use evidence-based order sets and CPOE
	
	• Apply clinical decision support at the point of care
		• Use CPOE for all orders[2]
		
		• Implement drug-drug, drug-allergy, drug-formulary checks
		
		• Maintain an up-to-date problem list of current and active diagnoses based on ICD-9 or SNOMED
		
		• Generate and transmit permissible prescriptions
			• 10% of all orders (any type) directly entered by authorizing provider (e.g., MD, DO, RN, PA, NP) through CPOE[2]
			
			• Implement drug-drug, drug-allergy, drug-formulary checks
			
			• Maintain an up-to-date problem list of current and active diagnoses based on ICD-9 or SNOMED
				• Report quality measures to CMS including:
				  o % diabetics with A1c under control [EP]
				  o % hypertensive patients with BP under control [EP]
				  o % of patients with LDL under control [EP]
				  o % of smokers offered smoking cessation counseling [EP, IP]
					• Use CPOE for all orders
					
					• Use evidence-based order sets
					
					• Manage chronic conditions using patient lists and decision support
					
					• Provide clinical decision support at the point of care
						• Use CPOE for all order types
						
						• Use evidence-based order sets
						
						• Record clinical documentation in EHR
						
						• Generate and transmit permissible discharge prescriptions electronically
						
						• Manage chronic conditions using patient lists and decision support
						
						• Provide clinical decision support at the point of care
							• Additional quality reports using HIT-enabled NQF-endorsed quality measures [EP, IP]
							
							• % of all orders entered by physicians through CPOE [EP, IP]
							
							• Potentially preventable Emergency Department Visits and Hospitalizations [IP]
							
							• Inappropriate
								• Achieve minimal levels of performance on quality, safety, and efficiency measures
								
								• Implement clinical decision support for national high priority conditions
								
								• Medical device inter-operability
								
								• Multimedia support (e.g., x-rays)
									• Clinical outcome measures (TBD) [OP, IP]
									
									• Efficiency measures (TBD) [OP, IP]
									
									• Safety measures (TBD) [OP, IP]

[1] The HIT Policy Committee recommends that incentives be paid according to an "adoption year" timeframe rather than a calendar year timeframe. Under this scenario, qualifying for the first-year incentive payment would be assessed using the "2011 Measures." The payment rate and phaseout of payments would follow the calendar dates in the statute, but qualifying for incentives would use the "adoption-year" approach.

[2] CPOE requires computer-based entry by providers of orders (medication, laboratory, procedure, diagnostic imaging, immunization, referral) but electronic interfaces to receiving entities are not required in 2011

[3] Race and ethnicity codes should follow federal guidelines (see Census Bureau)

Health Outcomes Policy Priority	Care Goals	2011[1] Objectives — Goal is to electronically capture in coded format and to report health information and to use that information to track key clinical conditions		2011[1] Measures	2013 Objectives — Goal is to electronically capture in coded format and to report health information and to use that information to track key clinical conditions		2013 Measures	2015 Objectives — Goal is to achieve and improve performance and support care processes and on key health system outcomes	2015 Measures
		Eligible Providers	**Hospitals**		**Eligible Providers**	**Hospitals**			
	• Generate lists of patients who need care and use them to reach out to patients (e.g., reminders, care instructions, etc.) • Report to patient registries for quality improvement, public reporting, etc.	electronically (eRx) • Maintain active medication list • Maintain active medication allergy list • Record demographics: ○ preferred language ○ insurance type ○ gender ○ race[3] ○ ethnicity • Record advance directives • Record vital signs: ○ height ○ weight ○ blood pressure Calculate and display: ○ BMI	• Maintain active medication list • Maintain active medication allergy list • Record demographics: ○ preferred language ○ insurance type, ○ gender ○ race[3] ○ ethnicity • Record advance directives • Record vital signs: ○ height ○ weight ○ blood pressure Calculate and display: ○ BMI	• % of patients with recorded BMI [EP] • % eligible surgical patients who receive VTE prophylaxis [IP] • % of orders (for medications, lab tests, procedures, radiology, and referrals) entered directly by physicians through CPOE • Use of high-risk medications (Re: Beers criteria) in the elderly • % of patients	(e.g., reminders, alerts) • Specialists report to relevant external disease (e.g., cardiology, thoracic surgery, cancer) or device registries, approved by CMS	(e.g., reminders, alerts) • Specialists report to relevant external disease (e.g., cardiology, thoracic surgery, cancer) or device registries • Conduct closed loop medication management, including eMAR and computer-assisted administration	use of imaging (e.g., MRI for acute low back pain) [EP, IP] • Other efficiency measures (TBD) [EP, IP]		

Health Outcomes Policy Priority	Care Goals	2011[1] Objectives — Goal is to electronically capture in coded format and to report health information and to use that information to track key clinical conditions		2011[1] Measures	2013 Objectives — Goal is to electronically capture in coded format and to report health information and to use that information to track key clinical conditions		2013 Measures	2015 Objectives — Goal is to achieve and improve performance and support care processes and on key health system outcomes	2015 Measures
		Eligible Providers	**Hospitals**		**Eligible Providers**	**Hospitals**			
		• Record smoking status	• Record smoking status	• over 50 with annual colorectal cancer screenings [EP]					
		• Incorporate lab-test results into EHR as structured data	• Incorporate lab-test results into EHR as structured data						
		• Generate lists of patients by specific conditions to use for quality improvement, reduction of disparities, and outreach	• Generate lists of patients by specific conditions	• % of females over 50 receiving annual mammogram [EP]					
				• % patients at high-risk for cardiac events on aspirin prophylaxis [EP]					
		• Report ambulatory quality measures to CMS	• Report hospital quality measures to CMS						
		• Send reminders to patients per patient preference for preventive/follow up care		• % of patients who received flu vaccine [EP]					
		• Implement one clinical decision rule	• Implement one clinical decision rule	• % lab results incorporated into EHR in					

Health Outcomes Policy Priority	Care Goals	2011¹ Objectives — Goal is to electronically capture in coded format and to report health information and to use that information to track key clinical conditions		2011¹ Measures	2013 Objectives — Goal is to electronically capture in coded format and to report health information and to use that information to track key clinical conditions		2013 Measures	2015 Objectives — Goal is to achieve and improve performance and support care processes and on key health system outcomes	2015 Measures
		Eligible Providers	**Hospitals**		**Eligible Providers**	**Hospitals**			
		relevant to specialty or high clinical priority • Document a progress note for each encounter • Check insurance eligibility electronically from public and private payers, where possible • Submit claims electronically to public and private payers.	related to a high priority hospital condition • Check insurance eligibility electronically from public and private payers, where possible • Submit claims electronically to public and private payers.	coded format [EP, IP] • Stratify reports by gender, insurance type, primary language, race ethnicity [EP, IP] • % of all medications, entered into EHR as generic, when generic options exist in the relevant drug class [EP, IP] • % of orders for high-cost imaging services with specific structured indications recorded [EP,					

Health Outcomes Policy Priority	Care Goals	2011[1] Objectives — Goal is to electronically capture in coded format and to report health information and to use that information to track key clinical conditions		2011[1] Measures	2013 Objectives — Goal is to electronically capture in coded format and to report health information and to use that information to track key clinical conditions		2013 Measures	2015 Objectives — Goal is to achieve and improve performance and support care processes and on key health system outcomes	2015 Measures
		Eligible Providers	**Hospitals**		**Eligible Providers**	**Hospitals**			
				• % claims submitted electronically to all payers [EP, IP] • % patient encounters with insurance eligibility confirmed [EP, IP]					
Engage patients and families	• Provide patients and families with timely access to data, knowledge, and tools to make informed	• Provide patients with an electronic copy of their health information (including lab results, problem list, medication lists, allergies) upon request[4] • Provide patients	• Provide patients with an electronic copy of their health information (including lab results, problem list, medication lists, allergies, discharge summary, procedures), upon request[4] • Provide patients	• % of all patients with access to personal health information electronically [EP, IP] • % of all patients with access to patient-specific educational	• Access for all patients to PHR populated in real time with health data • Offer secure patient-provider messaging capability • Provide access to	• Access for all patients to PHR populated in real time with patient health data • Provide access to	• % of patients with full access to PHR populated in real time with EHR data [OP, IP] • Additional patient access and experience reports using NQF-endorsed	• Patients have access to self-management tools • Electronic reporting on experience of care	• NPP quality measures, related to patient and family engagement [OP, IP]

[4] Electronic access to and copies of may be provided by a number of secure electronic methods (e.g., PHR, patient portal, CD, USB drive)

Health Outcomes Policy Priority	Care Goals	2011[1] Objectives *Goal is to electronically capture in coded format and to report health information and to use that information to track key clinical conditions*	2011[1] Measures	2013 Objectives *Goal is to electronically capture in coded format and to report health information and to use that information to track key clinical conditions*	2013 Measures	2015 Objectives **Goal is to achieve and improve performance and support care processes and on key health system outcomes**	2015 Measures
	decisions and to manage their health	**Eligible Providers** with timely electronic access to their health information (including lab results, problem list, medication lists, allergies)[4] **Hospitals** with an electronic copy of their discharge instructions and procedures at time of discharge, upon request[4] • Provide access to patient-specific education resources • Provide access to patient-specific education resources • Provide clinical summaries for patients for each encounter	resources [EP, IP] • % of encounters for which clinical summaries were provided [EP]	**Eligible Providers** patient-specific educational resources in common primary languages • Record patient preferences (e.g., preferred communication media, advance directive, health care proxies, treatment options) • Documentation of family medical history, in compliance with GINA • Upload data from home monitoring device **Hospitals** patient-specific educational resources in common primary languages • Record patient preferences (e.g., preferred communication media, advance directive, health care proxies, treatment options) • Documentation of family medical history, in compliance with GINA	HIT-enabled quality measures [EP, IP] • % of patients with access to secure patient messaging [EP] • % of educational content in common primary languages [EP, IP] • % of all patients with preferences recorded [IP] • % of transitions where summary care record is shared [EP, IP] • Implemented		

Health Outcomes Policy Priority	Care Goals	2011 Objectives — Goal is to electronically capture in coded format and to report health information and to use that information to track key clinical conditions		2011 Measures	2013 Objectives — Goal is to electronically capture in coded format and to report health information and to use that information to track key clinical conditions		2013 Measures	2015 Objectives — Goal is to achieve and improve performance and support care processes and on key health system outcomes	2015 Measures
		Eligible Providers	**Hospitals**		**Eligible Providers**	**Hospitals**			
Improve care coordination	• Exchange meaningful clinical information among professional health care team	• Capability to exchange key clinical information (e.g., problem list, medication list, allergies, test results), among providers of care and patient authorized entities electronically[5] • Perform medication reconciliation at relevant encounters and each transition of care[6]	• Capability to exchange key clinical information (e.g., discharge summary, procedures, problem list, medication list, allergies, test results), among providers of care and patient authorized entities electronically[5] • Perform medication reconciliation at relevant encounters and each transition of care[6]	• Report 30-day readmission rate [IP] • % of encounters where med reconciliation was performed [EP, IP] • Implemented ability to exchange health information with external clinical entity (specifically labs, care	• Retrieve and act on electronic prescription fill data • Produce and share an electronic summary care record for every transition in care (place of service, consults, discharge) • Perform medication reconciliation at each transition of care from one health care setting to another	• Retrieve and act on electronic prescription fill data • Produce and share an electronic summary care record for every transition in care (place of service, consults, discharge) • Perform medication reconciliation at each transition of care from one health care setting to another	ability to incorporate data uploaded from home monitoring devices [EP] • Access to comprehensive patient data from all available sources • 10 % reduction in 30-day readmission rates for 2013 compared to 2012 • Improvement in NQF-endorsed measures of care coordination.	• Access comprehensive patient data from all available sources	• Aggregate clinical summaries from multiple sources available to authorized users [OP, IP] • NQF-endorsed Care Coordination Measures (TBD)

[5] Health information exchange capability and demonstrated exchange to be specified by Health Information Exchange Work Group of HIT Policy Committee.

[6] Transition of care defined as moving from one health care setting or provider to another

Health Outcomes Policy Priority	Care Goals	2011[1] Objectives — Goal is to electronically capture in coded format and to report health information and to use that information to track key clinical conditions		2011[1] Measures	2013 Objectives — Goal is to electronically capture in coded format and to report health information and to use that information to track key clinical conditions		2013 Measures	2015 Objectives — Goal is to achieve and improve performance and support care processes and on key health system outcomes	2015 Measures
		Eligible Providers	Hospitals		Eligible Providers	Hospitals			
				summary and medication lists) [EP, IP] • % of transitions in care for which summary care record is shared (e.g., electronic, paper, e-Fax) [EP, IP]					
Improve population and public health	• Communicate with public health agencies	• Capability to submit electronic data to immunization registries and actual submission where required and accepted.[7] • Capability to provide electronic syndromic surveillance data to public health agencies and actual	• Capability to submit electronic data to immunization registries and actual submission where required and accepted.[7] • Capability to provide electronic submission of reportable lab results to public health agencies and	• Report up-to-date status for childhood immunizations [EP][7] • % reportable lab results submitted electronically [IP]	• Receive immunization histories and recommendations from immunization registries[7] • Receive health alerts from public health agencies • Provide sufficiently anonymized electronic syndrome	• Receive immunization histories and recommendations from immunization registries[7] • Receive health alerts from public health agencies • Provide sufficiently anonymized electronic syndrome	• % of patients for whom an assessment of immunization need and status has been completed during the visit [EP][7] • % of patients for whom a public health alert should have	• Use of epidemiologic data • Automated real-time surveillance (adverse events, near misses, disease outbreaks, bioterrorism	• HIT-enabled population measures [OP, IP] • HIT-enabled surveillance measure [OP, IP]

[7] Applicability to Medicare versus Medicaid meaningful use is to be determined

Health Outcomes Policy Priority	Care Goals	2011 Objectives — *Goal is to electronically capture in coded format and to report health information and to use that information to track key clinical conditions*		2011 Measures	2013 Objectives — *Goal is to electronically capture in coded format and to report health information and to use that information to track key clinical conditions*		2013 Measures	2015 Objectives — Goal is to achieve and improve performance and support care processes and on key health system outcomes	2015 Measures
		Eligible Providers	**Hospitals**		**Eligible Providers**	**Hospitals**			
		transmission according to applicable law and practice	actual submission where it can be received. • Capability to provide electronic syndromic surveillance data to public health agencies and actual transmission according to applicable law and practice		surveillance data to public health agencies with capacity to link to personal identifiers	surveillance data to public health agencies with capacity to link to personal identifiers	triggered and audit evidence that a trigger appeared during the encounter	• Clinical dashboards • Dynamic and Ad hoc quality reports	
Ensure adequate privacy and security protections for personal health information	• Ensure privacy and security protections for confidential information through operating	• Compliance with HIPAA Privacy and Security Rules[8,9], • Compliance with fair data sharing practices set forth in the Nationwide Privacy and Security Framework	• Compliance with HIPAA Privacy and Security Rule[8,9]. • Compliance with fair data sharing practices set forth in the Nationwide Privacy and Security Framework	• Full compliance with HIPAA Privacy and Security Rules • Conduct or update a security risk assessment	Use summarized or de-identified data when reporting data for population health purposes (e.g., public health, quality reporting, and research), where appropriate, so that important information is		• Provide summarized or de-identified data when reporting data for health purposes (e.g., public health, quality reporting, and research),	• Provide patients, on request, with an accounting of treatment, payment, and health care operations disclosures	• Provide patients, on request, with a timely accounting of disclosures for treatment

[8] The HIT Policy Committee recommends that CMS withhold meaningful use payment for any entity until any confirmed HIPAA privacy or security violation has been resolved

[9] The HIT Policy Committee recommends that state Medicaid administrators withhold meaningful use payment for any entity until any confirmed state privacy or security violation has been resolved

Health Outcomes Policy Priority	Care Goals	2011[1] Objectives — Goal is to electronically capture in coded format and to report health information and to use that information to track key clinical conditions		2011[1] Measures	2013 Objectives — Goal is to electronically capture in coded format and to report health information and to use that information to track key clinical conditions		2013 Measures	2015 Objectives — Goal is to achieve and improve performance and support care processes and on key health system outcomes	2015 Measures
		Eligible Providers	Hospitals		Eligible Providers	Hospitals			
	policies, procedures, and technologies and compliance with applicable law. • Provide transparency of data sharing to patient.			and implement security updates as necessary	available with minimal privacy risk.		where appropriate, so that important information is available with minimal privacy risk.	• Protect sensitive health information to minimize reluctance of patient to seek care because of privacy concerns.	payment, and health care operations, in compliance with applicable law. • Incorporate and utilize technology to segment sensitive data

INDEX